I0667678

WHY WE WANT TO KILL YOU

The Jihadist Mindset and How to Defeat it

Opens the door to a dark, hidden world
that few of us understand or can comprehend

By Walid Shoebat

Cover design: Graphics by Sher
Book design and layout: Cheryl Taylor
Editor: Norman L. Schulz, III

For information, please e-mail the author
at walid@shoebat.com

ISBN: 978-0-9771021-4-3

1st Edition

Printed in the United States

Acknowledgements

Over the last few years I have been compiling information and making many interesting observations and solutions concerning the threats of Islamic fundamentalism. In December 2006 I decided to write this book, as we believe that we need to face the realities of the fundamentalist Islamic threat now. Iran is fast moving to nuclear capability and our freedoms could not only be eroded but the lives of millions of people could be at tremendous risk. We must change our thinking and actions in order to deal with this real threat.

In order for me to achieve the prompt publication of this book, I owe a great deal of gratitude to several people, my manager Keith Davies and director of my Foundation, who also dedicates his life to help save this nation and the freedoms we all wish to preserve; to Cheryl Taylor and Norman L. Schulz, III for their many hours of overtime and dedication in the production and editing of the book; and finally to Rod Mitchell whose advise and council were of tremendous value.

Finally I would like to thank you the reader and supporters of our work for the tremendous positive response we have received over the last few years; people are crying out for the truth to be heard. I pray for our country, and that God will protect America, Israel and the rest of the world from the great evil that threatens us all.

Dedication

I first dedicate this book to my wife Maria, and my American family, who cared enough about my soul, to introduce me to the values of peace, love, and joy, and allowed me the opportunity to rediscover my life. If they had not done so, I possibly would be behind bars at Gitmo or have become a dead martyr. Secondly, I dedicate the content of this book to all American Patriots, with hope that the information and knowledge they gain will help to prevent terrorism from ever darkening our shores again.

– Walid

Table of Contents

Foreword

The information in this book, *Why We Want to Kill You,* is critically important for every American to understand. It explains what the media and many of our leaders fail to comprehend when they fret about "why they hate us" and try to explain terrorist "roots of anger" while our enemies sneer at our weakness and grow stronger. As the so-called "Global War on Terror" continues to be waged unabated we desperately need to understand the driving forces behind the ruthless jihadists who conduct terrorist operations under the ideological banner of fundamentalist Islam.

Author Walid Shoebat is uniquely qualified to write on the subject as he himself was once committed to the destruction of America, Israel, and the West as an active Palestinian terrorist. The clarity of view that Shoebat can provide from the perspective of one who was inside the movement is far more graphic and comprehensive than anything that we can glean from media talking heads and ivory-tower academic analysts.

You will not receive comfort from this book, for you will realize in a terrifying moment of clarity that our leaders really "do not get it" when it comes to understanding the elemental motives that drive our enemies to commit suicide for their ideology and to destroy us all – women, children, innocents – in an utterly conscienceless manner. Our leaders and the media either fail to grasp the reality of the situation or are unwilling to face cold facts.

But as a responsible citizen you must read this book. For the author articulately explains – in a most powerful and chilling prognosis – that while the threats are enormous, failure to act properly is unacceptable. For as Mr. Shoebat clearly states, the free world today must deal with challenges even greater than it faced from Nazi Germany.

This book opens the door to a dark, hidden world that few of us understand or can comprehend. Failure to heed Mr. Shoebat's warnings risks bringing that cruel dark world down upon us, while using solutions he offers can allow us to survive and triumph over this desperate challenge.

Why We Want to Kill You is a must-read, and a book you will return to often and will want to share with your family and friends. It is a vital piece of information for every citizen in a very difficult time.

– Lieutenant Colonel (U.S. Army Ret.) Gordon C. Cucullu

Introduction

The question I get asked all the time is, "What makes a Muslim fundamentalist?" What is Islamic fundamentalism? What makes Jihadists burn Americans in Fallujah, Iraq and drag their charred corpses through the streets? What makes a Palestinian mob kill two Jews who lost their way in Ramallah and dance with joy as they smash the bodies with whatever they could lay their hands on? What makes Muslim fundamentalists blow themselves up or decapitate civilian hostages in front of a camera so that the whole world can see?

Is it poverty? Is it an issue of human rights? Is it a desire for a state? Is it possibly a reaction to the occupation of their country?

The most important issue is how do we define this enemy? What are Western misconceptions when it comes to identifying this threat?

How big is this movement? How can we combat it? Can we change their minds? Is there anything we can do in order for them to accept us?

I should know this subject well, after all, I used to be a terrorist. I changed my mind in 1993 and decided to fight against Islamic fundamentalism. This was not an easy task for me, a Muslim from birth and a Palestinian terrorist.

You might ask what changed my mind and how this all happened. I documented my reasons in my book, *Why I Left Jihad*. Here, I will share my story and my findings of how Western misconceive the terrorist psychology and the motives of terrorists. I have done many interviews with news media and spoken at hundreds of seminars in the West and to millions through the media. Yet the question I am asked most often is, "Why?" Why would someone strap on a bomb and destroy his or her body to kill others?

When I explain it, people get it. Yet I have difficulty with the Western media when it comes to terrorism, they assume it always takes "two to tango." I can give one example:

"So what did the Jews do to 'tango' in Nazi Germany?" I asked my interviewers on the Jeremy Bowen show, Radio-5, on the BBC in London, "Did it take two to tango in Nazi Germany?" One interviewer blurted out immediately, "Yes!" Another panelist quickly concluded the interview grumbling, "The problem with today's world is fundamentalism, all religious fundamentalists." He was shocked when I looked straight into his eyes and said, "Yes indeed, but with a slight difference: Christian fundamentalists may give people a headache, since they love to proselytize, but Muslim fundamentalists will just take your head right off your shoulders, sir."

He was silent. I was quickly thanked for stopping by the BBC.

In an interview with Peter Graph, for Reuters in England, and with the same moral equivalency problems, I asked him if he could point out the difference between al-Qaeda and Hamas. He stated that Hamas and al-Qaeda were different. "Hamas," he said, "has a legitimate reason to fight for Palestinian rights, while al-Qaeda simply wants to kill anyone and everyone for no legitimate reason."

With such distinction between the two groups, justifying one that kills Jews while condemning the other that kills Westerners, I asked him if he knew the name of the man who was the inspiration for the Mujahideen that later became al-Qaeda. He responded as most people do, "Osama bin Laden."

"Wrong," I said. "It was Mustafa Azzam, a Palestinian from Jenin, who was Osama bin Laden's mentor and the inspiration for al-Qaeda (The Base)." I rarely find any Westerner who knows that. So, if Osama was inspired by a Palestinian Jihadist, why then do Westerners see a difference between Hamas and al-Qaeda?

We all live in some state of ignorance.

Before I enter into the meat of this subject of Islamic fundamentalism and the psychology behind the Jihadist mind, I must give a summary as to how I was challenged to study the Bible, Judeo-Christian culture, Jewish history, and such. After changing my mind, I spent ten years attempting to reason with many of my countrymen. I learned a lot. I learned to analyze how we thought, how we can transform our thinking, and how we can reach out to others. It was a difficult journey with very few converts along the way. Why did I have such little success? Was it because I lacked the ability to argue my views, or was it something else?

The purpose of this book is to answer these questions.

Chapter 1

The Confession

Yes, we confess we were terrorists, but only by confession can we begin to heal. For what good are we if we do not confess our wrongs and say what we truly feel and believe instead of the wishes of tyrants and the words of political correctness which are killing us all? It is this nation to which I pledge my allegiance to now, a nation that does its best to give us freedom, liberty, and justice for all. For this nation, I spit out the bitter herb from my past and partake in the truth that I so much believe and hold dearly to my heart, to which I am now committed, and I ask all to join. We are called traitors, scorned and rejected by our own families, yet that is not the most painful thing we endure. Rather, it's the pain we receive from the very ones who we are trying to protect, nevertheless, we risk our lives for them.

So, let me start from the beginning.

I was never caught. I am a terrorist who never paid for my crimes. You might ask why. Well, the Israeli government has released thousands of terrorists back to the streets as a result of international pressure. Israel releases more terrorists back to the streets than any other nation on earth. I have family members who had life sentences, but they have been able to return to their activism. I myself have confessed my terror connection, yet Israel does not want to press charges. Thousands of terrorists have been imprisoned, then released.

I was influenced to become a terrorist by my religious education at the school, the local mosque, and the Al-Aqsa mosque in Jerusalem. Some of the teaching that I recall in my Islamic studies at Dar Jaser High School in Bethlehem was given to us by Shaikh Zakaria and Naim Ayyad. Both were influenced by the Muslim Brotherhood in Egypt, and the Jihad ideology was greatly emphasized by them.

I remember that students had questions for our teacher, Naim Ayyad, after his discussion on the subject of eschatology and the end of days. He stated that when the Jews come back to the land we would kill them, and the *"trees and stones will cry out: here is a Jew hiding behind me, come O Muslim, come O slave of Allah, come and kill him."*

We supposedly would kill all the men, the women would be taken as concubines.

Ayad stated that we can have children with concubines.

We started to ask questions in class. "How? Wouldn't it be considered adultery?" I asked.

"No," he said.

"Is it marriage?" One of us asked.

"No," he said.

Then the tough question came – "Is it consensual?"

"It doesn't have to be," he responded.

"Then it's rape," I replied. "Is it permitted for Muslims to rape the Jewish women after we defeated them."

His response was, "The women captured in battle have no choice in this matter. They are concubines, and they need to obey their masters. Having sex with slave captives is not a matter of choice for slaves."

He said that sexual intercourse with Jewish captives does not have to be consensual.

I could not believe what I had heard. I asked my father for his opinion that same day, when I went home. During lunch, my father told me, "Son, Allah will provide you the strength to do it. We will take all Jewish women and rape them, and when we go to heaven, we will have the Al-Kawthar River and have sex with as many women as we like."

You might think, "Come on. Who is this guy telling us all of this – is he for real?"

You will see that this type of thinking permeated my religion and culture. It's as real as 9/11, the Iraq War, the genocide of Christians in the Sudan, and the war in Afghanistan. If these are not real to you, then I cannot help you.

The chapter of The Women in the Quran, verse 20, documents Allah's decree:

> Forbidden to you also are married women, except those who are in your hand as slaves, this is the law of Allah for you.

A Muslim can have sex with slave captives after a war.

The chapter of The Confederates (al-Ahzab verse 50) reads:

> O prophet; we allowed thee thy wives to whom thou hast paid their dowries, and the slaves whom thy right hand possesseth out of the booty which Allah hath granted thee, and the daughters of thy uncle, and of thy maternal aunt, who fled with thee to Medina, and any believing woman who hath given herself up to the prophet, if the prophet desired to wed her, a privilege to thee above the rest of the faithful.

The prophet had the best privilege, more than four wives, limitless concubines, and women who wanted to give themselves freely to him.

You might think that this is old, archaic stuff, that no one believes these things anymore. Read the rest of this book and then come back and argue with me later. You can write to me at walid@shoebat.com.

I was initiated into Yasser Arafat's Fatah terror group and recruited by a well-known bomb maker named Mahmoud Al-Mughrabi, from Jerusalem. I met up with him several times on Bab-El-Wad Street after our release from the central prison in Jerusalem's Russian Compound. The first discussions centered on whether to give my U.S. passport to one of the brothers for a plane hijacking mission. We rendezvoused a few days later at the Judo-Star martial arts club run by his father near the Temple Mount in Jerusalem's Old City. Instead, the decision was made to perform a bomb operation to be carried out by me with my cousin Nidal, who was injured years later when Israel launched a missile on Hussein Abiyat, one of the most wanted gunmen. The Israelis wanted to kill Abiyat during the Intifada. He died, along with two bystanders who were female relatives of mine, after helicopter missiles hit his car.

His relative Atef Abiyat, another one of the Israeli government's most wanted Palestinian fugitives, was also from my village in Beit Sahur-Bethlehem. Atef was directly responsible for the deaths of five Israelis. He was known as "Commander of the Al-Aqsa Martyrs Brigade" in the Bethlehem area. One can see from the photo below that the entire community sympathized with the terrorist and walked in his funeral.

Left: Funeral of Atif.
Right: Hussein Abiyat

Abiyat and two associates were killed after a car in which they were riding exploded in my village when the Israelis sniped him with a missile. Yet the Palestinian sources claim the incident was a targeted killing by Israel.

Many of the Abiyat family helped suicide bombers and purchased chemical compounds or explosives, planned the suicide bombing at the International Convention Center in Jerusalem, and even occupied the Church of Nativity, Christ's birth place, desecrating it and setting fires in it. Yet, The Vatican and the U.S. pressured Israel to set free the terrorists who violated the church. The terrorists now reside in Greece, Ireland, Italy, and Portugal.

In May 1985, over a thousand terrorists were released in exchange for three Israeli soldiers as part of the "Jibril deal." The terrorists who were released became the ideological and operational foundation for many terrorist activities in the years that followed. These releases occur constantly. My cousin, Mahmud Khalil Awad-Allah, was also released from prison after he was given a life sentence for planting a bomb and shooting an Israeli.

It's a revolving door, and the terrorists know it. International pressure eventually works, and terrorists are back on the street to kill more of the innocent. Such a war on terrorism is not a war at all!

Mahmoud and Nidal were not the only terrorists in my family. Mahmoud's younger brother, Raed, was killed on his way to plant a bomb in Ben Yehuda Street. Raed's mother, my Aunt Fatima, passed out sweets to everyone because he was martyred. In this resurrected Islamic tradition, the martyr's death is treated like a wedding celebration. Of course! Her son was instantly transported into the arms of the seventy-two virgins!

But why then, when Aunt Fatima was all alone at night, did she cry as though her heart would break? Her elder son, Ibrahim, taught about heaven and the seventy-two virgins at the Sharia school in Jerusalem's Al-Aqsa mosque, the source for religious guidance to the entire Muslim community in the Palestinian areas.

After my meeting with Mahmoud Al-Mughrabi, he gave me a sophisticated explosive device he had assembled. I was supposed to use the bomb – an explosive charge hidden in a loaf of bread – to blow up the Bank Leumi branch in Bethlehem. He helped me smuggle it with the aid of the Muslim Wakf, religious police on the Temple Mount, so that I could enter one of the world's most holy places.

From the Temple Mount, I walked on a platform with the explosives and a timer in my hand. Continuing to walk on top of the wall down the street, I avoided the checkpoints. I went to the bus station and took a bus to Bethlehem, fully ready to give my life if necessary. My hand was ready to throw the bomb when I saw some Palestinian children walking near the bank. Instead, I threw the bomb up on the bank's rooftop. I ran.

The bomb exploded as I reached the Church of the Nativity, walking down to Beit Sahur on my way home.

I was so scared and depressed that I couldn't sleep. I was only sixteen years old. I wondered if anyone was killed. That was the first time I came to grips with what it would be like to have blood on my hands. I felt both terrified and depressed. I didn't enjoy what I had done, but I had felt compelled to do it because it was my duty. I felt that some day I had to be a martyr, to kill Jews in order to go to heaven.

Dalal Al-Mughrabi
Terrorist who took part in bus hijacking and murder of 36 Israeli in 1978

The promise of seventy-two virgins in paradise was temptation enough to motivate most men, but not all terrorists were men. Even women carried out suicide missions. Westerners are unaware that national or spiritual salvation can be motivating factors to carry out suicide missions, even for women. Dalal Al-Mughrabi, the close relative of my bombmaker Mahmoud Al-Mughrabi, became the symbol of the Jihadist woman.

Dalal holds a special place of honor in Palestinian society. March 1978, a few months prior to my arrival in the U.S., she participated in a terror attack that claimed thirty-six Jewish lives, and remains one of the largest murderous attacks in Israel's history.

There are a number of girls' schools named for Mughrabi, and numerous TV programs and quizzes for children have glorified her life since the establishment of the Palestinian Authority. This recent article glorified her participation in the bus hijacking and with admiration, credits her with the killings:

> ...a hostage operation on the Palestinian shore. She (Dalal Al-Mughrabi) managed to get to the main road leading to Tel Aviv, she took over an Israeli bus and its passengers, who were soldiers and held them hostage...a real war took place, during which Dalal blew up the bus with all the passengers inside. They were all killed. (Al-Hayat Al-Jadida, November 7, 2006)

In my school much has been taught about Islamic heroism and even the encouragement for women to participate as heroines for Jihad comes from using references from the annals of Islam. During my education, perhaps the most talked-about woman in Jihad was Al-Khansa, the greatest poetess of elegiac poems in Arabic literature.

In the battle of Qa'dsia, she urged all four of her sons to take part and to fight bravely. When she heard the news of their martyrdom, she exclaimed, "All praise is to Allah who honored me through their martyrdom." (Hazrat Khansa, Zainab Siddique, July 22, 2005)

Al-Khansa was the symbol of the virtuous, Muslim woman whose main purpose in life is to produce more children to offer as a sacrifice for Allah.

Of course, my American mother was not virtuous, and wanting to escape to America made her situation worse, especially because her own children would turn her in at the notion of attempting to escape to America.

This concept of being a virtuous woman took hold of my entire society. Girls would do away with their western-style attire and cover themselves. I left for America in 1978, and when I returned to visit my home in Beit Sahur-Bethlehem in 1991, everyone had adopted the Sharia code of dress. All girls were covered from head to toe. Family relatives, who in the past socialized with male family members, were now dressed up in Hijab and would not even talk to me. Uncles who used to drink on occasion had repented and now prayed five times daily. Theatres were non-existent or had been burned. My mind which had adopted some Western concepts had no welcoming in any casual conversation. Everyone was consumed with talk about the occupation and martyrdom.

A new magazine, published by the Women's Information Office on the Arabian Peninsula, aims to teach women how to contribute to Jihad:

> Our main mission: push our children to the battlefield, like Al-Khansa, declares Umm Raad al-Tamimi in the magazine. The monthly publication champions the ideology of al-Qaeda terrorist chief Osama bin Laden: "Drive infidels from the Arabian Peninsula," or Saudi Arabia, the editorial in the first edition said. "The blood of our husbands and

the bodies of our children are an offering to god." (ABC News, September 4, 2004)

The participation of women in Jihad has no age limits. Fatima Omar Mahmud al-Najar is the oldest Palestinian woman martyr to date. She was fifty-seven years old when she decided to go on a suicide mission. She was the mother of nine children and grandmother of forty-one grandchildren. It is not unusual to have so many grandchildren in the Middle East where Muslims have more children per family than Westerners could manage. I myself had sixty-three first cousins, and my grandfather had four wives, yet we still accuse Israel of putting infertility drugs in the water in order to stop Palestinians from producing more children.

Fatima Omar Mahmud al-Najar suicide terrorist Al-Qassam website, Nov. 25, 2006

In the few known cases of Muslim female suicide bombers, most of the females were related by family to the male suspects and terrorist leaders. For example, an Iraqi woman, Sajida al-Rishawi, appeared on Jordanian television in November 2005, confessing her intent, as well as her husband's, to bomb a Western hotel in the capital city of Amman. (Khaleej Times, November 13, 2005) Having failed to release her explosives belt, her husband pushed her out of the ballroom and detonated his explosives. In recent years, several Palestinian female bombers – including Sana'a Shahada, Iman Asha, Abir Hamdan and Thawiya Hamour – had familial and personal links to male terrorists. (Israeli Ministry of Foreign Affairs, January 3, 2003)

Other examples of female suicide operatives include a nineteen-year-old Uzbek girl, Dilnoza Holmudora, who was married to the leader of the Islamic Jihad Movement of Uzbekistan. Two others were Egyptian women who shot at a tourist bus in Cairo in April 2005. Both women were in their 20s. The women were the fianceé and sister of the male perpetrators. (RCA No. 278, April 20, 2004)

Most recently, the Mujahideen Shura Council in Iraq issued a communiqué claiming responsibility for a suicide bombing on August 16, executed by a female member of the group's suicide brigade. The attack targeted a combined patrol of U.S. forces and Iraqi National Guards in al-Muqdadiyah. (Associated Press, September 28, 2005) According to the message, more than fifteen soldiers of the patrol were killed and others injured. Media reports indicate that the woman, wearing an explosives belt, detonated herself on the U.S.-Iraqi patrol near a bus stop, killing seven and wounding twenty, including civilians and military members.

Despite the recent participation of Muslim women in attacks, a Muslim woman's primary role is to offer moral and ideological support to male Jihadists. The wives of male militants demonstrate their support for their husbands, sons, brothers and other fighters through their communiqués and statements in jihadi magazines. Um Muhammad, the wife of deceased al-Qaeda leader in Iraq, Abu Musab al-Zarqawi, recently posted a letter on a jihadi website urging Muslim men to hold steady in jihad and warned the Iraqi government that the "great death is coming." (Mujahideen Shura Council website, July 2006) In the *al-Khansa* magazine, the propaganda arm of al-Qaeda in Saudi Arabia, articles focus on the role of women in jihad. Even on the internet, websites for Muslim women, such as http://www.mojahdat.jeeran.com, encourage them to support male jihadis in various conflicts worldwide.

In short, women are increasingly being called on for jihad. No longer invisible, Muslim women, with support from a new generation of male terrorists, are able to utilize modern technology and proclaim their voices on the global jihadi landscape. (Farhana Ali, Associate International Policy Analyst, RAND Corporation)

WOMEN IN PARADISE

While Westerners seem to focus more on the social aspects, the Hijab, and women's rights in the Middle East, they fail to focus on the major issue, the establishment of the Khilafa (Caliphate). Many Westerners ask me what Muslim women will do in paradise. Deputy Director of Al-Azhar's Center for Islamic Studies, Sheikh Abd Al-Fattah Gam'an stated:

If a woman is of the dwellers in Paradise but her husband in this world is not of the dwellers in Paradise, as in the case of Asia the wife

9

*of Pharaoh, she is given to one of the dwellers in Paradise who is of the same status…Regarding the woman who was married [during her life] to more than one man in this world, and all her husbands are dwellers in Paradise, she may choose among them, and she chooses the best of them. It is said that Umm Salmah asked the Prophet: "Oh Prophet of Allah, a woman marries one, two, or four husbands in this world and later she dies and enters Paradise, and they enter with her. Which of them will be her husband?" [The Prophet] answered: "She…chooses the best of them, saying, Oh Allah, this is the best of them that was with me in this world, marry me to him." Thus it is known that the women of Paradise also have husbands. Every woman has a husband. If her husband in this world is of the dwellers in Paradise [he becomes her husband in Paradise], and if her husband in this world is an infidel, she is given to one of the dwellers in Paradise who is suited to her in status and in the [strength] of his belief. (*www.lailatalqadr.com/stories/p1260503.shtml*)

MY SCHOOL RIOTS

During school riots against, what we called, the Israeli occupation, I would prepare speeches and slogans. In the middle of the night, I would sneak out of my home with spray paint and write anti-Israeli graffiti in an effort to provoke students to throw rocks at the armed, Israeli soldiers the next day.

We shouted, "No peace or negotiations with the enemy! Our blood and our souls we sacrifice to Arafat! Our blood and our souls we sacrifice to Palestine! Death to the Zionists!"

I vowed to fight my Jewish enemy, believing that I was doing Allah's will on earth. I remained true to my word as I tried to inflict harm by any means I could devise. I would participate in any riot: in schools, in the streets, and even in the holiest place, the Temple Mount in Jerusalem, called by Arabs, "Al-Masjid Al-Aqsa."

Throughout my high school years, I was one of the first to provoke a riot. We used terror tactics and bombs, and we organized armed assaults against Jews in an attempt to force them to leave Israel. But we never succeeded.

Do you think this only happens in Israel? Like drug pushers, hate pushers have neither sight nor insight. Sheikh Umar Abdulrahman was blind when he instigated the first bombing of the Twin Towers in New York. Blind men like Abdul-Hamid Kishk from Egypt, gave me my weekly dose of "hate drugs" through tapes recorded in Egypt and sent to me by my father, calling for America's destruction.

There was another incident when I was only sixteen. I joined in with other Palestinian youngsters, throwing rocks at an Israeli truck driver who had accidentally struck a Palestinian girl. We broke the glass of the truck to kill him while he was still calling for help for the girl. Finally, he started up the truck to escape with his life.

When we returned to Dar-Jaser High School in Bethlehem, a man who had been blind since birth and was part of the student association, gave a fiery speech, shouting that the accident was intentional. "Allah Akbar! Death to all Jews!" he shouted. It now seems unbelievable to me, but one thousand students believed him then. He nearly sparked an intifada. The Israeli military came, and many people were hurt.

Recalling the scene twenty years later, I wonder why an entire school followed a blind man who obviously could not have seen what really happened.

The intifada started from a similar incident. It was an accident in Gaza, when an Israeli Jeep accidentally struck and killed a boy.

Hatred is like a hydrogen-filled balloon, awaiting any spark, and the rest is tragedy. Now, some trigger-happy governments in the Middle East are pushing for rights to build nuclear bombs, not hydrogen balloons.

I remember my first attempt to lynch a Jew. Stones were flying everywhere like swarms of locusts. We set fire to a row of tires, making a blockade. One Jewish soldier tried to catch the kid who hit him with a rock. Instead, we caught the Jew. I had a club and pounded him in the head until the club broke. Another teenager, Jamal Hanouneh, had a stick with a nail sticking out, and he kept whacking the soldier's skull with it. We nearly killed him. Incredibly, (perhaps the adrenaline that's stored up for facing wild animals kicked in) he lunged across the fire to the other side of the blockade. The incident made the eight o'clock headline news that night.

I guess there is a curse for attacking Jews. Jamal's brother, Basem Hanouneh, suffered a horrible fate. His body was found dead near the military camp in Beit Sahur, mutilated and with his penis cut off. When the news circulated through town, everyone blamed the Israeli military for the crime. Twenty years later, his real killers were discovered. The sons of Bishara Qumsieh while drunk, confessed the whole gruesome details. Of course, no one acknowledged the lie perpetrated against the Israelis who had nothing to do with the crime. It got worse, the two brothers also confessed to another unsolved mystery – the murder of my first Bible teacher in third grade, an elderly single lady Mrs. Christa from Germany, who was raped and mutilated by the two brothers.

Not only was Basem's murder a lie, so was the murder of Muneer Abu Sayb'a, our landlord's son. Muneer was a nice young man who made repairs to the property we rented from his father. The home we lived in had cracks and when it rained, it would drench the house. Muneer would come and patch the roof. His father, Muhammad Amin Abu Sayb'a, was a known thief, and an excellent one at that. If there were any robberies in town Muhammad was always a suspect, but there was never enough evidence to convict him. Muneer, who worked hard and did all the chores, ended up in prison. The rumor was that Muneer was a member of an illegal terror organization. He was killed during his prison term, and Israel, of course, was accused of his murder. Later, the killer's brother, my friend from Dehaisheh refugee camp, confessed to me that Muneer was suspected of being a collaborator for Israel, and several inmates took a sink and cracked his head open and spilled his brains. Being accused of collaboration with Israel brings certain death. Again, Israel was accused of the killing and the whole community believed it. The irony was that the discoveries of the true criminals never caused me to question our honesty or integrity. I continued to work as a terrorist.

GAINING ENOUGH MERIT

The other irony was that, while terrorizing others, I terrorized myself with my beliefs that required me to gain enough merit and good deeds to go to heaven. But I never was sure if, when Allah judged me, my good deeds would outweigh the bad. Of course, to die fighting the Jews would ease Allah's anger toward my sins, and I would be assured a good spot in heaven, enjoying the Al-Kawthar River with beautiful wide-eyed women to fulfill my most intimate desires. Either way, it's a win-win ending, as long as I terrorized my enemies.

I remember one time in Bethlehem, when the entire audience in a packed theater clapped their hands with joy, watching the movie, "21 Days in Munich," the story of how eight members of the PLO faction, Black September, murdered the entire Israeli wrestling team that had gone to Munich to compete in the Olympic games. The moment we saw the Palestinians throwing grenades into the helicopter, killing the Israeli athletes, hundreds of viewers yelled, "Allah Akbar!" (Allah is the greatest!) This is the slogan of joy used by Muslims for victorious events.

MY LIFE IN AMERICA

After finishing high-school, it was typical for students to go overseas. Some went to Egypt, others to Greece, but most of us ended up in America. Many parents would advise their sons to marry American girls temporarily in order to obtain resident status and plan to come back and take an Arab wife permanently.

Immigrants from Muslim and Arab countries have a difficult time adjusting, especially when one belief system encounters a different one. My first wife was Jewish, or so I found out later. I was eighteen years old, and without her parents approval we got married. I knew that her parents hated the fact that their daughter had married an Arab Muslim, but I never knew why, until the day I visited Cheryl, her aunt in San Diego. I noticed a Mezuzah on the door. I asked later if that truly was her aunt and was she a blood relative. My wife assured me that she was. I asked then, what is a Mezuzah doing on your aunt's door. That's when she told me she was Jewish. She never told me before, because she never thought it would make any difference. I had never gotten along with her and was quite abusive. She had officially converted to Islam with the help of my first mentor Sheikh Abdul Qader Al-Najjar from Syria at my local mosque which was part of the Islamic Society in Garden Grove, California. She of course was asked to cover her hair. She had a difficult time doing that while working at the Pup-N-Taco fast food in Fullerton, the Hijab hair covering seemed to interfere with her work uniform. She tried as much as possible to cover every strand of hair, but I was never satisfied. I could never make this "Jew" fully behave, and since she was no virgin, she received a daily dose of beatings from me. "A woman who denies her husband's wishes, will never breathe the fragrance of paradise," I'd say, always quoting from the prophet. I would slap her any time she said the word "no" to me. One day she finally ran to her parents home covered with bruises from the beatings. I went there to get her, but her father, who was the head of the Santa Monica Harbor Patrol, grabbed me by the throat, and threatened to kill me. I left her and moved to Chicago. That's where all the mess began.

IN CHICAGO

I enrolled at the Loop College in Chicago where I became president of the Palestinian Student Association which was raising funds for the PLO and recruiting volunteers to fight in Lebanon. I worked with others to organize events and to smuggle a shipment of United States military outfits to Lebanon. We were all activists. Very few were really doing any studying. It was just a ruse to allow us to stay here and accomplish our real work. Most of us worked on obtaining green cards from American girls who were unaware that they were simply pawns for a greater cause. If anyone of us fell in love with his green card wife, the others would chastise him, reminding him he should divorce her later to marry a "homegrown" Muslim.

Other women served the cause, too. I became a friend of Mary Edwards, who was an activist, serving on a board alongside James Zoghby for the defense of Ziad Abu Eain. Ziad was a terrorist seeking asylum in the U.S. and was wanted for extradition to Israel for a 1979 Palestine Liberation Organization (PLO) bombing.

The United Nations ruled against taking action regarding Ziad, who murdered two boys and injured thirty-six other people with a bomb operation similar to mine in which the bomb was timed to go off when many children would be there, near the start of Lag b'Omer celebrations. Ziad was later released and became a member of the Supreme Committee of the PLO. He was a well-known terrorist, who ironically became Secretary of the Palestinian Ministry of Prisoners' Affairs. Yet, James Zoghby, the founder and president of the Arab American Institute (AAI) in Washington, D.C. makes statements that Israel implements "systematic discriminatory policies towards Arabs and Arab Americans." (Ma'an News 7/11/2006)

Having a relationship with Mary Edwards for the "cause" was justified – as long as the girl did her part to help our colleague, Ziad. Chicago was notorious for its influx of Arab students. The Loop College cafeteria looked like an Arab coffee shop (Qahwah); Islamists, PLO, PFLP (Popular Front to Liberate Palestine), DFLP (Democratic Front to Liberate Palestine), were all competing against each other. Jordanians hated the Palestinians for Black September; the Lebanese had not forgotten the massacres committed by the PLO in Damur. No one got along with the other. But when it came to hating Israel, they were united. Now began what I thought would be a return to Islam.

I was introduced to the Muslim Brotherhood by Ghazi Dhabaybeh from Jordan, who worked with Shaikh Jamal Said, a well connected activist with Mustafa Azzam, Osama bin Laden's mentor. I had asked permission to keep my girlfriend since she was of use to us to try to get the release of Ziad Abu Eain. Their response was to dump her. Then I joined the Muslim Brotherhood. I was recruited by Sheikh Jamal Said, who worked with a network of scholars from Jordan and elsewhere to recruit students in the United States to train for future jihad (holy war) operations against America and Israel. This was the boot camp from hell. The training was underground. I lived in an abandoned home next to an old Bethlehem Steel factory on the south side of dangerous Chicago in a basement infested with rats the size of cats. No music was allowed. I had dumped Mary Edwards, following my instructions from the Muslim Brotherhood. We had to wake up in the middle of the night with Sheikh

Said for vigorous training, martial arts, and chanting the slogans of hate and indoctrination.

The Brotherhood would rent hotels and plan large events, and I traveled with Ghazi to help him muster students from all over for these events. The hotel was exclusively for Muslim students. No one was allowed unless they were Muslim, and every window was covered. The anti-America chanting and fervent speeches went on day and night until three in the morning, ending with martial arts training by Jamal Said. I have video tapes from the IAP (Islamic Association of Palestine) showing what type of programs they were offering the Muslim community in the U.S. In addition to Jamal Said, there were reports from terrorist leaders describing killings in detail, and Quranic recitation calling to behead unbelievers wherever they were found. Then young men would dance on the stage with knives, in full view of the Muslim community that had been invited. Speakers were brought in and some were even related to Abdullah Azzam, Osama bin Laden's mentor.

Throughout much of 2006 I have issued press releases for the media to view these tapes in an effort to inform the public of what we are dealing with, but no one was interested.

However, in November 2006, my mentor, the Hamas terrorist affiliate Jamal Said joined the Mayor of Chicago and other city officials, in a ribbon-cutting ceremony for a new park, "Mosque Foundation Garden." The park is a "gift" from the Bridgeview Mosque Foundation, whose prominent member, Mohammed Salah, is *on trial* for terrorism and membership in Hamas. How very timely! However, this donation should be seen for what it truly is – a bribe – a ploy to show to judge, jury, and the community that Muslims are peaceful, good, and generous, not terrorists! Not only was the press present, but in a further show of support, scholars at the event included Professors Scott Alexander of the Catholic Theological Union, and Harold Vogelaar of the Lutheran School of Theology.

If these facts frighten you, **they should**. Here is an account of Steven Emerson's visit to the mosque:

Later, he took Khalid and me to the Bridgeview Mosque, where Jamal Said was the imam. I could tell immediately that we were deep in the heart of Hamas territory. The walls of the vestibule were covered with Hamas posters and recruiting literature showing masked gunmen brandishing automatic weapons. It was all in Arabic, but you could see daggers plunged into Jewish hearts wrapped up in American flags. They even had a library filled with militant terrorist videos and books. Khalid was there to translate for me. The Friday service was a rather strange experience. Out of 800 people, I was the only one wearing a red ski jacket. When the service was over I approached the imam and asked him if he had known Abdullah Azzam. He was very defensive. "I never met with him," he said quickly and then dismissed me. Earlier that year, two Hamas operatives, congregants of the mosque, were arrested in Israel for transferring money from the United States to terrorists in the West Bank. One of these men, Mohammed Jarad, told the Israelis that he was sent on his mission by Jamal Said.

Talat Othman, is the co-founder of the Council of Islamic Organizations of Greater Chicago, whose director, Talat Sunbulli, sits on the board of the Bridgeview Mosque Foundation, (a known terrorist headquarters). Othman has also been linked to Mohammed Salah, who was convicted of helping to finance the murder of the American teenager David Boim who was shot to death by Hamas terrorists while waiting for a bus to go home from school in the West Bank. The U.S. courts awarded the Boim family $156 million dollars.

How could the U.S. forget the mental indoctrination button that Jamal Said used to turn Muslims into extremist robots, ready to carry out any order. These people are on your children's college campuses. There are also "Peace Weekends," sponsored by the Palestinian Solidarity Movement, whose agendas look like a day at Bible school. But then comes the party line. At campus events, they will speak of peace in English and talk about infiltration in Arabic.

For example, Abdurahman Alamoudi, an official of the American Muslim Council, a friend and sometime adviser on Islamic affairs to Hillary Rodham Clinton, who proudly stood before a Muslim crowd in Lafayette Park across from the White House and passionately declared his support for the terrorist organizations Hamas and Hezbollah. He was revealing the true face of "moderate" Islam.

In 1998, AMC (American Muslim Council), CAIR (Council of American Islamic Relations) and AMA (American Muslim Alliance) hosted a rally at Brooklyn College, where Islamic militants exhorted the attendees to carry out jihad and described Jews as "pigs and monkeys." In 1999 these same groups, together with MPAC, sponsored a rally in Santa Clara, California, where speakers accused Israel and the U.S. of carrying out a conspiracy to kill Muslims. One speaker called for the death of Jews.

On Oct. 13, 2000, CAIR and the AMC sponsored a rally outside the Israeli Embassy in Washington where the speakers led the crowd in a chant: *Khybar, Khybar, ya, ya Yahood, jesh Mohammed sofa ya'ud.* Translation: *Khybar Khybar, oh Jews, the army of Mohammed is coming for you.* It is a refrain used by Hamas, threatening the annihilation of Jews as was done to the Jewish tribe in Khybar, Saudi Arabia, by Mohammed the prophet of Islam in the year 628. At another Washington rally, on Oct. 28, 2000, the AMC's Mr. Alamoudi led the thousands in attendance to chant their support for Hamas and Hezbollah. "Hear that, Bill Clinton, we are all supporters of Hamas," he declared. "I wish they argued that I am also a supporter of Hezbollah." (When the New York Daily News asked about these comments, Mr. Alamoudi denied making them, telling the reporter: "You better check your Arabic." When the reporter noted that he had given the speech in English, Mr. Alamoudi replied, "It was in English? Oh my God, I forgot!")

Even though Alamoudi would slip when speaking in English every now and then, so-called Muslim moderates would know that what they say in Arabic is truly from their heart. In a June 2000 interview for the Arabic paper *al-Zaitonah,* Alamoudi said, "[AMC's] position with regard to the peace process is well known. We are the ones who went to the White House and defended what is called Hamas." Now Alamoudi is in jail, caught heading to Syria with $340,000 that came from Libya. According to FBI counterterrorism chief Steve Pomerantz, "It's very hard to explain in any innocent way a suitcase full of money going from one terrorist-sponsoring nation to another terrorist-sponsoring nation." (MSNBC, Oct 22, 2003)

Americans need to be aware of the usual lies in English and the truth in Arabic. The idea is to galvanize the Muslims and to win over naïve, idealistic students who believe their David and Goliath stories, but with the wrong Goliath. They collect enormous sums of money. And they have far-reaching access to the Western world through the Internet. The Muslim Brotherhood in America, which Jamal Said help start, soon gave birth to a new organization, the IAP (Islamic Association of Palestine). The IAP was a front group for Hamas since the people back home needed much support from American Muslims. This movement first began by setting up social infrastructure as was done by Shiekh Ahmad Yassin, a leader of the Muslim Brotherhood in Gaza. The Islamic Centre, which was opened in 1973, was the base for administration and control of religious and educational institutions that aimed to promote a return to Islam, to eradicate "immoral" behavior. We didn't have many of these social problems. Instead, the focus was on small bars, theatres, and weddings that used modern music because Islam forbids listening to anything with musical instruments. The leaven soon grew to spoil the whole batch with recruitment centers and an open training of children on terror camps. A birth of new style struggle began with Yahya Ayyash, the engineer by implementing the suicide belt. In 1987, Hamas was essentially the launching pad of an armed wing of the Muslim Brotherhood in Palestine. Hamas, in order to have any social base, had to bridge the divide between Palestinian nationalism and Islamism; no easy task given Qutb's preachings against nationalism as idolatry because it divides the *umma* and replaces a *sharia*-centered consciousness with ethnic pride (the *sharia* is the body of law based on Islamic teachings).

Hamas bridged the contradiction in its charter with a more pragmatic interpretation of Qutb's theory, namely that the success of each (national liberation and the creation of the *umma*) depended on the advance of the other. Thus, Hamas embarked on a twin-track policy of Jihad and nationalist struggle.

MOVED TO CALIFORNIA

I soon left Chicago and moved to California, where I began my career in computer programming. I held a position at the Linford Company in

Oakland, California. It was then that the first real war began between the U.S. and an Arab state – the first Gulf War.

I must confess that lying was our nature. Do you remember when Saddam Hussein sent scuds flying over Saudi Arabia in the first Gulf War, disregarding the high risk it would pose to the Islamic "holy land?" Yet as Muslims, we never objected since Saudi Arabia is one of the most hated nations in the Muslim world. Arabs attacked by Arabs seemed to have little impact on us as Kuwait was raped as a nation prior to that event. Yet Americans fighting Arabs made us furious. When I was at work surrounded by Americans as they huddled during lunch break to watch the news, I would express regret for any American losses. That was in front of Americans. When I went into my car and got on the freeway I would relieve my frustration not being able to voice my true feelings by rolling down my window and yelling as loud as I could "Allah Akbar" (Allah is great). This is the call made when Muslims are victorious. As soon as I got home, all of the Arabs within my building complex in Alameda, California would get together and cheer for Iraq.

After being in America for several years, and getting use to the American lifestyle, I went back home in 1991 for an arranged marriage with my second wife. This time I wanted to marry a Muslim.

On my flight from Rome to Tel Aviv's Ben Gurion airport, I sat next to a Jewish lady. I didn't want her to know my Palestinian origin, so I faked my name and introduced myself as "Bill visiting the Holy Land." Getting acquainted with this lady I asked if she had any children. She replied she had two girls in the IDF (Israeli Defense Forces). I then bluntly remarked, "So how do you feel when your daughters shoot Palestinians and kill them? Does it feel good?" She immediately said, "No. Thank God my daughters never killed any Palestinian. We Jews value life more than anything else." She started to sob in sadness.

When I got to the airport I was excluded for questioning because my passport showed that I was born in Jordan. Then they let me off at a different section. When my family connected with me, we started to talk about how badly we were treated. Why would we be let out at a different section than anyone else? It was the occupation of course. We blamed everything on the occupation.

On one occasion, my uncle decided to take me on a tour throughout all of the Palestinian areas. The first thing that one would notice is the graffiti all over the walls. There wasn't one square meter in the whole country that didn't have graffiti. I even made a bet with my uncle to find one square meter without graffiti or white-washed graffiti. I won the bet. You might wonder what kind of graffiti. No, it's not simple gang graffiti. One example sticks out: "We knock on the gates of heaven with the skulls of Jews." – this was written everywhere. I asked my uncle why we needed to kill Jews or die in order to enter Paradise, and what does this slogan have to do with the 'occupation?'

After living so long in the States, my mind had become somewhat infected with liberal thinking. The serious critical thinking began when I encountered a situation in which Palestinians began throwing stones at a civilian Jewish bus in Hebron. The bus had wire mesh throughout to repel the stones, and bars to prevent larger rocks or boulders from getting in. It was quite a scene. The Jewish passengers, going home to Quriat Arba within Hebron, were being stoned just for living in Arab areas.

I asked the Taxi driver, "Why?"

He said, "well, they're Jews."

"No," I said. "I am not asking why we stone them, but why aren't Jews allowed to live among us? We have 1.2 million Palestinian Arabs living in Israel proper, yet Jews are not allowed to live in Arab areas? Why?"

We were racists. I have no better term to apply to this phenomenon. Now after changing my views and speaking out, I am being labeled a racist. I began to wonder why when I <u>hated</u> Jews and wanted to kill them I was labeled as a freedom fighter by the world community. Now, that I <u>love</u> Jews and Americans, I am being labeled as a racist.

There was another thing I needed to confront after leaving Islam: it took me years to realize that I had to deal with my untruthful nature, and recognize this habit of lying was still acceptable with most of my countrymen. As a Muslim, how could I understand that I had a serious problem? This realization came after I was out of Islam and had adopted a different faith. I became a Christian in 1993. To my Muslim brethren, of course, this was my first crime. Not only in the Middle East but also here in the West I quickly learned that once you were labeled as a Christian you were considered a *radical*. Many have accused me of going from one extreme to another.

MY MOTHER

After my conversion, my American-born mother and grandmother were the only relatives to stand by me. Initially, though, even my mother didn't suspect my change of heart and mind, and it was much too dangerous to talk to her about it. She was living in the West Bank and was effectively held prisoner by my father for thirty-five years. Every time she would try to escape back to America, we were too eager to drag her back to the "house of obedience" where a woman belongs in that part of the world. I was never told that she was a Christian. Yet I had my suspicions. I remember that once, my mother tried to escape with me, my brother, and sister, but the neighbors, always looking out from their balconies, reported her leaving with her children and their suitcases. When we arrived in Jerusalem, my Muslim relatives were waiting for us at the entrance of the United States Consulate. Then they forced us to go home. Years later, when I re-united with my mother in America, I found out for sure she was a Christian. I discovered she had been influenced by an American missionary couple who she secretly asked to baptize her as she wanted to go back to her true faith. When she refused to be submerged in a pond full of green algae, the missionary, Edmond Davis from Texas, had to plead with the people at the YMCA in Jerusalem to clear their pool of men, and my mother was baptized there. Years later, I searched for Mr. Davis in Texas and he told me her story. No one from our family knew.

I recall when my mother would take me on trips to museums in Israel and I fell in love with archeology. I was fascinated with it. In my many arguments with her, I would bluntly say that the Jews and Christians had corrupted the Bible. She responded by taking me to the Israel

Scroll Museum in Jerusalem and showing me the scroll of Isaiah, still intact. She often answered my questions with silence. She had to be careful, because the Islamist culture can even cause a child to turn on his mother. I remember when I tormented my mother by calling her an "infidel." I had doubted her profession of faith to Islam and viewed her as an American imperialist. I'd show her the pictures in the newspaper of all the teenagers supposedly martyred because of violence, demanding that she respond to me. At times, we all hated her and the family would ask my father to divorce her and marry a "good Muslim woman."

One time, my father cracked my mother's skull with a hammer. Fed up because my father ignored her and spent most of his time with friends, she barged in on a game of Shesh-Besh backgammon, and, in front of the men, she threw the game to the floor. "I am an American and I am not used to this life," she cried out. The crack of the hammer was her sympathy. In 1995 I was finally able to rescue my mother. I thank God, since today, Bethlehem has become so dangerous, no one is safe.

The whole of my society was built on conjecture, beginning with our lullabies. Jew-hatred is an integral part of daily life for all Palestinian and Muslim children in many countries around the world.

When I was a child, my hungry young cousin picked up a piece of bread off the ground in front of the house. My grandmother caught her just before she could put it in her mouth. Grandma reprimanded, "Don't you know the Jews are putting bread in front of Arab houses that is tainted with poison?" I never knew that grandma's suspicions would turn into national accusations. In school, we were sometimes warned that the Jews put chemicals in the school water to cause sterility.

Today's reality is much worse than my grandmother's fairy tale. The volumes of accusations against Israel include arson attempts on the Temple Mount area, destruction and the digging of tunnels, creation of artificial earthquakes. Absurdly, they even accuse Jews of terrorist attacks on Jewish civilians. It is said they spread spoiled corn oil in the West Bank, sold English Cadbury chocolate tainted with the Mad Cow disease, used a chemical agent in attempted assassinations, sold sexually stimulating gum, spread cancer agents, and even injected Palestinian infants with the HIV virus causing AIDS. As with the Nazi-controlled media, the news organizations throughout the Middle East have been co-opted by Islamism. Regarding weapons in the hands of Arab terrorists, Arafat said, "These weapons could be obtained only from high authorities with great influence on the Israeli side." (Jerusalem Post, Feb. 1996.)

When I was a young boy in Jericho, the American Consul sent representatives from Jerusalem when they heard that a major war was about to erupt. They started evacuating all Americans in the area; and because my mother was an American, they came to rescue her. My father, however, refused the offer to leave because he loved his country. For my American born mother, marrying into Islam was like entering the Hotel California: "You can check out anytime you like, but you can never leave." Out of fifty-five Muslim states, not one is a signatory to the Hague Convention regarding abducted women.

Islamic males may marry Christian and Jewish women, but if an Islamic woman marries a Christian or Jew, "honor killing" by her relatives is permitted.

CHANGING MY VIEWS

I am no longer a terrorist. I am a Christian. I am a man who is dedicated to peace and truth. What gave birth to my profound change of heart and mind? How did I shed the mantle of the terrorist? How did I escape from the prison of thought that had held me for so long – the drug of hate that is so addictive? The answer was a self-detoxification program. It started in America, with a question my wife asked me while I was attempting to *convert her* to Islam. She would not accept my hatred of the Jews. "Show me in the Bible the textual corruption the Jews have made," she demanded.

By accepting her challenge, I walked into a new world. For the first time, I studied factual history, the Bible, Jewish history and Jewish songs and art, but I couldn't find anything about the murderous, terrible Jews that had been in my mind for so long. In fact, I could not find the words "kill" or "war" in Jewish songs! When I finally found one Jewish song with the word *Milchama,* one of the few Hebrew words I knew that meant war, I said, "Ha! There it is!" But I was stunned when the translation from Isaiah 2:4 was: "And man will not learn war any more…"

But in this new world, the United States, I was studying, for the first time, factual history regarding the Holocaust and much on Jewish history. I discovered that Jews did not start wars, did not take over other nations, and did not commit genocide. There were no calls for mutilation or degradation. On the contrary, it was all about following God's Commandments, sticking to the laws of living provided by the Torah, and maintaining Jewish ethics such as *tzedakah* (charity), *tikun olam* (repair of the world), and *mitzvot* (good deeds). They also had a remarkable way of atoning for any wrongdoing. They did not just ask God to be forgiven; they were required to go out and make right what was wrong. If you hurt someone, go to him or her and apologize or repair the damage you caused. If he or she is no longer around, then perhaps do something for that person's family. If not that, then do something for the community. For Jews, to be a good person means doing, not just talking. I wondered, how did they live like this when they were always in a self-defense mode throughout Biblical history, and as they are, unfortunately, again today? Suffering attacks by the Babylonians, Assyrians, Amorites, Philistines, and Edomites, always needing to think in terms of self-defense. Who are these people?

Little did I know that someday I would find out the answer to that question. At home in the West Bank, I was taught that when the Jews come back to the land, we would kill them, and the *"Trees and stones will cry out: here is a Jew hiding behind me, come O Muslim, come O slave of Allah, come and kill him."* We would be on the attack; they, again, would be in self-defense mode.

I studied Jewish art and music. I began with "Fiddler on the Roof."

This was Jewish culture 101 – I must have watched it over 350 times.

One day, I saw some Holocaust footage, but I saw it through new eyes, not the way I had viewed it when I was living in Israel. Back there, in an attempt to change the hearts of Palestinians, the Israeli TV station would show Holocaust documentaries. Just like the rest of the community, we would sit and watch, cheering the Germans while we chewed on popcorn. At that time, it was impossible for us to change our minds or hearts concerning Jews; only a "heart transplant" could have accomplished that. I saw that the Jews have suffered the true refugee problem, not the Palestinians.

As time went on, I prayed to God that if love was indeed an infection, that I would be plagued with it and never recover. Yet, the day I expressed my new views to my own family and people, I was hated.

Was it a sin that I began to love Jews, as well as Hindus, Buddhists, and Muslims? Is it a sin to love life, to want to protect both Jewish and Arab children? To Islamists, the answer is yes.

Westerners might think that leaving the Islamic religion was easy. To Westerners, one can leave drugs or alcohol. Consider what Islam does to a family member who changes his faith. When my family learned I had converted to Christianity, my brother made his last call to me – through my wife. "I know what your husband is doing against Islam; I also know where you live." My father's threats came at odd hours of the night – "You will die by shooting."

Blood may be thicker than water, but for those who leave Islam, blood is spilled as easily as water.

I had written to a Christian lawyer in Jerusalem, Jonathan Kuttab, regarding a case I had to resolve back home, and I received this reply: "If you ever come back, not only will you lose your property, but your son will be taken as well, since in Islamic law, he was born Muslim." In Arabic, the term is "murtadd fitri," which means an apostate who was born to Muslim parents. Islam allows no rights whatsoever to those who were born Muslim and then leave the faith – including the right to life. So I was warned.

Chapter 2
Islamic Fundamentalism
Definition, Goals & Psychology

DEFINITION

In this chapter I will provide what I believe is the most important part of any practical study of Muslims and Jihad, the definition of Islamic fundamentalism. After years of analyzing my life and the web of Islamic terror, I have concluded that Islamic Terrorism is:

> *Religious conditioning taught to Muslim masses, by using allusions of misery, historic manipulation, and illusion of the virtues of a distant past by continual reflection on glory days long ago, in order to convert masses into angry, pride-filled, remorseless killers and seekers of salvation by death. The goal is to intimidate non-Muslims by fear and threats, in order to re-establish a utopian theocratic world order in which Islam and Muslims are dominant and all non-Muslims are subservient. This conditioning becomes the sole focus of both the spiritual leaders, and the followers in every aspect of their daily lives.*

That's what Islamic fundamentalism is, and you will find that everything in this dangerous movement fits within that definition. It's crucial to keep that definition in mind. It will help you when you watch news media coverage, and you will be able to understand the mindset.

GOALS

A Jihadist's view breaks the world into two classes, the Muslim class and the non-Muslim class, which, in turn, will survive under the rule of Islam, paying a jizzieh tax (protection money). The non-Muslims, called Dhimmi, are relegated to second-class non-citizens, lacking any legal or human rights, living nearly as slaves for the benefit of Muslim survival.

This Muslim utopia has already occurred in history, only not exactly as described by Islamic anals. For the Jihadists today the goal is to regain the glory days of the 7th Century when, following the establishment of a government under The Caliph, who is viewed as the Vicar of Muhammad on earth, Arab Muslim armies conquered Syria, Palestine, and Mesopotamia. They imposed their rule over the indigenous Christian Armenians, Arameans, Assyrians, Syriacs, Chaldeans, and Jews.

Coptic Christian Egypt, Nubian Northern Sudan, Berber Cyrenaica (Libya), and Numedia (Algeria) were also conquered at that time, followed by Spain, Southern France, and Sicily. The Arab Muslim armies also invaded Persia and Central Asia, reaching as far as India. In all of these lands, an Islamic state was established against the will of the native populations and imposed by Arab governors under the Caliph.

Today, the same dreams are coming back, not only to re-conquer these lands but the whole globe.

We have seen the beginning of that war: Hezbollah's initial trigger of the War with Israel in July 2006; The UN Nuclear crisis with the Ahmedinijad regime; the concerns of Tehran and Damascus; the fruitless democracy experiment in Iraq; Islamic conflicts in Afghanistan, Palestine, Iraq, Egypt's Muslim brotherhood, Algeria, Lebanon, Chechnya and Somalia. Jihad militancy exists in India, the Southern Philippines, Indonesia and Southern Thailand.

This is a huge problem.

PSYCHOLOGY – PROFILING

Christopher Reuter's "expert" research on suicide bombing challenges us to rethink our response to the mindset behind a human bomb. Reuter debunks several myths by providing well-documented qualitative data, drawn from eight years of interviews with the families and organizations behind Islamic-motivated "martyrs" in the Middle East. (Christopher Reuter, *My Life is a Weapon: A Modern History of Suicide Bombing,* [English-Language translation and abridgment], New Jersey, Princeton University Press, 2004)

Reuter's research reveals that a "terrorist profile" does not exist, a conclusion which applies even more to suicide bombers, especially in the Middle East:

> *The original assumption – that suicide bombers were exclusively isolated, young, poor, ultra-religious people with no prospects – might have applied in some degree to the first attackers. But nowadays "none of this is right anymore," admits Ephrahim Kam, a retired major of the Israeli military secret service who heads the Jaffe Center for Strategic Studies in Tel Aviv.* (p. 109)

Thus, according to Reuter, trying to pick the suicide bomber in the crowd is a naïve and futile task. Reuter mentions the biographies of dozens of suicide bombers which confirm that there is no longer any way to draw a reasonable profile of today's would-be attacker (p. 109). He cites psychologist Ariel Merari of Tel Aviv University, who puts forth the argument that the more you look into these biographies, the more the expected factors, such as poverty or loneliness, are dismissed as playing any major role in determining the profile of a suicide bomber. The truth is, suicide bombers come from poor and wealthy families, from among the working class and university graduates.

While I agree that profiling based on biographies is fruitless, I must stress that visual profiling based on observation, in airports and public areas, is crucial. The perception of death as an alternative and a more attractive state-of-being is the main attraction promoted by religious and educational groups, which act as facilitators of the Jihad agenda. The suicidal act often involves a variety of disassociated processes, such as narrowing of vision, altered states of attention, absorption in the act, detachment from feelings and the body, semi-hypnotic ecstasy, and the self-surrendering sense of merging with a transcendental power. I know this to be true, since it is exactly what I experienced during my bomb operation. I was disconnected from reality.

Some of these processes are actually induced into the state of mind of the shaheed-to-be. In fact, many suicide operations were stopped as a result of bus drivers in Israel not allowing certain passangers to board the bus. The bus drivers had been trained on terrorism awareness and avoided passengers who were later caught with suicide belts.

Reuter concludes that the key motivating factor behind Palestinian suicide bombers is not poverty nor even religious fanaticism but rather, their sense of powerlessness – "the thwarting of these expectations" (p. 10); expectations for their own land, their own state, their independence and freedom. For Reuter, a terrorist mind is far from crazy or fanatical. Suicide bombers exhibit "a calculated rationality which has concluded that armed struggle is the only way to get back their dignity and independence." (p. 110)

ONLY MUSLIMS DO IT

Yet, even Reuter, who debunked some Western assumptions about suicide bombers, still doesn't get it himself. If Reuter's analysis is correct, that the bombers commit suicide as a result of expectations for a homeland, then where are the Palestinian Christian suicide bombers? They simply do not exist. Christians live in Iraq, where the desire is to get rid of the American occupation, yet only Muslim Iraqis, and Muslims from surrounding countries, commit suicide bombings.

One might claim that Christians, in general, are not as accustomed to terrorism as Muslims. However, one of the strongest, active terror organizations in the world is The PFLP (Popular Front to Liberate Palestine), which grew out of the Harakat al-Qawmiyyin al-Arab, or Arab Nationalist Movement (ANM), and was founded in 1953 by Dr. George Habash, a Palestinian Christian. Whereas Hamas completely dominates the slums of Gaza, Qalqilya, and Hebron; the PFLP has its roots among the urban middle class, mostly Christians, like their founder George Habash, who fear Islamization of the Palestinians and the erasure of the rights of minorities within a Hamas theocracy.

The PFLP was responsible for several suicide bombings, yet in each case they used Muslims to carry out the missions. The bombing in a pizzeria in Karnei Shomron was carried out by Sadak Ahad Abdel-Haq of Qalqilya, a Muslim. The bombings in Ariel, Netanya market, and a bus station in Geha Junction in Petah Tikva were all committed by Muslim suicide bombers.

Consider that, in our time, every martyrdom operation committed by Palestinians, or by people of any nation, is carried out by Muslims not Christians, Buddhists, Hindus, or even atheists. This point alone should debunk all the Western analyses of suicide bombers who attribute other reasons than Islamic fundamentalist beliefs.

WHY SUICIDE?

There is a twofold purpose of a suicide bomber. First, he or she is a guided missile, and second, he or she transits from this world to the next instantly, without judgment, and with an assurance of salvation. This second purpose is evident in every video clip of martyrs, every statement made by clerics regarding suicide, and the volumes written in the Hadith interpretation of Allah's edicts regarding Jihad.

While Reuter fails to show the definite religious reasons; he argues that martyrdom operations distort Islamic texts. His conclusion that the Islamic text was distorted is obviously the point of view of a Westerner who lacks understanding of Islam.

The "shaheed," Fida'e sacrificial lamb, in Islam, is a warrior who sacrifices himself for a religious holy war (Jihad) or national cause. He or she is ready to fight the enemy, even if death is certain. If Reuter is correct, then *all* the wars of early Islam from the founding father, the prophet Muhammad himself, were the result of textual twisting. It would further mean that all of the documented history in Islam is, in reality, legends of acts of heroism and were falsely canonized in the Islamic tradition.

In fact, such conclusions are an insult to anyone's intelligence. Growing up as a Muslim, I learned several examples of martyrdom operations. A popular historical narrative of the Mu'ta battle, dispatched by the prophet Muhammad himself, tells the story of 3,000 Muslim soldiers who opposed 100,000 Byzantine soldiers. Ja'far Ben Abi Talib, the prophet's cousin, took over command and raced onto the battle-field alone, seeking martyrdom, and his right hand was cut off. He raised the flag he was carrying with his remaining left hand, but his left hand was then cut off too. He continued holding the flag with the stumps of his hands until his body was sliced in two. Fifty staves were later found in his body, and not one of them was in his back. Muhammad called him Ja'far Al-Tayyar, "the flying Ja'far," because Allah gave him two wings in heaven, replacing his two amputated hands. (Battle of Mu'tah, Wikipedia.org)

Reuter concludes that Jihadists use "Words of Mass Distortion" and "are formed by radicalizing the fundamentals of a religion or ideology."

His solution to the problem is to simply wait out the process:

> The moral dictatorship turned inspired believers into a jaded, disgusted, and fed-up populace. The Khomeini era's praise for, and popular acceptance of, martyrdom was beaten down not by military means – the preferred (and not terribly successful) method of Israel and the United States vis-à-vis their Palestinian and al-Qaeda Jihadist foes – but by the Islamic state's own limitations and contra-dictions (p. 172).

Yet, while we await this turnaround, Iran could have a nuclear arsenal, which, like Hitler, could cause the death of millions. If that happens, the Reuters of this world will be the first to call on Israel and the United States to intervene – militarily.

Reuter's assessment that the "thwarting of these expectations for their own land, their own state, their independence and freedom," (p. 10) doesn't account for all of the martyrdom operations from Algeria to the Philippines, from Tanzania to Central Asia and from Europe to America. Are they all a result of the Muslims' desire to gain independence?

Indeed, they want to establish an Islamic state across the whole globe.

They are not merely interested in killing Zionist occupiers of "Palestine." They also pursue what they call, the global war on international Zionism. In the Jihadist view, the international Zionist movement con-trols all evil, from the Congress to Hollywood. Muslims attribute their calamities and failures to international Zionism. Islamists everywhere are unified by the idea that there is a huge global conspiracy by the Jews aimed at eradicating Islam from the face of the earth.

Al-Watan, November 18, 2003
In Arabic: "Oh, the best of all nations,"
depicting Israel on top of the U.S. and
death is under both of them.

Al-Watan, November 8, 2003
In Arabic: "The European Survey" showing how Zionism
seems to choke the world.

Chapter 3
The Psychological Conditioning

MYTH VS. FACT

Myth – Terrorists are Dysfunctional and Live Isolated Lives

In my extensive review of the Western analysis of terrorists, I have found certain flaws. In general, Western psychologists believe that terrorists are usually members of cults which are frequently located in isolated environments.

This is not the case with Islamic terrorists.

The other error of Western analysts is that they believe that those who join these groups agree to live in these isolated environments, in order to make it easier for them to give up membership in any of their previous group affiliations, often including their families.

In Islamic terrorism, usually the culture and family support the activity, as you will see in this study. Analysts also assert that "it appears that terrorist group joiners from dysfunctional family backgrounds are particularly susceptible to the seductive messages of charismatic leaders." (Anthony Stahelski, Ph.D., *Terrorists Are Made, Not Born,* March 2004)

It is true that terrorist leaders usually request and receive unquestioning obedience from their followers. Yet, in the Middle East, the followers are conditioned in religious and educational institutions, and followers have the support of their society. In Islam, when science conflicts with religion, religion always takes precedence, as the text is reanalyzed to fit science. Psychologists in the Palestinian areas would be better off supporting the Jihadists rather than lose their jobs, or lives.

However, the more I study the Western psycho-analysis of terrorism, the more I find the need to correct much of what I read. Here is but one argument:

> The basic premise of the frustration-aggression (FA) hypothesis is two-fold: (1) Aggression is always produced by frustration, and (2) Frustration always produces aggression. (Randy Borum, Psychology of Terrorism I, 2004)

Yet, when it comes to Islamic fundamentalism, Randy Borum should add that most of their "frustration" is not real but superficial. The Islamic frustration is without longsuffering, justified reasons, or reasonable goals.

Based on the case examples shared in this book, one should realize that in the Muslim fundamentalist mind, the perceived frustration is often times self-created by crafty manipulations of facts and simplistic analysis of social problems. This can be found at all levels of education within the Islamic society in which terrorists-to-be live.

Also, the induced frustration in terrorist societies is, at times, caused by legitimate reasons – poverty, joblessness, and hopelessness. Yet, instead of directing the blame on the real culprit, which is usually the bad decisions made by national leadership, a collective accusation is made about a perceived enemy, anyone else but the jihadist society itself.

Jihadist ideologies are considered supreme. This, in itself, is not the main problem. However, the difference between Judeo-Christian cultures and Islamic cultures is that questioning religious edicts in most Muslim societies is illegal and considered sacrilege, but in the West, we are free to question religious edicts and even cancel them altogether.

In terrorist societies, questioning the ideology is not accepted or expected from followers. My Islamic studies teacher, Naim Ayyad, would always quote Muhammad's words: "Allah hated questions." Questioners can be viewed as traitors because the actions of terrorists are based on a subjective interpretation of the world that surrounds them, rather than an understanding of objective reality. Perceptions of the political and social environment are filtered through beliefs and attitudes that reflect history and faith. Usually, these beliefs are handed down by popular teachers and leaders, who become the welcoming father figure, and the leader's group provides a close-knit family atmosphere. In the Middle East, groups follow certain clergy, sect, or tribe.

Researchers have generally concluded that most terrorists are not initially psychopaths. (Andrew Silke, "Cheshire-Cat Logic: The Recurring Theme of Terrorist Abnormality in Psychological Research," *Psychology, Crime and Law,* Vol. 4, pp. 51–59) Most terrorists are not obviously or consistently mentally ill. (Martha Crenshaw, "The Psychology of Terrorism: An Agenda for the 21st Century," *Political Psychology,* Vol. 21, No. 2, June 2000, pp. 405 – 420) While this is a true and valid argument, former C.I.A psychiatrist, Jerrold Post, built on the earlier models that sought to explain terrorism as a form of psychopathology or personality defect. He argued that two different forms of dysfunction produced two different patterns of terrorist behavior. The first type was the Anarchic-ideologue. These individuals were hypothesized to have come from severely dysfunctional families, where they likely had suffered severe abuse or maltreatment, leading them to have hostile feelings toward their parents. (Randy Borum, *Psychology of Terrorism I,* from Jerrold Post, 2004, Chief Scientist, Political Psychology, Notes on a psychodynamic theory of terrorist behaviour. *Terrorism,* 7, pp. 241-256)

One could easily argue that such an opinion lacks validity. The majority of Muslim terrorists receive the blessings of their parents and record their thoughts and deeds to be aired on public media, in order to encourage other parents to give their children to martyrdom. I myself would obtain the doses of religious martyrdom instructions, via tape cassettes of Abdul-Hamid Kishk from my own father, or I could have obtained other recorded sermons everywhere in my community, abroad, and even in the U.S. The tapes contained religious incantations of glory days when Islam was triumphant, along with instructions to the mujahideen on martyrdom. These tapes are usually sold every-where in Muslim communities worldwide. Video tapes were sold openly in Muslim and Arab stores in the U.S. Sales have been cut down drastically since 9/11, yet you can still listen to them online. Try, http://audio.islamweb.net and access:

http://audio.islamweb.net/audio/index.php?page=lecview&sid=374& read=0

I recall the tapes sent to me by my own father, recordings of Abdul-Hamid Kishk of Egypt's Muslim Brotherhood. These tapes would contain repetitions:

Oh Allah...Oh Allah...Oh Allah

Give victory to Islam and Muslims

(repeated many times)

May we taste martyrdom...

Where art thou Oh Umar

Then the call for Jihad *Wa-Islamah* – Oh Islam.

This is the call to the days in which Islam ruled the ancient world. Everything you will find in every sermon, will fit our definition of Islamic fundamentalism.

You will find that the titles of these tapes are deceptive – "The Importance for Believers in Understanding Their Faith," or "Obedience to Allah and His Prophet," and "Judgment of Making Fun of Islam."

However, if you understood Arabic and listened to these tapes, you would find that they're all about Jihad – the desire for the glory days, and how Muslims need to reclaim what was lost, by declaring Jihad war. Of course, the punishment for anyone who makes fun of the faith is execution, without the right of burial in a Muslim cemetery or prayers by the community. He or she is excommunicated in death and even after death.

The sermons all have one thing in common, the repetition of the glory days of Umr bin Al-Khattab, Muhammad's companion, who invaded Jerusalem and took it. He was the one who established the Umar Declaration, which made non-Muslims subservient dhimmis, (lower class non-citizens) who were required to pay the jizzieh tax, a tribute to Islam.

The sermons are poetic. The instructions and teachings rhyme and are spoken in a combination of soft, loud, piercing, and screaming voices, designed to induce fear in the unbeliever and comfort for the believer. They are void of intellectual dialogue or critical exchange. You would never hear, "Come now, let us reason together, says the Lord." (The Bible, Isaiah 1:18) There is no reasoning by question or by doubt. Every teaching is considered to be holy and unquestionably true. In order to get into the Jihadist mind, I present a typical poetic sermon for a Muslim fundamentalist.

In a poem entitled "Jihad Warrior," a Jihadist writes regarding his piety:

> People look at him, not knowing him for who he really is.
> His true soul invisible to all but Allah.
> His deeds known to none but the One above.
> By night when all have gone home
> Does he clean the toilets and scrub the floors of the Masaajid (mosques)
> By day does he work for his family with his hands
> Halal money to feed Halal to the little mouths
> Never does a person come to him and not go away in smiles.
> Gentle and loving is he to the children as they run towards him
> Screaming in delight.
> He shares the silence of the Fuqara' (poor)
> And is no stranger to the troubles of the Yateem (orphans).
> Unbeknownst to him, Allah said:
> "I love my servant."
> And thereupon Jibrael called out to the creation:
> "Love him"
> And the creation loves him.
> Little does he know.
> He held tightly to his Deen (faith) when it was
> Like a piece of shining gold.
> He held it even tighter when it became

Like a piece of burning hot coal.

Yet, there is another side to him besides his gentleness, meekness, and love during the day:

At night does he fight sleep
And arises from his warm bed
In the midst of Tahajjud prayers in tears
Does he call out unto his Lord:
"Allahummar zuqni Shahadah!" (Allah give me martyrdom)

Martyrdom is his main focus and to die for Allah in Jihad becomes the utmost aspiration in his life. Yet, he must always come up with perceived Muslim suffering to justify Jihad:

Defender of the Nisaa' (women)
Protector of the oppressed
Supporter of the weak

He would never see how Muslims oppress women, or the root causes of their weakness. Neither does he ever examine the problems that are from within. To him, his oppression comes from external forces. He fails to see that he plunges his people back towards the middle ages. He fails to move forward in a modern world.

Al-Imad alDeen (Guardian of the Quran)
His heart has no space for nifaaq or riyaa (hypocrisy)
Jealousy or hate
He knows no hate or bias against any Believer anywhere.

Jihadists would never consider that their hatred of the West is a result of jealousy. They see that Muslim nations have not gained dominance, and instead of emulating the West, they hate it and declare war against it. The reality is that they are quite the opposite of what they claim. Instead of looking forward and modernizing, they look back towards the glory days of Islamic victories in battle. The Jihadist transformed Arabia into an Islamic state:

He was present at Badr battle
Felling the Unbelieving criminals

Alongside the Rasulallah (prophet of Allah)

At Uhud battle he stood his ground on the mountain

Raining arrows of death down on Khalid's charge.

He was there at Mutah when the three commanders fell one by one

'Till Saifullah led the Believers back to safety

He was there right next to his brother Al'Barra

In the Garden of Death as they fought the Liar's army

To open the gates of that bloody oasis.

He (the Jihadist) ruled over the non-Arabs. Yet he would never call this aggression, occupation, or even war. The need to force the spreading of Islam is not war *(harb)*, a word that is used only to describe the use of force by non-Muslims. Islamic wars are not *war*, but acts of "opening" the world to Islam. In this case, the jihadist in reality liberated Persia:

He was there with Sa'id as they crossed the river

To face the Persians across the vast expanse.

His heart was firm as the horses tread above the water.

Saying nothing but "Husbunallahu waNa'mal Wakeel" (we trust in Allah)

In his mind he also "liberated," not occupied, Spain for Islam, as Tariq bin Ziyad declared to his army, when he burned the ships after crossing the Gibraltar. *"O People! There is nowhere to run away! The sea is behind you, and the enemy in front of you: There is nothing for you, by God, except only sincerity and patience."* (as recounted by al-Maqqari). By this the **Opening of Andalusia** commenced on 28th Ramadhan 92 Hijri. So the Jihadist poem proudly exclaims:

He was there as Commander Tariq bin Ziyad ordered the boats to be burned

Fighting the Disbelieving Goths fearlessly

And marched past the Pyrenees to establish the banner of Islam.

He was the first in the smoky pack as Bin Qasim and the others poured down

The mountain slopes, racing towards death with a smile on his face

The Jihadist immitates Salah al-Diin al-Ayyoubi (Saladin from Kurdistan) when he conquered the crusaders in the battle of Hittin, throwing them back to Europe, then frees Jerusalem:

He avenged his slain brethren at Hittin

For what the savage heathens did in 1099

And was there when Salahuddin (Saladin) opened the gates of Al-Quds (Jerusalem).

The famous Muslim cries for Jihad – "Wa Islamah" and "Wa Mu'tasimah" are the cries for heroism. Jihadists always refer to Kosovo where Muslims suffered by the Serbs. Yet, they would never see what Christians suffered in Serbia by the hands of Muslims. In this poem, the Jihadist refers to the glory days when Muslim *Khalifas* took up arms and dispatched a huge army to rescue just one woman who cried out for his support saying. *"Waa **Mu'tasimaah!**"* (i.e., "O ***Mu'tasim!*** Help me!").

Truly he was there on that rock

In the Valley of Ayn Jalut, yelling

"Wa Islamah! (O Islam) Wa Islamah! (O Islam) Ya Shababul Islam!! (O youth of Islam)"

As the Mameluke army smashed their way through the Mongol waves.

He was amongst the first to march out when the Muslimah (Muslim woman) was dishonored

She cried "Ya Mu'tasim where are you?!"

America, in the Jihadist view, is not America, but a re-incarnation of the Crusader's. The Jihadist mind-set is to have no guilt for the dead. They are remorseless killers:

He rode with the shababb ul-Islam (young Muslims) to detonate the Crusader army at Khobar Tower (Americans in Saudi Arabia)

To clear al-Jazirah (Arab Island), true to the command of the Rasul (prophet) as he lay on his deathbed

Anyone who is not Muslim is depicted as Kaffer (unbeliever) treated as Haram (non-Kosher) dogs or pigs:

Indeed, Shababbul-Jannah (Youth of Heaven), and not cowards as the Kuffar (unbelievers) accuse

When his brother Jibrael Abu-Adam from Atlanta

Fell on the streets of Kashmir, he was there to avenge him

Sending a deadly force of lead bullets back at the filthy Hindu dogs.

He went to Grozny once again to teach the Russian pigs

What it means to mess with the best.

You tangle with the Mujahideen and off you go to that eternal-burning place

He held down the Kuffar (unbelievers) as his brother Abu Maryam went to slay that Philippine dog.

Laughing his way through the blizzard of bullets, crying Allahu-Akbar, Allahu-Akbar, Allahu-Akbar.

Jihadists are die-hard anti-Semites.

He'll return to Philistine (Palestine) once again, that Ancient Land

Running to the Gate of Ludd,

To see none other than Ibn Maryam slay that Yahuudi (Jew) Liar.

For each bullet he takes, he sends back a dozen more.

With each Kuffar that he slays, he knows that

Another one of the Believing women will not be humiliated

Another one of his Muslim brothers will not be shot in front of his little ones.

In the end of his poem – the grand finale – is his martyrdom, and it comes without pain or anguish. By the first drop of his blood, he is redeemed, sinless, and obtains salvation. He then enters the abode Allah prepared for him, with all the wordly pleasures he could not have:

Allah decides which bullet has his name on it

He feels it not as at it goes deep into his flesh

As he falls, with that joyous smile on his face

"La Ilaha Ilallah Muhammad arRasulallah! Allah Akbar!

(There is no god but Allah, and Muhammad is Allah's messenger)

Look in the sky! Look what I can see! Allah Akbar!"

Even before the first drop of that fresh blood falls
Allah with His Mercy wipes the slate clean
The angels bearing his soul straight to Al-Firdaus (heaven)
His soul, like the inside of green birds,
Glides around the 'Arsh (Throne) as it pleases.
On that big Day, when his blood, still fresh
Smelling as sweet as the musk of Jannah,
Will flow from his wounds, badges of honor
That none will fail to recognize the warrior
On that Day, when he shall have no fear nor shall he grieve
A Day on which the Book in his Right hand shall be heavy
As the angels send their salutations
On the Day when the Hur al'Ayn (virgins) give him the sweet drink
From Al-Kawthar River with their own soft hands,
laughing and bursting with pleasure
Indeed, this and more is what he bargained for
As he sold the World for that which was better.
And on this day verily does he receive his Rank.
"…the Prophets, the Siddiqûn, the Martyrs, and the righteous. And how excellent these companions are!" (Quran 4:69)
Who is he?
He is the fighting spirit of Iman (faith) that is in all Mujahideen (Jihad warrior)
He was, and is present, inside the hearts of all the Shaheed (martyrs).

~ The End ~

Terrorist ideologies tend to provide a set of beliefs that justify and mandate certain behaviors. Those beliefs are regarded as absolute, and the behaviors are seen as serving a meaningful cause. Anyone who questions or doubts the cause is considered a traitor. The Umma (Muslim Nation) are the defenders of the cause of Allah, to which all must submit and obey. In other words, the Muslim is not only obliged to enforce civil laws to which Western societies are accustomed, but they also must enforce the Islamic moral code – the way everyone dresses, the times to pray, business hours, dietary laws. Every aspect of life in the society must adhere to the Sharia Islamic law.

Some suppose that Muslim terrorists are not strictly interested in material rewards. However, the rewards of the here and the life ever after are all carnal and material.

Martha Crenshaw (1985), for example, suggests that there are at least four categories of motivation among terrorists: (1) the opportunity for action, (2) the need to belong, (3) the desire for social status, and (4) the acquisition of material reward.

The genius of Islamic fundamentalism is that the offer for material reward is not only obtained on earth but also in heaven. It's mind-boggling to Westerners that Muslim people are willing to pay so much when their leaders offer nothing in return. But consider that eternal lusts and carnal desires can be pursued in the life after death.

Such a system was necessary because, in the "glory days" of Islam, there was not much to offer except booty if the battles were won or an after-life if the battles were lost. The system worked and recruited a lot of terrorists indeed.

WHAT IS FORBIDDEN ON EARTH
IS PERMISSIBLE IN HEAVEN

What the Muslims complain about with the West – being run by international Zionism, it's Hollywood mentality and sexual licentiousness – all seems to exist in abundance within the Muslim paradise. Angels and (handsome) young boys as pearls well guarded (Quran 52:24), perpetual freshness (Quran 56:17) thou seest them, thou wouldst think them scattered pearls (Quran 76:19) rivers of wine (Quran 47:15) served with goblets filled at a gushing fountain, white and delicious to those who drink it. It will neither dull their senses nor befuddle them, (Quran 37:40-48) rivers of milk of which the taste never changes; a joy to those who drink; And rivers of honey pure and clear (Quran 47:15) bosomed virgins for companions: a truly overflowing cup (Quran 78:31), these virgins are bashful undefiled by man or demon.

Sexual enticements play an integral role in the recruitment of Jihadists. The late author and journalist Muhammad Galal Al-Kushk. Al-Kushk wrote:

> The men in Paradise have sexual relations not only with the women [who come from this world] and with 'the black-eyed,' but also with the serving boys." (Not to be crude, but it is stated) Al-Kushk also said, "In Paradise, a believer's penis is eternally erect. (Al-Quds Al-Arabi, London, May 11, 2001)

A Hamas youth leader in a Gaza refugee camp told Jack Kelley of USA Today that "most boys can't stop thinking about the virgins." (USA Today, June 26, 2001)

Sheikh Abd Al Fattah Jam'an speaking to Muslims in Palestine stated:

> What is waiting for the suicide bomber in paradise is a harem of beautiful virgins who are delicate and pure, esthetic, passive, with no personality or self or ego, whose only role is to sexually satisfy the shaheed and be ever ready to fulfill his desires. (The Jerusalem Post Internet Edition, 9,6,2001)

Some delights do not have to wait until paradise:

> Ibn Fahd asked Al-Hajjaj, "I have some slave girls who are better than my wives, but I do not desire that they should all become pregnant. Shall I do azl (withdrawal) with them?" Al-Hajjaj replied, "They are your fields of cultivation. If you wish to irrigate them do so, if not keep them dry." (Malik 362:1221)

There are many references to sex in the Quran pertaining to sexual entitlement which belong only to Muhammad:

> Forbidden to you also are married women, except those who are in your hand as slaves, this is the law of Allah for you.

And Sura: Confederates (al-Ahzab verse 50):

> O prophet; we allowed thee thy wives to whom thou hast paid their dowries, and the slaves whom thy right hand possesseth out of the booty which Allah hath granted thee, and the daughters of thy

uncle, and of thy maternal aunt, who fled with thee to Medina, and any believing woman who hath given herself up to the prophet, if the prophet desired to wed her, a privilege to thee above the rest of the faithful.

We had no problem with Muhammad taking advantage of this privilege. He married many wives and took several slave girls as the booty he collected from his victorious battles. We never knew how many wives he had, and that question was always a debatable issue for us. We could debate the numbers but never question the moral justifications. One of Muhammad's wives was taken from his own adopted son, Zaid, because Allah declared that she was to be given to the prophet. Others were Jewish captives, forced into slavery after Muhammad beheaded their husbands and families.

Banu Al-Mustaliq had a similar fate, as Muhammad's army lusted after their women and raped them:

We were lusting after women and chastity had become too hard for us, but we wanted to get the ransom money for our prisoners. Therefore, we wanted to use the 'azl' (Coitus Interruptus where the man withdraws before ejaculating). We asked the Prophet about it and he said:

"You are not under any obligation to stop yourselves from doing it like that..." Later on the women and children were given for ransom to their envoys. They all went away to their country and not one wanted to stay although they had the choice...(Narrated Abu Burda, Volume 9, Book 84, No. 58)

Abu Sa'id al-Khudri said:

The Apostle of Allah sent a military expedition to Awtas at the battle of Hunain. They met their enemy and fought with them. They defeated them and took them captives. Some of the Companions of the Apostle of Allah were reluctant to have intercourse with the female captives in the presence of their husbands who were unbelievers.

Therefore, Allah, the Exalted, sent down the Quranic verse: 'And all married women are forbidden unto you save those (captives) whom your right hand possesses.' (Narrated Anas Bin Malik, Hadith Sahih Bukhari Vol. 1 No. 387)

The Quran and Muhammad confirms:

Thus (shall it be), and We will wed them with Houris, pure, beautiful ones. (The Evident Smoke, 44:54 Shakir, Shakir, M. H., The Quran, Tahrike Tarsile Quran, Inc, Elmhurst, NY, 1993)

They shall recline on couches lined with thick brocade, and within reach will hang the fruits of both gardens...Therein are bashful virgins whom neither man nor jinnee will have touched (...with sexual intercourse) before...Virgins as fair as corals and rubies. (The Beneficent, 55:54-58 Dawood, Dawood, N. J., "The Koran," Penguin, London, England, 1995)

In each there shall be virgins chaste and fair...Dark eyed virgins sheltered in their tents whom neither man nor jinnee would have touched before. They shall recline on green cushions and fine carpets...(Quran, *The Beneficent,* 55:70-77)

We created the Houris and made them virgins, loving companions for those of the right hand...That Which is Coming," (Quran, 56:36)

As for the righteous, they shall surely triumph. Theirs shall be gardens and vineyards, and high-bosomed virgins for companions: a truly overflowing cup. (The Tidings, 78:31-33 Dawood)

The very same Quran and Sunna which served as the rules of conduct in the seventh century remain the basis for Islamic law today, although many Muslim countries have banned such laws as a result of Western inquisitions. Today, the cry of the Muslim fundamentalist is to reinstitute them, including slavery:

A slave is the property of his or her master. He or She is subject to the master's power, insomuch that if a master should kill his slave he is not liable to retaliation. With female slaves a master has the 'mulk-i-moot'at', or right of enjoyment, and his children by them, when acknowledged, have the same rights and privileges as his children by his wives. A slave is incompetent to anything that implies the exercise of authority over others. Hence a slave cannot be a witness, a judge, an executor or guardian to any but his/her master and his/her children. A slave cannot inherit from anyone, and a bequest to him is a bequest to his or her master. (p. 367, *Digest of Islamic Law*, N. Baillie, Premier Book House, Pakistan).

You might ask how people can believe this. The Muslim attitude towards sex, though bizarre, is a stubborn reality that eludes many in the modern, secular West.

Terry Mattingly – a syndicated religion columnist, and scholar of media and religion at Palm Beach Atlantic College – explains, "If your world-view is essentially materialist, then to be 'real' something has to present itself in a form that makes sense in a laboratory, or on Wall Street, or in the New Hampshire primary, and anything that can't be explained within those templates doesn't count. Thus we can't seem to understand why people behave in ways that don't serve their self-interest." (National Review Online, April 11, 2002)

Boston University's Landes agrees, saying that the American cultural elite tend to disdain religion, although it is a major factor in modern history.

Landes explains:

"When 9/11 happened, one of the questions people asked was, 'Is it religious, or is it political?' People are more comfortable explaining it as politics. The very fact that people asked that question shows how little they understand.

"Since September 11, we have all been brought to the point of recognizing the pervasive power of religions to shape all kinds of events," Weber adds. "We are dealing with ancient religious convictions and memories, and they are driving forces in the modern world. The secular press just doesn't get it, but it seems to me there's no other way to understand this." (National Review Online, April 11, 2002)

THE PHASES

Terrorists are completely dependent on individuals who will do whatever it takes to retain membership in the group. The Middle East encourages this dependency because everyone there relies on their tribal, organizational, and religious affiliation. Most Westerners think that terrorist conditioning takes place in isolated environments, but that is not the case. Although terrorist conditioning is similar to that of a cult, it's more like Nazi Germany, where the German masses were conditioned in public squares, the boy scouts, and open arenas.

Anthony Stahelski in Terrorists Are Made, Not Born, proposes five phases of recruitment:

- Phase 1 – Depluralization: stripping away all other group member identities

- Phase 2 – Self-deindividuation: stripping away each member's personal identity

- Phase 3 – Other-deindividuation: stripping away the personal identities of enemies

- Phase 4 – Dehumanization: identifying enemies as subhuman or nonhuman

- Phase 5 – Demonization: identifying enemies as evil

(Anthony Stahelski, *Terrorists Are Made, Not Born, The Five Phases of Social-Psychological Conditioning*, August 21, 2005)

Stahelski argues that "studies of cults demonstrate that many cults cease to exist once the original founder or leader has been somehow removed from the group."

While this paradigm would certainly apply to small cult groups in the West, it would be ludicrous to presume that Osama bin Laden's death would eliminate al-Qaeda or that Khomeni's death would end the Iranian Revolution. It is doubtful that Nazism ended as a result of Hitler's death. If Hitler had died suddenly or by an assassination, Nazism would still have flourished, since many in the Nazi party would still have allowed the legend to continue. Nazism ended in Germany when Nazis witnessed the futility and falsehood of their ideology. This realization came about after the massive destruction of Dresden, at which point the Nazis realized they were not a perfect, indestructible, invincible, superior race.

Chapter 4
Psychological Motives

SALVATION

Jihadism is a message of salvation. For one to die in the cause of Allah is an assurance of salvation and entry to paradise. It's a corruption of Christian dogma. The difference is that the *shaheed* (Martyr) can atone for sin. A martyr in Islam can be an intercessor for 70 members of his or her family.

Dying in Jihad is the ultimate way to ensure one receives instant passage of one's soul to paradise.

In order to become a martyr *(shaheed)*, one must be killed, thereby obtaining an assurance for salvation. It may appear that Christianity and Islam have similarities – both accept that they need a death for salvation. However, the major difference is that Christians understand that salvation comes from the death of one man, Jesus Christ, so that whoever believes in and accepts Him obtains salvation. Islam rejects the idea that Christ died for all humanity. It's not the death of Christ that sends you to heaven, but your own death. That, or you better work to obtain enough merit to outweigh your sins. But how much merit do you need? This is the dilemma that confounds Muslims.

There is one interesting similarity between the Islamic and Christian concepts of salvation. A suicide martyr is called "Fida'e," which is similar to the word Fidyeh (sacrificial lamb), used in Christian doctrine.

The Islamic salvation occurs upon death and with the first drop of blood spilt:

> *A martyr has six bounties: He will be forgiven with the first drop of his blood that is spilt; He will see his place in paradise (at the time of death); He will be saved from the 'great horror' (on the day of judgment); A crown of dignity will be placed on his head, which contains many corundum's, each one being more precious than this life and all that it contains; He will have seventy-two Women of Paradise; And, he will be allowed to intercede for seventy of his family members (who would have otherwise gone to hell).* (Muhammad, the prophet of Islam, narrated by Al-Miqdaam Ibn Ma'di Karib, Tirmidhi & Ibn Maajah).

Allah in the Quran gives this assurance regarding salvation:

> *And never think of those who have been killed in the cause of Allah as dead. Rather, they are alive with their lord, receiving provision.* (Quran, Al-'Imraan: 169)

And to alleviate the thoughts of any pain:

> *The pain that a martyr feels at the time of death will be reduced so greatly that he will only feel as if he was stung by a mosquito. Abu Hurayrah narrated that the Prophet said: "A martyr only feels from the effect of being killed that which one would when being stung by a mosquito."* (Tirmidhi, Nasaa'i and others)

Martyrdom is, indeed, the highest aspiration of even the dwellers in heaven:

> *Anas bin Maalik, narrated that the Prophet said: "Nobody who enters Paradise would ever wish to return to this life again, even if he was to be given the whole world and everything in it – except for a martyr; for he would wish to return and get killed ten times due to the honour that he received (in Paradise)." and in another narration: "For what he finds as virtues of martyrdom."* (Al-Bukhari & Muslim)

As I mentioned in my example of my cousin Raed who was killed by the Israelis for the attempted bombing of Ben Yehuda Street, my Aunt Fatima passed out sweets to everyone. In this revived Islamic tradition, her son's death was treated as a wedding celebration. This is to be expected! She believed her son was in Paradise, in the arms of the seventy-two virgins!

The death announcements of martyrs in the Palestinian press are often full of joy and celebration. "Blessings will be accepted immediately after the burial and until 10 p.m., at the home of the martyr's uncle," read one suicide bomber's death notice. (Al-Ayam [Palestinian Authority], July 21, 2001)

Twenty-two year-old Saeed Hotary was a Jordanian suicide bomber who lived in Qalqilya. Saeed's father, Hassan, told the Associated Press, "I am very happy and proud of what my son did and I hope that all the men of Palestine and Jordan would do the same." According to Saeed's brother, Saeed "was very religious since he was young; he prayed and fasted." (Middle East Media and Research Institute, or MEMRI, June 25, 2001)

"With great pride, the Palestinian Islamic Jihad marries the member of its military wing...the martyr and hero Yasser Al-Adhami, to 'the black-eyed'" read another. (Al-Istiqlal [Palestinian Authority], October 4, 2001)

The goal of Jihad is to gain salvation, as shown in the following story:

> A Bedouin came to the Prophet, accepted Islam and said: "I wish to migrate (to Madeenah)." So the Prophet asked some of his companions to take care of him. Then after a battle, the Muslims had gained some booty so the Prophet divided it and gave the Bedouin's share to some of his companions to look after, as the Bedouin was still at the rearguard. When the Bedouin returned, they gave him his share, so he asked them: "What is this?" they replied: "It is your share from the booty which the Prophet gave us to hold on to for you." So the Bedouin took the booty and went to the Prophet and asked: "What is this?" The Prophet answered, "Your share of the booty." The Bedouin said: "This is not why I believe in you and follow you; rather, I follow you so that I can get shot by an arrow right here, (and then he pointed to his throat) then die and enter Paradise." The Prophet said, "If you are sincere then Allah will grant you your wish." After a short while, fighting resumed and the Bedouins body was brought to the Prophet with an arrow in his throat at exactly the spot where he had pointed to the Prophet. Thereupon The Prophet

said, "He was sincere so Allah granted him his wish." Then using his own garment, the Prophet shrouded the Bedouin, prayed the funeral prayer over him and was heard by his companions to say during the prayer: "O Allah! This is your slave who migrated for your sake and was killed as a martyr – and I testify to this." Which testimony could ever be more honorable, sincere and truthful than this great one given by the Prophet?

Unlike Christian doctrine, which admonishes followers to present their body as a *living* sacrifice (Romans 12:1), Islam teaches an aspiration for death as an intricate part of its doctrine.

Some Westerners find it difficult to comprehend that Muslims aspire to die. So, they blame suicide bombings on poverty or human rights issues. But if poverty and human rights issues are the cause of suicide bombings, again we must ask, why do we never hear of a Palestinian Christian suicide martyr? After all, it is claimed that both suffer equally from the Israeli occupation.

The answer is that a traditional Christian is not raised on a doctrine of suicide bombings and death. Similarly, when I spoke at the University of South Florida, where professor Sami Al-Arian, (a suspect for terror involvement) taught, I received an objection when I presented my case as to what I thought were the true causes of terrorism. One unhappy professor raised his hand and disagreed and stated that poverty is the main reason which causes such frustration that men blow themselves up.

I felt someone else better give input to the discussion, so I asked the audience if there was anyone from India.

One student, with an obvious Indian accent, said, "I am from India."

I asked him if they had poverty in India.

He remarked, "We have lots of poverty in India, lots of poverty."

I asked, "Do you have a lot of suicide bombings as a result of poverty?"

His response was so timely, "No sir, we do not blow ourselves up as a result of poverty, but they sure come from Pakistan and blow us up." The crowd broke into laughter, and nothing further needed to be said.

The reason Westerners do not get this is simple, and I will repeat this throughout the course of this book – what Muslims say in English is usually different from what is said in Arabic. Arafat's words in English at Oslo were completely opposite from his words in Arabic. The same is true for all the Iranian ambassadors and such.

Also, expressions and agreements made with non-Muslims are usually considered by Muslims to be non-committal. When dealing with non-Muslims, Muslims tend to be evasive and are known for breaking contracts. Muhammad Sa'id Tantawi, sheikh and mufti of Egypt's famous al-Azhar Mosque and University, signed the Alexandrian Document in January 2002, with other religious leaders, both Christian and Jewish, stating, "We declare our commitment to ending the violence and bloodshed that denies the right to life and dignity." In 2003, he was unequivocal about the issue of suicide bombers. He declared that the Sharia (Islamic law) "rejects all attempts on human life, and in the name of the Sharia, we condemn all attacks on civilians." (Middle East Quarterly, Spring 2003)

Unaware of Tantawi's intent to dupe the non-Muslim committee, harsh rebuttals came from Egyptian-born Sheikh Yusuf al-Qaradawi, known as the theologian of the Muslim Brotherhood.

Dr. al-Qaradawi is described by the Muslim Council of Britain as the moderate umbrella group representing the majority of Muslims in Britain. He is "the most authoritative Islamic scholar in the world," and currently he is head of the Sunni studies faculty at Qatar University. Dr. al-Qaradawi declared, "I am astonished that some sheikhs deliver fatwas that betray jihadists, instead of supporting them and urging them to sacrifice and martyrdom." He argued that "Israeli society was completely military in its make-up and did not include any civilians ...How can the head of Al-Azhar incriminate jihadists who fight against aggressors? How can he consider these aggressors as innocent civilians?" (Ibid)

Westerners listen to what al-Qaradawi says in English. Speaking to the West, Qaradawi fiercely condemned the atrocities carried out by al-Qaeda and similar groups. He called upon Muslims to give blood to the victims of 9/11. He has denounced attacks on synagogues. He has repeatedly denounced hostage taking in Iraq and, as a consequence, has been publicly attacked by the terrorist leader Abu Musab al-Zarqawi. (Ken Livingston, published by Labour Left Briefing, Feb 2005, criticizing Thachell's *Islamic Conspiracy Theory*, quoting Qaradawi speaking to Channel 4 News, The Guardian Newspaper, City Hall)

Tantawi began to equivocate. He started issuing contradictory statements, finally declaring and effectively abrogating his earlier fatwa:

> *My words were clear…a man who blows himself [up] in the middle of enemy militants is a martyr, repeat, a martyr. What we do not condone is for someone to blow himself up in the middle of children or women. If he blows himself up in the middle of Israeli women enlisted in the army, then he is a martyr, since these women are fighters.* (Middle East Quarterly, Spring 2003).

Of course he can change his fatwa, renege on his deal, and abrogate his declarations. Such is permissible in Islam.

Yet, the evidence for approval of martyrdom operations comes from others than Al-Azhar. Former President of Al-Azhar University Ahmad 'Omar Hashem refers to suicide bombers in a Friday Sermon, April 23, 2004, Channel 1 Egyptian TV from a Sinai mosque:

> *We ask of our believing brothers not to forsake Jerusalem. We want our believing brothers to see their brothers in the occupied land, who have no support and no weapons, no money, and no (assistance) in the struggle. They have nothing except for their souls and their bodies, which they turn into a weapon and blow themselves up before the enemy, in defense of their honor and their stolen land. Shall we not stand by them as Mujahideen?* (MEMRI.ORG)

Professor Franz Rosenthal, the great American scholar of Islam, who fifty years ago translated Ibn Khaldoun's classic "Introduction To History," also wrote a seminal essay entitled "On Suicide in Islam" in 1946. In it he observed:

> *While the Qur'anic attitude toward suicide remains uncertain, the great authorities of the hadith leave no doubt as to the official attitude of Islam. In their opinion suicide is an unlawful act…On the*

other hand, death as the result of "suicidal" missions and of the desire of martyrdom occurs not infrequently, since death is considered highly commendable according to Muslim religious concepts. However, such cases are not suicides in the proper sense of the term. (Franz Rosenthal, "On Suicide in Islam," Journal of the American Oriental Society, 66 [1946], pp. 243, 256)

Muslim apologists argue rightly that both suicide and the taking of innocent lives are expressly and unequivocally forbidden in Islamic teaching. Dr. Eric Ormsby, Professor of Islamic Studies at McGill University, wrote a book review of Feisal Abdul Rauf's *"What's Right with Islam."* In the review, Dr. Ormsby stated: "That is, of course, if one kills oneself without purpose. Why else is there all this talk about dying in Jihad?"

In summary, in order to become a martyr, one must die, and by becoming a *shaheed,* one would have an *assurance* of his or her salvation. In Islam, the idea of Christ dying for all humanity is rejected and is one of the reasons why Islam was founded. This is the major difference between Muslim salvation and Christian salvation; it's not the death (and resurrection) of Christ which provides entrance into heaven, but your own death.

A martyr is a sacrificial lamb, a sacrifice to obtain salvation, which is evident from the cultural term given to a terrorist – "Fida'e," which literally means "the sacrifice." The Islamic argument against blood atonement is somewhat contradicted when it comes to the concept of martyrdom in Islam. Blood atonement is hardly absent in Islam. In fact, blood atonement makes it possible to intercede on the behalf of others, since the Shaheed takes on Christ-like abilities, interceding for seventy members of his or her family, who would otherwise have entered hell's fire. So, in order to alleviate the suffering in hell, at least one family member is encouraged to be given as a sacrifice.

Chapter 5

The Rewards

VIRGINS

Many in the West think that the concept of seventy-two virgins in heaven is only accepted by those who are Muslim radicals. Yet when one investigates the highest authority in the Muslim Sunni world from the Islamic education dept. at Al-Azhar University of Egypt, the answer, provided by the deputy director of Al-Azhar's Center for Islamic Studies, Sheikh Abd Al-Fattah Gam'an, reads:

> *The Quran tells us that in Paradise believers get the "black-eyed."*
> *As Allah has said, "And we will marry them to the "black-eyed." The*
> *black-eyed are white and delicate, and the black of their eyes is*
> *blacker than black and the white [of their eyes] is whiter than white.*
> *To describe their beauty and their great number, the Quran says*
> *that they are "like sapphire and pearls" (Al-Rahman 58) in their*
> *value, in their color, and in their purity. And it is said of them:*
> *"[They are] like well-protected pearls in shells" (Al-Waqi'a 23), that*
> *is, they are as pure as pearls in oysters, no hands have touched*
> *them, no dust or dirt adheres to them, and they are undamaged. It*
> *is further said: "They are like well-protected eggs" (Al-Safat 49),*
> *that is, their delicacy is as the delicacy of the membrane beneath*
> *the shell of an egg. Allah also said: "The 'black-eyed' are confined*
> *to pavilions" (Al-Rahman 70), that is, they are hidden within, saved*
> *for their husbands. (MEMRI.ORG, October 30, 2001, No. 74 '72*
> *Black-Eyed Virgins: A Muslim Debate on the Rewards of Martyrs)*

Most of the "black-eyed" were first created in Paradise, but some of them are women [who came to Paradise] from this world, and are obedient Muslims who observe the words of Allah: "We created them especially, and have made them virgins, loving, and equal in age." This means that when the women of this world are old and worn out, Allah creates them [anew] after their old age into virgins who are amiable to their husbands; "equal in age" means equal to one another in age. At the side of the Muslim in Paradise are his wives from this world, if they are among the dwellers in Paradise, along with the "black-eyed" of Paradise. (Ibid)

In sharp contrast to the promised sexual potency and sexual goods, there is the spiritual gift of closeness to god which is given to the shaheeds. Although the relationship between the transcendental transformation and closeness to god is not specified, the suicide act, in and of itself, symbolizes closeness to god. The shaheed immediately receives god's love, as death by suicide is a faithful service to god in purifying the world of evil. It is the culmination of a wish to satisfy god's will.

This is echoed in the words of Ahmed Yassin, the Hamas leader who inspired the suicide bombers:

Love of martyrdom is something deep in the heart. But these rewards are not in themselves the goal of the martyr. The aim is to win Allah's satisfaction. (From an interview of Yassin by N. Hassan, The New Yorker, November 19, 2001, pp. 36-41; see Stein, 2002)

Satisfying god brings not only forgiveness for all the sins, but it immediately puts the shaheed on god's paradisiacal lap and unites the shaheed with the cosmic power and with omnipotence. (Ibid)

SOCIAL AND FINANCIAL REWARDS

Recognition, materialistic benefits, and devotion are most important values in the cohesive, paternalistic Islamic family. Islamic sons and daughters feel a sense of commitment and responsibility with respect to their parents, brothers, and sisters. The children usually stay at home until they get married. Strong family ties extend beyond the immediate family to close and even distant relatives.

Women who dishonor the family by participating in improper sexual relations can still be put to death by male members of the family.

The suicide bomber brings many benefits to his or her family. Many suicide bombers come from poor families, and it is a well-known fact that these families are compensated financially. The families of the shaheeds also gain a special status, glorified with respect and honor. The religious advantage is that the shaheed can choose seventy people, usually family members, for whom god has promised a secured place in heaven. In addition to the financial, social, and spiritual benefits, the shaheed gains the love, idealization, and admiration of his mother, father, sisters, brothers, and also extended family members.

As we have seen from the media, the family members of the shaheed enthusiastically accept his or her shahada (testimony for Allah by giving one's life) after the fact. In some cases, it is even evident that they encourage the suicide in advance. Following are the words of shaheed Muhammad Farhat's mother:

> Jihad is a commandment imposed upon us. We must instill this idea in our sons' souls all the time...and this is what encouraged me to sacrifice Muhammad in Jihad for the sake of Allah. Because I love my son, I encouraged him to die a martyr's death for the sake of Allah. I sacrificed Muhammad as part of my obligation...This is an easy thing...I, as a mother, naturally encouraged the love of Jihad in the soul of Muhammad and in the souls of all my sons...[two days before the operation] he asked me to be photographed with him...I personally asked to make the film so as to remember. He spent the night with his friends...I was in contact with him and asked him about his morale. He told me he was very happy...But I worried and feared greatly that the operation would not succeed...[I] asked Allah to make his operation successful and give him the martyrdom...After the martyrdom [operation], my heart was peaceful about Muhammad. I encouraged all sons to die a martyr's death, and I wish this even for myself. After all this, I prepared myself to receive the body of my son, the pure shaheed, in order to look upon him one last time and accept the well-wishers who [came] to us in large numbers and participated in our joy over martyrdom...(Al-Sharq Al-Awsat, London, June 5, 2002)

Sacrificing children to and for god has its roots in the mythical study of the Quran, which tells us of a woman named Khansa, who fought in the battles of the prophet Muhammed and who encouraged her four young sons to sacrifice themselves along with her.

However, not all families act or respond in the same way, and there is some evidence that privately, the parents experience pain and anguish. In a few rare cases, we see the heart-breaking protests against the terrorist leaders who snap up the children for the Shahada. One father wrote:

> *From the blood of the wounded heart of a father who has lost what is most precious to him in the world, I turn to the leaders of the Palestinian factions, and at their head the leaders of Hamas and Islamic Jihad and their sheikhs, who use religious rulings and statements to urge more and more of the sons of Palestine to their deaths – knowing full well that sending young people to blow themselves up in the heart of Israel deters no enemy and liberates no land. On the contrary, [it] intensifies the aggression, and after every such operation, civilians are killed, homes are razed, and Palestinian cities and villages are reoccupied."* (Letter to the editor 'Who Gave Them the Legitimacy to Send Our Children to Their Deaths?' appearing in Al-Hayat, London, Ocober 1, 2002)

Suicide bombing has become a rite of passage closely akin to a cult, and a very popular one at that. Seventy percent of Palestinians approve of suicide bombings, and there is, apparently, a considerable waiting list for those eager to become martyrs. Without farewells to family or friend, the shaheed says some heroic last words for the videotape, which are followed by final prayers, and then a recorded sermon on martyrdom. Immediately after detonation, the shaheed is proclaimed a martyr; and this is announced in no uncertain terms from loudspeakers mounted on the very minarets of the mosques. Candy is distributed in the streets. Women passing by often greet the news, we are told, with joyous shrieks. Spontaneous marches set out for the bomber's house, which later becomes an impromptu youth center or social club. The house walls are instantly and almost entirely covered with slogans. "Shadi, we shall never forget you," one slogan reads. Another reads, "Shadi, enjoy paradise." Within hours, posters of the bomber go up on walls throughout the community. The poses on the posters are like those of Rambo, but with a Quran displayed alongside some extravagant weapon. Saddam Hussein would give $25,000 to a bomber's family – a king's ransom. (*Palestine/Israel and Suicide Bombers* – an Essay, by George Meegan, July 22, 2006)

"Martyrdom has become an ambition for our children," says Fadl Abu Hein, lecturer in psychology, Gaza. (The AP – Apr 30, 2002)

Chapter 6
Funding

While the subconscious believes in heaven, the conscious wants the yields in the here and now. As a result of Israel's "Operation Defensive Shield," new documents from Palestinian offices have been uncovered that directly link the Kingdom of Saudi Arabia with financial backing of terrorist attacks against Israel. The Saudis have repeatedly denied such connections. However, in the past, Saudi state television held a telethon for the families of "Palestinian martyrs" which raised over $100 million.

Responding to charges that Saudi Arabia was backing terrorism through the telethon, Adel Al-Jubeir, foreign policy adviser to Saudi Crown Prince Abdullah, told Fox television, "We have made it very clear in terms of where Saudi funding has gone to provide humanitarian assistance to the families who have suffered as a result of the Israeli occupation and the recent Israeli aggression." Adel Al-Jubeir added, "We do not support suicide bombers. Our objective is to put food on people's tables and medicine in their pharmacies." (Fox News, April 28, 2002).

As usual, aggressive behaviors are excused by pointing to "victims" of the "occupation." When it comes to the Israeli-Palestinian conflict, in almost every interview with an Arab apologist, you hear about the occupation. Yet, Saudi Arabia, with it's financial backing of suicide bombers is, in reality, murdering Palestinian youth.

Among the documents found in Tulkarm was a table from Saudi Arabia itemizing the tenth set of payments to the "Martyrs of the Al-Aqsa Intifada." The table details how $545,000 was allocated to 102 families. The logo at the top of the table reads, "Kingdom of Saudi Arabia, the Saudi Committee for Aid to the Al-Quds Intifada." This committee was established in the fall of 2000 under the Saudi Minister of the Interior, Prince Nayef bin 'Abd al-Aziz. Prince Nayef's organization was also responsible for collecting Saudi contributions during the April 11th Saudi state television telethon for Palestinian "martyrs." (*Washington Misled: Saudi Arabia's Financial Backing of Terrorists,* Jerusalem Center for Public Affairs, Jerusalem Issue Brief, Vol. 1, No. 23 May 6, 2002)

The table explains the type of activity that entitled a family to receive Saudi assistance.

- According to the document, Abd al-Fatah Muhammad Musalah Rashid, No. 15 on the list, died in a "martyrdom act." The individual involved was a member of the pro-Iranian Islamic Jihad and died in a car-bomb attack at Beit Lid on September 9, 2001, for which he was responsible. Eight Israelis were wounded.

- Abd al-Karim Amr Muhammad Abu Na'sa, who appears as No. 17 in the Saudi table, is described as having died in a "martyrdom act in Afula." This is a reference to his suicide bombing on behalf of Islamic Jihad and the Al-Aqsa Martyrs Brigades in Afula on November 27, 2001. Forty-six Israelis were wounded.

There is no doubt that when the document refers to a "martyrdom act" – *amaliyeh istishhadiyeh* – it is referring to suicide attacks. A martyr, or "*shaheed*" in Arabic, is an individual who gave his life in a holy war – or Jihad – and is therefore entitled to automatic entry into Paradise after his death, according to Islamic tradition. The term "martyr" has thus become synonymous with suicide bombers or those who died attacking Israelis. Israel has been able to determine that at least eight of the beneficiaries of Saudi aid are the families of suicide bombers.

Other "martyrs" on the Saudi list may not have been suicide bombers, but they are well-known for their past involvement in terrorism. Thus, No. 68, Mahmud Abu Hanud, was the commander of Hamas for the

West Bank. No. 8, Atef Abiyat, was a terrorist from Bethlehem. His name was well-known to those who engaged in peace process matters after Yasser Arafat promised the European Union that he was in prison, on the while Abiyat moved about freely until his death.

When a potential suicide bomber knows that his family will be handsomely rewarded with financial aid after his death, his motivation to undertake suicide operations increases. Thus, Saudi aid directly promotes terrorism. (Ibid)

ZAKAT AND TERRORISM

Along with Jihad (holy war) and Hudna (cease fire), another word that should be known by Westerners is the word Zakat. The fundraising for terrorism uses one of the holiest tenets of Islam – Zakat.

Zakat is one of the five pillars of Islam. It is intended for charity and Jihad for the cause of Allah. Muslims honor Allah in Zakat, which is a percentage of gold, silver, or finances from every Muslim. Osama bin Laden has used Zakat fundraisers. In Afghanistan, Riyadh and Washington together, he collected some $3.5 billion to fund the Mujahideen – the Afghan fighters who took on the Soviets. At the same time, men like bin Laden served as fundraisers for the thousands of foreign jihadists streaming into Afghanistan. By persuading clerics across the Muslim world to hand over money from Zakat, the charitable donations that are a cornerstone of Islam, they collected huge sums. They raised millions more from wealthy princes and merchants across the Middle East. Most important, they joined forces with the Saudi charities, many of which were already moving aid to the fighters. Saudis, rich and poor, responded with donations at thousands of Zakat boxes in mosques, supermarkets, and schools; doling out support for besieged Muslims in Algeria, Bosnia, Kashmir, the West Bank, and Gaza. Millions of dollars poured in. (Saudi Arabia Accountability Report, NORPAC)

Starting in the late 1980s – after the dual shocks of the Iranian Revolution and the Soviet war in Afghanistan – Saudi Arabia's quasi-official charities became the primary source of funds for the fast-growing Jihad movement. In some twenty countries, the money was used to run paramilitary training camps, purchase weapons, and recruit new members.

The charities were part of an extraordinary $70 billion Saudi campaign to spread their fundamentalist Wahhabi sect worldwide. The money helped lay the foundation for hundreds of radical mosques, schools, and Islamic centers that have acted as support networks for the jihad movement, officials say.

U.S. intelligence officials knew about Saudi Arabia's role in funding terrorism by 1996, yet for years Washington did almost nothing to stop it. Examining the Saudi role in terrorism was "virtually taboo," according to a senior intelligence analyst. Even after the embassy bombings in Africa, moves by counterterrorism officials to act against the Saudis were repeatedly rebuffed by senior staff at the State Department and elsewhere, who felt that other foreign policy interests outweighed fighting terrorism.*

---

* The Freedom of Information Center, The Saudi Connection, How billions in oil money spawned a global terror network, By David E. Kaplan; Monica Ekman; Aamir Latif, U.S. News & World Report, December 15, 2003.

Chapter 7
The Hypnotic State and Psychoses

I recall my first demonstration in our village in Beit Sahur. We all gathered in the town square by the municipality, all of us demonstrating in a hypnotic ecstasy, opening our shirts to the Israelis who fired bullets in the air, daring them to kill us.

One of the immediate, striking impressions of the suicide attackers is the enthusiastic determination with which all of the Intifada is carried out. The Palestinians demonstrating in the streets – children, women, men, and old people alike – appear to be in a hypnotic ecstasy and completely engulfed by the al-Aqsa Intifada. One commentator stated:

> In the thirty-five years of the Israeli occupation, we have never witnessed such a sweeping, ecstatic determination by the Palestinians. No retaliatory action by the Israeli army has yet proven an immediate effect in cooling down the heated emotional excitement. Each successful suicide attack brings in many new volunteers for the Shahada. The Palestinians feel that now, more than ever, their long-lasting nationalistic dreams and aspirations are about to be actualized: For the first time in history a Palestinian state is being envisioned concretely and they feel they actually have the power to destroy the State of Israel, "the Zionist dwarf," as they refer to it.

Palestinians feel confident that they have found the perfect means to finally achieve their goals. They believe that suicide attacks are the only means to shake the Israelis' confidence in their own home and that every suicide attack causes more people to emigrate from Israel and fewer Jews to immigrate to Israel. El Sudki, a columnist for the Egyptian newspaper Al Akhbar, wrote, "The rats who come from the U.S., Europe, and Russia will run away." (Al Akhbar, June 11, 2001)

In spite of economic difficulties, casualties, and destruction, they feel that the suicide attacks have filled their lives with meaning, replacing the long-lasting desperation and helplessness they have experienced.

The enthusiastic determination is not only reflected in the faces of Palestinian street demonstrators at funerals or in joyous crowds following a suicide attack, but it is also delivered through cultural and literary avenues. The following is part of a poem that recently appeared in the Palestinian Islamic Jihad weekly, Al Istiqlal (see MEMRI special dispatch series No. 318, December 21, 2001), entitled *"Because I am a Palestinian."*

Because I am a Palestinian

Because I am enamored of fate

And my fate is to have my blood

Turn into songs.

Then sketch out the road to freedom

My fate is to become a human bomb

Because I am a Palestinian.

(*Terror Suicide: How Is It Possible?* Israel Orbach, Department of Psychology, Bar-Ilan University, Ramat-Gan, Israel)

What began as the struggle to establish a state has transformed into a state of psychoses. This hypnotic, psychotic state and euphoria can best be explained by viewing a mob reaction in Ramallah. When Jihadists catch an enemy, it creates feelings of mass joy, euphoria, and ecstasy.

Norzitch, thirty-three years old, and his fellow reservist Yossi Avrahami, thirty-eight years old, had taken a wrong turn and ended up in Ramallah. They were spotted by local Arabs and attacked by what quickly became a large mob. The grisly footage, aired worldwide, was filmed by an Italian film crew whose news agency later apologized to the Palestinian Authority for doing so. Several photographers who also filmed the scene that day were beaten by P.A. officers and had their cameras and film destroyed. (*Charity and Resolve,* 11, 25,2004)

The two Jewish men were taken to the central police station, where mobs carried out a festival of blood. One of the killers was seen standing at the police station window after Norzitch's body was thrown out of it, proudly displaying his blood-soaked hands to the murderous mob below. Then the mob was carried into a frenzy of joy and cheers of "Allah Akbar!" One could almost see an entire city enjoying the festivity and jumping up and down with joy.

Another example of this frenzy is seen when collaborators are killed. Their intestines, heart, and kidneys are displayed on a platter, while children hold on to the pieces of tissue and flesh, screaming out with joy and incantations of Islamic slogans.

After Israel pulled out, my country has become the night of the living dead – literally.

Muslims falsely accuse the Jews and manufacture so much media against them, yet it is the Muslims who actually carry out the type of brutal, bestial, murderous activities for which they libel the Jews. The Ramallah community stood there jumping and dancing for joy as if they had won the lottery, after they strangled, stabbed, disemboweled, two men, tearing them limb from limb. However, the Western media bias is inexcusable! This same story was covered by the Washington Post as follows:

> The young man was very ill when he was a baby, he stuttered, he was shy...maybe it really wasn't him photographed in the window...people's emotions were boiling over because of Palestinian teens shot by Israeli soldiers...Israel's settlements and occupation were on Salha's mind...he was a calm, good-natured and athletic kid...

Hockstader adds, for good measure, that the Palestinians have their own picture to compete with the bloody hands image: the video of "terrified twelve-year-old Muhammad Dura, cowering behind his father seconds before he was raked by Israeli machine-gun fire."

Even if the story of Dura is true, no Jews have been recorded standing with such joy over blood and death. There is no moral equivalency between the Judeo-Christian culture and the culture of Jihad. One would never find such public behavior when terrorists are caught in Israeli areas. In fact, injured terrorists are taken to hospitals and given treatments in Israel.

If the claim is that Palestinians behave in this fashion because of their suffering, would anyone in the world claim that Jews do not also suffer?

LET THE WEAK SAY I AM STRONG

"Beat your plowshares into swords, and your pruning hooks into spears: let the weak say, I [am] strong." (Joel 3:10)

The new Palestinian is transformed from a helpless, hopeless, passive and fearful captive into a determined, powerful doer who takes control of his or her life. A thought comes to mind: that becoming a shaheed, by means of self-explosion, is also symbolically a form of metamorphosis – the destruction of the old, shameful self-image of a helpless, depressed, and fearful being and the birth of a determined, powerful entity.

The breeding ground for autocracy is not only hunger and disease but also national amnesia and ignorance. The culprit is, then, a state of mind in which millions lose their senses, and in their hypnotic state they allow liars and criminals to blame others for their own largely self-inflicted ills – or at least, they lack the courage to seek solutions from within. (Victor D. Hanson, "Breeding Ground," National Review Online, January 22, 2002)

During Germany's Nazi era, the Germans did not want Hitler (he received a minority of the votes in 1932), but they did not want to face up to their real military defeat in 1918 either. Nor did they want to confront the fools and the bogus beliefs that had led them down the road to catastrophe in 1914. (*Little Green Footballs,* 1,22, 2002)

How is it possible for people, who apparently do not suffer from the kind of distress or pathology usually attributed to individuals who commit suicide, to become people who commit violent, cruel suicides? (*Terror Suicide: How Is It Possible?* Israel Orbach, Department of Psychology, Bar-Ilan University, Ramat-Gan, Israel)

The following sheds some insight into this phenomenon.

THE GLORIFICATION OF DEATH

Palestinian media is plagued with death glorification. The Voice of Palestine, which was the inspiration for my Jihadist upbringing during my teen years, still broadcasts daily in the Palestinian areas:

> *The Muslim believer loves death and the 'Shahada' (death-sacrifice) as you [the Jews] love life. There is a big difference between the one who loves the next world and the one who loves this world. The Muslim who loves death and is requesting the Shahada does not fear the oppression by the arrogant ones [the Jews] or their bloodshedding weapons."* (The Voice of Palestine radio, May 25, 2001, from *Terror Suicide: How Is It Possible?* Israel Orbach, Department of Psychology, Bar-Ilan University, Ramat-Gan, Israel)

Sheikh Abed Al Halim from Jerusalem stated that "the shaheed has a very high standing in Islam in this world and in the next world. The wish to die as a shaheed is highly valued in Islam, but not everybody is capable or worthy to do so. The one who seeks to die as a shaheed has to be a person of virtue, a dedicated believer, determined and loyal to the highest religious and national causes." (Al-Ayam, the Palestinian Authority, March 15, 2001).

Thus, the Shahada is strongly rooted in the Islamic faith and the history of Arab nationality. It is defined and valued as the highest moral, ethical, spiritual, and heroic stand. Death by Shahada is valued more than life itself. (*Terror Suicide: How Is It Possible?* Israel Orbach, Department of Psychology, Bar-Ilan University, Ramat-Gan, Israel)

DEATH SONGS

As a youth, I recall memorizing all of the Jihad songs. Yet, in those days, most of the PLO songs came out of Egypt and had a Nazi-style beat. Today's songs sung by Jihadists, called Anasheed songs, are much different and have lethal potency. They are rhythmic chants that use no instruments, since Islam has forbidden musical instruments.

I even used to be in contests – if you gave me any word, I would know a revolutionary song with that word in it. I recall some of the songs from the early seventies, before suicide martyrdom began to come into action. These were the years of preparation, and today we see the results, the eggs that have been incubating since the seventies have hatched.

SHARPEN MY BONES

Arabic:

"Sinnu Ithamy sinnuha sinnuha syoof,

a'boni a'boni qunbula Molotov

Ana Sha'b Elddam weshug el-layl

we-yisna' min lahmu ganabil"

English:

Sharpen my bones and sharpen them
and make them swords

Fill me up a Molotov Cocktail

We are a nation of blood

who break through the night

And transforms their flesh into bombs

KOSHER BLOOD

Another song which goes as follows:

Arabic:

Ya Gatileen

Damkum halahl a'layna

Waynan tifirru

min l'gabna wayna

English:

[Jews] O killers,

your blood is halal [kosher] to us
Where will you hide from us in that day?

"That day," is the day of judgment when the trees and stones cry out revealing the hiding place of the Jew.

Yet, the songs in today's world are not restricted to Palestinians. Terrorist songs have engulfed much of the Arab world and non-Arab Muslim countries. A very popular song in the Middle East, goes as follows:

Singer:

If the martyrs of Palestine are terrorists

If Hizbullah are terrorists,

If any resistance is terrorism,

I scream at the top of my lungs,

I scream at the top of my lungs:

I'm a terrorist. I'm a terrorist.

This slogan is written on every available wall in the Palestinian areas:

Arabic:

Naqra'u abwab al-Jannati
bi-jamajm Al-Yahood

English:

We knock on the gates of heaven
with the skulls of Jews.

In Iran, a song goes as follows:

Yes, it's the global Jerusalem Day, the day all the precious Iranians go out to march and protect the oppressed, defenseless Palestinians. Children of Palestine! We are with you. You don't have home, school, or food, and can't live properly. We love you. Yes. Today is the global Jerusalem Day. We await the day Palestine will be liberated.

Everyone has a home on the Lord's land, and everyone loves his home very much. Nobody has the right to stay in someone else's home and to consider it his own.

The Iranian news channel IRINN TV broadcast a between-program music video produced by the television department of the Iranian Revolutionary Guard. Thais was a Greek courtesan who joined Alexander the Great on his campaign, and, according to one story, persuaded him to set fire to Persepolis. The Iranian Revolutionary Guard's song shows the Statue of Liberty as Thais. The following is an excerpt:

The accursed Macedonian courtesan,
in a nocturnal attack of wine and fire

At the dawn of rage and blood – The scheme of Thais.

That promiscuous saint of Athens And her temple in Nice –

A she-demon measuring slightly less than 320 feet And 6 inches, In her hand a torch and on her head a crown, plundered from the kingdom of Persia.

Perhaps she was expelled from Paris a year or two ago

And abandoned on the red waves of Atlantis –
The scheme of Thais.

There she is, the unique symbol of freedom

That temptress by the banks of the Sea of Freedom

The scheme of Thais

The scheme of Thais,

That accursed paramour of Alexander

The scheme of the cry of women seeking a mate
at the mouth of the port

The scheme of Thais and the torch.

A scheme of plunder

A scheme of rage to burn Mandana and Farvahar

And even the candlestick unto dust.

A scheme of freedom despite a life of slavery

A scheme of heresy and polytheism

A scheme of humanism that brags of its birth in the arts.

A scheme of the final invasion of man's faith

A scheme of Thais, bearer of the torch,

A scheme of satan,

A she-demon that remains on the waves of Atlantis,

The scheme of Thais.

That which you see is neither Babylon nor Athens. It is Attica.

Even more so, it is Attica of Greece, haughty Babylon, America.

America is the enemy of god's Unity and an affront to god.

America is a mad demon; for the moment she slumbers, in chains.

She is the shadow of the tyrant, the anti-christ. She is not dead.

And now, in the end of days, in our days of iron,
she is plotting a great conspiracy.

O men of the seven continents, awake! awake!
Light the pure flames to destroy the serpents;

This impure octopus with seven heads is always boasting

And its dark lies cause the eyes to cry without cease

It must be killed – that would be a mercy

Or else each man must be on his guard against the werewolf.

This is the scheme of Thais, of the devil, of the satan from Attica

It adds another stain on the world's disgrace - America's shame.

(MEMRI.ORG)

This passage parallels the beast of Revelation 17 in the Bible, yet Revelation 17 speaks of a woman coming out from a desert region with a cup of wine from which the world drinks and gets drunk. America is addicted to a wine from the desert. It is interesting that they mix biblical references with Greek mythology to depict the statue of liberty.

The common theme in most of these songs is a united effort to concentrate on Jerusalem and the destruction of all the Jewish populations. The Saudi-based religious TV channel, Iqra TV, aired a monologue by Palestinian Sheikh Ahmad Qattan in memory of Sheikh Ahmad Yassin. Following, are excerpts from his comments:

*Oh mothers and fathers, you must train your children every night,
before they go to bed, to go on raids in order to liberate Jerusalem
and Al-Aqsa, and when he goes to sleep, after reading the Quran
and the bedside verses, he should recite together with you the
prayer for martyrdom:*

"*Allah, I pray to you, in all honesty, to be martyred for your sake.*"
Do this every night.

Ahmad, Ahmad, Oh Yassin,

We seek martyrdom.

Ahmad, Ahmad, Oh Yassin,

We continue on the path of Jihad.

Ahmad, Ahmad, Oh Yassin,

For Al-Aqsa we are steadfast.

Respect and honor to every Mujahideen in Hamas.

Respect and honor to every Mujahideen (fighting) for al-Aqsa.

You son of an ape, you opium fiend,

Hide the others, Oh Sharon,

Khybar, Khybar, Oh Jews

Muhammad's army will return

With a sling and a slingshot

With a sling and a slingshot

Shake, shake…

Shake the Qaynuqa' tribe

With a sling and a slingshot

Shake the Qaynuqa' tribe.

(MEMRI.ORG)

Qattan reminds of Khaybar, when Muhammad slaughtered the Jews, and he is always reminding them that the day will come when Jews will be slaughtered throughout the world. Repetition in unison is a very effective way to condition people. Indeed, it converts masses to become remorseless killers.

The induction of the new Palestinian self-image begins at a very early, age. Jack Kelley of USA Today visited Hamas schools in Gaza City, where he saw an eleven-year-old boy say to his class, "*I will make my body a bomb* that will blast the flesh of Zionists, the sons of pigs and monkeys...I will tear their bodies into little pieces and will cause them more pain than they ever knew." His classmates shouted, "Allah Akbar" and his teacher shouted, "May the virgins give you pleasure." (USA Today, June 26, 2001)

The depiction of Jews as being monkeys is from the Quran "We transformed the Jews [The Sabath breakers] into detestable monkeys." Muhammad's Endloesung was accompanied by dozens of suitably grim "revelations" in the Quran. The Jews have drawn on themselves wrath upon wrath, and their just reward in the form of "disgracing torment" yet awaits them. (Quran, 2:88-90) They break covenants, "and you will not cease to discover deceit in them." Allah "caused you [Muslims] to inherit their lands, and their houses, and their riches, and a land which you had not trodden before. (Quran, 33:26-27) The Jews are cowards: "If they fight, they will show you their backs." They are doomed to "humiliating agony." (7:167) Allah has put "enmity and hatred amongst them till the Day of Resurrection." (5:64) Even when they seem united, their hearts are divided. (59:14) They are cursed by Allah, who transformed them into monkeys and swine. (5:60) Indignity is put over them wherever they may be because they transgress beyond bounds. They cling greedily to this life, even if it is humiliating and villainous. (3:112) (*Ahmadinejad and Islamic Judeophobia,* by Srdja Trifkovic 23 Mar 2006)

The self-image metamorphosis is not only a personal change in the shaheed; it carries with it a glorification of the entire Palestinian people. The single shaheed turns his entire nation into heroic beings. After a detailed description of a suicide attack in the town of Kfar Saba in Israel, the editor of the weekly Al Asboua, Mustafa Bachri, writes, "This is the mighty Palestinian nation, a nation that does not fear death, a nation that does not know how to surrender and how to be defeated. This is a nation of heroes that never gives in to despair." (Al Asboua, Egypt, April 23, 2001)

As these songs have the elements of our definition of an Islamic terrorist – the cult-like conditioning, allusions of misery and injustice. The poetic rhyme and chanting of the song without music, simply a group of men singing these in one voice, converts normal individuals into angry, pride-filled, remorseless killers, for the purpose of intimidating an enemy in the hope to re-establish a utopian, theocratic world order, where Islam is dominant and all non-Muslims are subservient. This is obvious from today's Jihadist's favorite song:

The word is the word of the sword

Until the wrongs are righted.

The despicable ones have even cursed

The Messenger of the people of strong will

Our sanctuaries would not have been desecrated

Had the lions surrounded them

The filthiest of bandits has attacked us

So where are the swords?

They have forgotten we are the defiant ones

Who defend like lions.

We are those who trampled with our steeds

The thrones of the empires.

We are those who built our forts

Out of skulls

Which we brought from the land of Chosroes

By force and on top of the booty.

Our messenger is the one who made us

Noble builders of Glory.

Our Messenger is the sun of truth

Who lit the face of the world.

He lit the lamp of a night

Black from misguidance

And created from a few people

A generation coming from the dawn.

So they destroyed the head of aggression

And humiliated every oppressor.

War against every oppressor

And peace for every peaceful one.

THE SKULLS WE BROUGHT FROM THE LAND OF CHOSROES

As one can read from this Nashed song, Muslims pride themselves on Jihad conquests with Chosroes and Hiraclius. Muhammad instructed his followers to call people to Islam before waging war against them – the warfare would follow from their refusal to accept Islam or to enter the Islamic social order as inferiors, required to pay a special tax:

> *Fight in the name of Allah and in the way of Allah. Fight against those who disbelieve in Allah. Make a holy war...When you meet your enemies who are polytheists, invite them to three courses of action. If they respond to any one of these, you also accept it and withhold yourself from doing them any harm. Invite them to (accept) Islam; if they respond to you, accept it from them and desist from fighting against them...If they refuse to accept Islam, demand from them the Jizya [the tax on non-Muslims specified in Qur'an 9:29]. If they agree to pay, accept it from them and hold off your hands. If they refuse to pay the tax, seek Allah's help and fight them.* (Sahih Muslim 4294)

There is therefore an inescapable threat in this "invitation" to accept Islam. Would one who converted to Islam under the threat of war be considered to have converted under duress? By non-Muslim standards, yes, but not according to the view of this Islamic tradition. From the standpoint of the traditional schools of Islamic jurisprudence such a conversion would have resulted from "no compulsion."

Muhammad reinforced these instructions on many occasions during his prophetic career. Late in his career, he wrote to Heraclius, the Eastern Roman Emperor in Constantinople:

Now then, I invite you to Islam (i.e., surrender to Allah), embrace Islam and you will be safe; embrace Islam and Allah will bestow on you a double reward. But if you reject this invitation of Islam, you shall be responsible for misguiding the peasants (i.e., your nation). (Bukhari, 4.52.191)

Heraclius did not accept Islam, and soon the Byzantines would know well that the warriors of jihad indeed granted no safety to those who rejected their "invitation." (Robert Spencer, *Jihad Watch,* 08,30,2006)

Muhammad did not get a satisfactory answer from Chosroes, ruler of the Persians. After reading the letter of the Prophet of Islam, Chosroes contemptuously tore it to pieces. When news of this reached Muhammad, he called upon Allah to tear the Persian emperor and his followers to pieces (Bukhari, 5.59.708). He told the Muslims that they would conquer both empires: "When Khosrau [Chosroes] perishes, there will be no (more) Khosrau after him, and when Caesar perishes, there will be no more Caesar after him. By Him in Whose hands Muhammad's life is, you will spend the treasures of both of them in Allah's Cause" (Bukhari 4.53.349).

Orders for conversion were decreed under all the early Islamic dynasties – Umayyads, Abbasids, Fatimids, and Mamluks. Additional extensive examples of forced conversion were recorded under both Seljuk and Ottoman Turkish rule (the latter until its collapse in the 20th century), the Shiite Safavid and Qajar dynasties of Persia/Iran, and during the jihad ravages on the Indian subcontinent, beginning with the early 11th century campaigns of Mahmud of Ghazni, and recurring under the Delhi Sultanate, and Moghul dynasty until the collapse of Muslim suzerainty in the 18th century following the British conquest of India. Since these Muslim rulers and armies all revered Muhammad as an "excellent example of conduct" (Quran 33:21), this is not surprising. (Andrew Bostom, Front Page Magazine, August 29, 2006)

Chapter 8
Identifying a Jihadist Mind

THE VICTIMCRAT

It is obvious when one reads statements by Muslim terrorists in search of justifications for their actions, the arguments almost always used by terrorists are that *they* were victims. Following the bombings of two American embassies in Africa, Time magazine interviewed Osama bin Laden. Time asked, "What can the U.S. expect from you now?" Bin Laden replied, "Any thief or criminal or robber who enters another country in order to steal should expect to be exposed to murder at any time. For the American forces to expect anything from me, personally, reflects a very narrow perception. Muslims are angry. The Americans should expect reactions from the Muslim world that are proportionate to the injustice they inflict."

Ramzi Ahmed Yousef, an acquaintance of bin Laden, is serving a life sentence for the 1993 attack on the World Trade Center. Before his sentencing, Yousef told the court, "The government in its summations and opening said that I was a terrorist. Yes, I am a terrorist, and I am proud of it. And I support terrorism so long as it is against the United States Government and against Israel, because you are more than terrorists; you are the ones who invented terrorism and use it every day. You are butchers, liars and hypocrites." This angry, historically warped worldview spells one thing – victim. (Larry Elder, Jewish World View, 9,21,2001)

A person who is raped is a victim, but the rapist who blames his crime on his abused childhood is a "victimcrat." I am hoping to coin this term.

LOYALTY COMES BEFORE TRUTH

Dr. Muqtedar Khan, director of International Studies at Adrian College in Michigan, challenges American Muslims to set the masses straight:

While we loudly and consistently condemn Israel for its ill treatment of Palestinians, we are silent when Muslim regimes abuse the rights of Muslims and slaughter thousands of them. Remember Saddam and his use of chemical weapons against Muslims (Kurds)? Remember the Pakistani army's excesses against Muslims (Bengalis)? Remember the Mujahideen of Afghanistan and their mutual slaughter? Have we ever condemned them for their excesses? Have we demanded international intervention or retribution against them? Do you know how the Saudis treat their minority Shias? Have we protested the violation of their rights? But we all are eager to condemn Israel; not because we care for rights and lives of the Palestinians, we don't. We condemn Israel because we hate them. (Dan Canon, Posted: Fri. July 4, 2003 3:24 pm. Post subject: *A Muslim on Muslim hypocrisy*)

In other words, *loyalty comes before truth,* and in the Middle East, one is called to be loyal to the cause, and the cause comes before everything – lives, facts, work, goals…everything.

U.S. uses Islamic world to slaughter Iraq as it is
being held by U.N. inspectors

The victim mentality is evident in most media in Muslim countries from TV, songs, art, and newspapers. Al Hayat Al Jedida, Jan. 5, 2003, shows this caricature:

Everybody wants a piece of Iraq.
Al Hayat Al Jedida, Dec. 19, 2002.

If one compiled the Muslim reactions to misery into a flowchart, the statements would always seem to point at anyone except the supposedly victimized Islamist society. Muslims seems to pardon themselves from any blame, and they do it in several ways.

CONSPIRACY THEORIES

A victimcrat is created when this type of mental flowchart is infused with many years of conditioning the people to believe in conspiracies – International Zionist conspiracy, American conspiracy, even internal conspiracy.

Conspiracy theories are accusations made against anyone who opposes the Muslim point of view. Muslims use conspiracy theories to write off their opponents' arguments, in lieu of any valid counter argument.

The use of conspiracy theories is evident in the early years of Islam. When Muslims compiled the works and deeds of Muhammad into the Hadith, the sections that they didn't like were attributed to *Israeeliat* (Israelite inventions), lies invented by Jews in order to defame Islam.

Remember that on the flowchart, blame will always be directed somewhere else, anywhere except towards the Muslims. The favorites on this flowchart are Israel and the U.S.

Even when Anwar Sadat was assassinated by Muslim Jihadists, and the media directed the blame on the U.S., as in the following report:

> *Tal'at Al-Sadat: Some countries had an interest in President Al-Sadat's disappearance from the political scene. I gave the U.S. as an example. President Al-Sadat had reached the stage at which he would regain Sinai, and then he would have the time to run the Arab region of the Middle East. This was not in the interests of the U.S., and what exacerbated the situation was President Al-Sadat's declaration that Egypt supported the Afghanistan rebels and supplied them with arms.* (MEMRI.ORG)

While Americans think that U.S. policies are the reason for America-phobia and continual hatred of Americans in the Middle East, most Americans are unaware of how these policies are interpreted. Lebanese Shiite Leader Muhammad Hussein Fadhlallah states:

> We say to President Bush: *You have succeeded in becoming the most barbaric model of tyranny, because you and your despicable, extremist administration continue to threaten the Middle East, and to indiscriminately accuse those who oppose your policy, using ludicrous logic when talking about the danger Iran poses to America. All the while, everybody knows that the [real] danger is to the entire world, and comes from the imperialistic American power, with its plans for more than just a preemptive war. This is especially true now, with <u>the commemoration of the events of 9/11, which were exploited by the American administration in order to impose its domination over the world,</u> while everyone can see that these events were not subjected to any legal process. It's been said that the Jews and some American powers may be behind this. But they concealed this very well. Everybody can see that these events were not subjected to any legal process in America, which would determine clearly who is responsible.* (MEMRI.ORG)

This statement clearly states that the suicide attacks were not carried out by Muslims but by America itself, and the suicide attacks were an invention to excuse America to attack Muslim lands.

Conspiracy theories are not only a phenomena in Arab countries. Indonesian cleric Abu Bakar Bashir has accused America's main intelligence agency of involvement in the 2002 Bali suicide bombings, which claimed the lives of 202 people, including 88 Australians. Bashir, the spiritual leader of Jemaah Islamiyah (JI), was released from prison in June after having served almost two years for involvement in the planning of the attack.

The cleric has told the ABC's Foreign Correspondent program that the Bali bombs were "hijacked" by the Central Intelligence Agency (CIA). "So the bomb that killed so many Australians was an American bomb," he said. "It wasn't the bomb made by Amrozi and his friends...I don't know whether the Australian Government pretends not to know this, or really doesn't know...If they don't know, then they're stupid. But I think they're just pretending not to know." Bashir described the device used in the bombing as a "micro-nuclear bomb," and he said the bomb originally intended for use in the attack "would not have killed people, only injured them." *(Bashir links CIA to Bali Bombings,* By ABC, 08/29/06)

Regardless of what Westerners do, Muslims view those actions as aggression, even if they are purely self-defense. In the eyes of the Muslim Jihadist, Westerners are subservient and shouldn't dare to fight back. In Islamic culture, Westerners fall into the class of dhimmi status and cannot be viewed as morally higher than Muslims. Muslims believe they are never at fault, and others are always blamed.

Muslims employ the mentality of a rapist who accuses the victim of showing too much flesh. A Muslim might accuse the murdered Jewish child of being a future soldier who might kill Arabs!

Even my exposition here, would be blamed on hatred, bigotry, and racism. Muslims project their own blemishes onto their opponents. Islamic culture suffers from a pandemic lack of introspection. They fail to examine the log in their Islamic eye, while always picking on the spec in the eye of the West.

One finds a perceived misery sprinkled all over the newspapers in the Middle East, as if misery is some holy-water necessary to cleanse Arab souls. That misery, however, is always blamed on anyone else but Muslims.

"For [many] months we respected a cease-fire, expecting to see changes in the lives of the Palestinian people, but we received from the Israeli side more assassinations…and above all we received the Hamas victory, *which seems to be the result of an Israeli and international conspiracy*," Abu Nasser told WND. "They believe that Hamas will give up easier our lands and rights. I think that they are right, but we will not allow this to happen. We will fight and we will blow up the new Intifada." (WorldNetDaily.com, By Aaron Klein, June 7, 2006)

This type of propaganda is widespread throughout Islamic circles. In Columbus, Ohio, Dr. Sallah Sultan stated, "9/11 Attacks Planned by Americans on the Basis of the Film 'The Siege.'" The following excerpts are from an address given by Dr. Sallah Sultan, president of the American Center for Islamic Research in Columbus, Ohio, which aired on Al-Risala TV on May 17, 2006:

The film "The Siege," starring Denzel Washington, portrayed the Muslims in a very bad light. They are shown calling for prayer, performing the ablution, praying, and then planning multiple bombings – a government building, a security agency, the FBI, a bus carrying young men and women, adults and children. They bombed shops. The film came out in April 1999. It paved the way for 9/11, since it was filmed in Brooklyn, New York. The truth is that immediately after 9/11, I said people should view these events in the context of "The Siege," because these events were identical.

This scenario…I still believe to this day…The scenario still baffles me. I share the view of many Americans, French, and Europeans, who say that 9/11 could not have been carried out entirely from outside [the U.S.] – by Muslims or others. The confessions of some people could have been edited. But even if they were not edited, I believe that these people were used in a marginal role. The entire thing was of a large scale and was planned within the U.S., in order to enable the U.S. to control and terrorize the entire world, and to get American society to agree to the war declared on terrorism, the definition of which has not yet been determined. The U.S. remains the only country to determine who is a terrorist, and what is the definition for terrorism, and it can pin it on anyone. The most recent instance is the case of Dr. Al-Zindani, who has been accused of terrorism, even though he is known worldwide for his refinement, virtue, and broad horizons. (MEMRI.ORG, also see Jihad Watch Sunday, May 21, 2006)

THE VOICE OF REASON

The Middle East needs the element of confession. Confession is the beginning of healing – to search out the log in one's own eye, before we pick on the spec in everyone else's eye.

Some confession occurs at times, especially from Arab gulf states in which some degree of freedom still exists. The following excerpts are from an interview with the former Kuwaiti Minister of Education, Ahmad Al-Ruba'i, which aired on Al-Ruba'i TV on March 27, 2006:

Ahmad Al-Ruba'i: *Today, we have the concept of modern conspiracy. In most Arab countries, everybody is a victim of a foreign conspiracy.*

[…]

Interviewer: *[Some proclaim:] "No Iraqi would kill another Iraqi," "We love one another, we are great." They begin to review thousands of years of Iraqi history, and say: "but there are some who have entered Iraq in order to destroy it." How would you respond to such a person?*

Ahmad Al-Ruba'i: *Abu Tareq, this [the following comments] is the prevalent talk everywhere, I'm sad to say. "Is it conceivable that Muslims did the killing on 9/11?" Yes, they did. They killed 3,000 people. But it wasn't Islam – they were criminals. "No, it must have been an <u>American conspiracy</u>…As the plane was flying, there was an American that…" With regard to the occupation of Kuwait, they say: "The American ambassador told Saddam to enter Kuwait." So America brought Saddam into Kuwait and then took him out, why? In order to gain control of the region. But America has been in control of the region and its oil for a long time."*

<u>*The concept of conspiracy has spread in a very organized and efficient way, and many Arabs, even intellectuals, believe they are victims of conspiracy.*</u>

[…]

Interviewer: *Ahmad, what is the solution to this crisis?*

Ahmad Al-Ruba'i: *I believe that the solution, without oversimplifying things, is that we stop dealing with politics, and establish economic [cooperation] among the Arabs. We have been destroyed by the politicization of everything, and it is high time we agree on an economic program for revival. People have no food, no jobs, and no capabilities. Two neighboring countries, Kuwait and Iraq, have had closed borders for thirteen years, but this has not been detrimental to either market – to ours or the Iraqi one. What kind of nation is this, if it does not have common interests?*

What kind of nation is this – if a ruler can wake up at any moment, decide to invade his neighbors and then invades them, and nobody gets hurt? In Europe, no country would dare invade its neighbors, because 3,000 trucks loaded with merchandise cross the border every day. This would harm the farmers and the industries, because people's interests are intertwined.

[…]

As I've said before, we need a summit to discuss how to wipe out illiteracy. Illiteracy grows every day, yet we talk about liberating Palestine? All the Arab leaders who talk about liberating Palestine should liberate their citizens from oppression and prosecution.

Well put. I love to hear clear-minded people like the former Kuwaiti Minister of Education Ahmad Al-Ruba'i. I pray and hope that he infects others.

Chapter 9
Reasoning with Jihadists

THEY MUST WRITE YOU OFF

A Muslim fundamentalist mind-set has no real ammunition with which to argue. Almost always, as soon as you start a dialogue, make an argument, state a fact, or expose Islamic injunctions, they will write you off. I debated Anjum Choudhary on Irish TV. He is a leader of Al-Muhajirun, one of the most notorious, openly pro-terror, jihadist organizations in England. After I shared my story, Choudhary immediately stated, "This man was never a Muslim. He is a Falangest Lebanese Christian in disguise as a Muslim."

Expressing an opposing view to Islamists was so fruitless. I spent ten years attempting to reason with them to no avail. I was always accused of being a Lebanese phalangest, Zionist agent spy, lunatic, Islamophobe. I was even accused of being paid by Zionists.

I started to recognize that if these people were right, then I must have somehow repressed my memory, or been hit with amnesia, especially when my origin was in question.

This method of applying labels is not exclusively Muslim. Although it is becoming common in the West, especially in universities, it is not to the level we see in the Middle East. Unfortunately, as soon as I begin to speak against terrorism at any university, I am labeled an Islamophobe.

I speak quite frequently at universities across the U.S. My speaking engagement at Colombia University in November 2006 was interesting. I performed an experiment there, and what I found confirmed my suspicion that we face a dangerous trend. At that speech, I made a special attempt to critique not only Islam, but Martin Luther and his writings, "The Jews and Their Lies." My speech was a balanced critique of both Christian and Muslim history, yet the first student from the audience to comment on my speech criticized it as anti-Islam, bigoted, racist, and Islamophobic. Why wasn't I accused of Christian-phobia when I critized Christendom? Only when you criticize Islam do you gain such titles.

Ironically, when I was a terrorist, the world labeled us as freedom fighters. While I was a "freedom fighter," I was free to say that "Jews are shylocks, Israel is a racist state, Jews run the Congress and the media…" In those days, I hated Jews, but when the day came that I changed my mind and loved everyone, I was labeled as a racist and Islamophobe. Go figure!

This dangerous trend is escalating in all sectors from political to educational. To critique a religion is not racism, yet critique of Islam is regarded as racist in most academic circles. No president, or even the Pope, dares to quote the historical attrocities committed by Islamists. *We are loosing not only our will to fight for what is right but our freedom as well. We cry out for balance by executing truth.*

HELPING JIHADISTS

I have had, literally, hundreds of dialogues with Jihadist minds and ignorant Jihad supporters who mean well. I have sat for thousands of hours analyzing their mindsets, as well as my own. The secret to changing Jihadists is not to start off by attacking their faith. Let them examine their own faith later. Your job and mine is to give them the mechanism to do some critical thinking. This is done with a series of check-mates, but first ask him to pass judgments regarding certain issues that are not related to the subject at hand. Never go straight to the heart of the subject you want him to understand. Always speak of unrelated subjects first. Here is one example. Ask him what he thinks of trials and jury duty. Should we examine both sides of the arguments – the defense and the prosecution?

Or, should we only accuse the defendant and have the judge call the sentence without listening to the defense? The Jihadist's response should be a fair one – the defense must present its arguments on behalf of the defendant. Then when you start bringing forth facts, and with his inability to accept any of them, you can then revert to his own statements – a good jury examines the facts without prejudice. Thus, you have proven beyond doubt that the terror mentality plays the roll of prosecutor, jury, and judge, with no defense.

You must first establish the rules before you can begin discussion. Then you can apply his own rules to the debate. Ask him about a case of genocide not related to Muslims, then apply the same example with genocide committed by Muslims.

ARGUING WITH A VICTIMCRAT

Jihadists all start as victimcrats. The main arguments used against the U.S. throughout the whole of the Middle East have the same context, which can be summed up in one concept – American imperialism. Muslims cite the bombs we dropped on Hiroshima and Nagasaki; the enslavement of blacks; American support of Israel; and our support, for national security reasons, of unpopular regimes in the Middle East. (Jewish World Review, Larry Elder, September 21, 2001)

The fact is that Arab slave traders brought more slaves to South America and the Middle East than European slave traders brought to North America. In "Conquests and Cultures," Thomas Sowell writes, "By the time the Europeans discovered the Western Hemisphere at the end of the 15th century, Muslim merchants already dominated the slave trade in West Africa, as they did in East Africa and North Africa. The Islamic jihads of the 18th and 19th centuries created new Muslim states in West Africa, which in turn promoted enslavement on a larger scale. Altogether, between 1650 and 1850, at least 5 million slaves were shipped from West Africa alone." And while slavery ended in the West, says Sowell, "In some Islamic countries in Africa and the Middle East, slavery lasted even longer. Saudi Arabia, Mauritania, and Sudan continued to hold slaves on past the middle of the 20th century." (Ibid)

Sunera Thobani, assistant professor of women and gender studies at the University of British Colombia, was among the first outside of Gaza to revel in the murder of thousands of Americans at the hands of al-Qaeda's killers on September 11, 2001. Only weeks after the 9/11 attacks, she told an Ottawa feminist conference that Americans were the real terrorists. She said that the U.S. is "the most dangerous and powerful global force unleashing horrific levels of violence...U.S. foreign policy is soaked in blood." Even British Colombia's Premier condemned the speech as "hateful." Still, universities are buying what this firebrand feminist is selling. Thobani was president of the National Action Committee on the Status of Women. She is a rising star, having been appointed Ruth Wynn Woodward Endowed Professor in Women's Studies at Simon Fraser University in 1996 before she even finished her doctoral dissertation. She gained her current post in 2000. Though Thobani hails from Tanzania – where sharia law is still practiced – she's said that Americans are the real misogynists (women haters), stating that: "there will be no emancipation for women anywhere on this planet *until the western domination of this planet is ended.*"

Another typical argument I often hear goes as follows:

"You claim that Islamic extremists have but one demand – the destruction of modern secular society. Really? Don't Chechen terrorists care about Chechnya becoming independent? Don't Palestinian terrorists care about getting Israel out of the West Bank and Gaza? Don't Iraqi insurgents care about the American occupation of Iraq? Islamic extremists do despise modern secular society, but to claim that is all that motivates them is dangerous nonsense. It implies that the only thing we can do about Islamic terrorists is kill them. In fact, if ordinary Muslims have legitimate grievances against the U.S. and other Western countries and we fail to address them, we strengthen the terrorists' support and act as their recruiter."

RESPONSE

People who make such arguments usually ignore important elements in history. While the argument could typically come from a terrorist mindset, it could also come from many Americans who are unaware of the facts. Most Americans, both conservative and liberal, reject terrorism, yet they do not understand that, at times, they borrow the terrorists' arguments and ignorantly support their enemy's cause.

Remember, a *terrorist mind-set is concerned with occupation.* To them, everything is an imperialist or Zionist conspiracy. The reality is that the terrorist mind is occupied with half truths. Although many times the terrorist knows the truth, he simply ignores it. The reason is simple – he is usually a racist, filled with bias. He views everyone who is non-Muslim as Kafir, an unbeliever. Whereas, the usual problem with many Westerners is that they have a very narrow view of traditional, conservative people.

Are there legitimate Muslim grievances? Yes, of course. For instance, Afghanistan was attacked by Russia. However, America liberated Afghanistan and aided the mujahideen with stinger missiles. So, the U.S. aided Afghanistan to gain an advantage over communism. This is the way it is in the world of politics, but does that justify a war against the U.S.? It was not the U.S. who invaded Afghanistan. Yet, the Taliban aided Osama bin Laden and turned Afghanistan into a hell hole. How can the pro-jihadist ignore these factors?

It would be unfair to say that the problem of unbalanced reasoning only occurs in the Middle East. We have it here too, but here, it's more out of ignorance than anything else. The following is a response to a typical Palestinian, pro-Jihad objection. It shows all the elements I've mentioned and fit's a common pattern that shows the cookie-cutter mentality:

> **Ramzi:** *Mr. Shoebat, I am totally opposed to your positions!*
>
> **Walid:** *I am glad that we have people who can object – it's only in a free world that two parties can oppose each other and live in peace. Today, we have Hamas and the P.A. killing each other. How is that a free society?*
>
> **Ramzi:** *You are a person who has lost all his roots!*
>
> **Walid:** *I disagree for several reasons:*
>
> 1. *Jesus was from Bethlehem. However, most Muslims in "Pales-tine" chose to follow a desert religion far away in Arabia. My*

roots are connected to the land where Jesus walked. I follow a faith of a Bethlehemite and not an Arabian.

2. Why is it that when Jews stand with "Palestine," you don't accuse them of loosing their roots? What about Germans who died as a result of standing up against Hitler. Do you accuse them of loosing their roots? Why is it that if anyone objects to the Palestinian dogma, then they are accused of loosing their roots?

3. I am from the Holy Land. I was born there. No one can take away my roots. It seems to me that you feel free to uproot people as you wish. You want to expel Jews from Palestine, yet you want to keep only Palestinians in Israel. Why should Arabs have a right to live in Israel, yet Jews are not allowed to live in Palestine?

4. What roots are we talking about? Before 1967, we were Jordanians, and before that, we considered ourselves Syrians, and only since 1967 have the people living in historic Judea clinged to being Palestinains. So, what roots are you talking about?

5. The Palestinian Charter never included Judea or Gaza as part of "Palestine." Only after loosing the war in 1967 was the charter changed. Why?

6. We all had Jordanian passports all along. Why is it that we wanted to establish a Palestinian state in Jordan? When King Hussein decided to throw out that brat named Yasser Arafat, they lost that hope of creating a state there. Why are Palestinians not trying to create a Palestinian state in Jordan? Why is it only in historic Judea?

7. I still listen to Arab songs – I love George Wassuf, Abd Alhalim, Um-Kulthum, Fairuz…I still eat falafel and hummus. I still speak Arabic…So, I am still well connected to my culture. I hate your terror war songs, Hamas Anasheed…

How have I lost my roots?

What roots are you talking about? My terror roots? My racist roots? My old bigoted opinions?

Do Americans loose their roots for being liberal? Conservative? Pro Abortion? Pro civil rights? Pro Palestinian? Pro Israel?

How does one loose their roots, Ramzi?

Ramzi: *As a Palestinian born and raised IN PALESTINE, in Bethlehem, I never was told to hate anybody!*

Walid: *Then why do you hate me so much?*

So, do you mean to tell me that what Naim Ayyad, my Islamic teacher in high school taught us, that killing Jewish civilians is o.k., is a lie I made up?

Are you telling me that it is a lie that Arafat went to mosques and asked women to give him their children for suicide?

Is it a lie that Hamas teaches that in the end of days "the stones will cry out, there is a Jew hiding behind me, come Oh slave of Allah, come and kill him?"

Are you saying that these are all fabrications?

Have I fabricated the hate filled cartoons, Holocaust denials, suicide bombings, or the writings on walls calling for the murder of Jews?

Oh my, can it be? Have I been deceived?

Thank you so much for helping me to re-discover my roots.

Ramzi: *Your positions about Israel show clearly that you are biased and that you don't know much about what is happening!*

Walid: *So far, you have not shown or proven anything except your hatred for anyone who opposes your views. You have not shared anything worth discussing.*

Ramzi: *I suggest that you come and live one week in Bethlehem! Maybe then you will know what being a Palestinian nowadays means!*

Walid: *Does being a Palestinian nowadays include killing Arab teenagers and dragging their bodies down the streets of Bethlehem, or are the executions of Palestinians, by Palestinians, fake?*

I have seen them on video. Are all these videos fake? Did the Zionists make these up?

Ramzi: *I hope that you don't hold the Palestinian nationality accountable, and count on me to prove you wrong no matter what you say!*

Walid: *I think you misunderstand me. I want you to prove me wrong. For if you do, then indeed, we would have peace.*

Peace at last, peace at last, peace at last.

Ramzi: *I went to Ramallah and held a Poster condemning Terrorism! I held the same poster in Bethlehem and in Jordan!*

Walid: *Can you send me photos of that so I can post them on my website? I would love to show the peaceful side of Palestinians. I think you do not understand me.*

I would love to see Palestinians marching for true peace. I shall await these photos.

Ramzi: *On CN8 you said that you can't do it! [Marching for peace and against terrorists!] It is your problem!*

Walid: *Prove me wrong, and I will apologize on TV. I have another request. Can you send me a photo of you in Gaza carrying the same poster?*

I want you to have a poster stating, "Suicide Bombing is Evil" and another which states, "Killing Innocent Jews in Buses is Evil." I do not want a photo of you after the fact – and in a coffin. I want a photo with you still alive.

Ramzi: *You don't know who we are or what we stand for. I hope deeply from the heart that you will spend the rest of your life in the USA or in Israel.*

Walid: *So, anyone who would object to your views should not live in your state? How does that express any freedom? How is that peaceful?*

It seems to me you think that anyone who does not agree with your party line should not be allowed to live in your country.

Truth can be read between the lines. What kind of a country is it when conscientious objectors cannot express their views and have no right to live in that society. Are conscientious objectors traitors? If so, are they to be evacuated?

Ramzi: *We absolutely don't need you back here!*

Walid: *So then, would you approve that my land be confiscated as well? I own land there. Who are you? Are you God? Is it for you to decide who can and who cannot live in our country?*

Ramzi: *By the way, for your information, rootless person…*

Walid: *Rootless person? Now you are resorting to insults.*

Ramzi: *I will never forget the house of my grandfather in Mamila, Jerusalem, occupied since 1948 by a certain Jewish family! There is something called compensation, and I am waiting for it to come!*

Walid: *That's fair. But would you also say that Jews who lost their homes in Iraq, Libya, Lebanon, Egypt, Syria, and so on, should also get compensation?*

When we used to get together as Arabs, we would confess to each other that we had sold our land to Jews, yet, when Westerners ask us, we say that Jews stold everything.

Ramzi: *And again, count on me to burn you politically!*

Walid: *I can't wait. Actually I am looking forward to it. When would you like to take me on?*

In fact, I will be publishing our debate. It helps to serve my argument that in Palestine, there is only one party line. Islam is the state religion. There is no tolerance for minority opinions. There are no rights for Jews to live freely in "Palestine" and no rights to be Jewish or for Jewish holy places to exist. All Synagogues must be converted to mosques. The people suffer harassments and desecrations of Christian holy places…I could go on and on.

Ramzi: *People like you don't deserve any kind of attention!*

Walid: *It seems like you are giving me attention here. I did not write to you. You wrote to me. Ask yourself why you are paying attention to me?*

You state that I should count on you to burn me politically. I bet you would love to burn me physically as well, wouldn't you?

Ramzi: *I will never allow you to ruin our image!*

Walid: *Why are you accusing me of ruining your image?*

You are already destroying your own image. No one has to do that for you. The world already views Palestinians as terrorists thanks to your political leadership which espouses terror, educates children to become suicide killers, teaches intolerance to anyone who opposes the main stream opinions.

Look at yourself, Ramzi. You are burning your image already by your hatred of me. You do not want me to come home. You hate me because I have a different view than yours. Had this been a public dialogue, it would be evident that you have zero tolerance for any other view except yours. This would devastate your image.

But don't burn yourself Ramzi. You have been burned for decades. You have been burned by being used as a pawn by Arab countries, keeping you as refugees for decades while blaming the Israelis.

You have been used as pawns when Arab leaders ordered your people to evacuate in 1948 and again in 1967. You have been used as pawns by your own leadership, yet you keep blaming Jews for everything under the sun. Wake up Ramzi, lest you drown yourself in your own hatred.

Ramzi: *We are VICTIMS!*

Walid: *Only racists claim victimhood when they ignore what they do to others.*

We chased 850,000 Jews out of Arab lands. Are they not victims, too? Suck it up. Grow up. Quit your belly-aching, and stop that victimhood paranoia. Arabs lost homes. Jews lost homes. Arabs want their homes back. Jews don't. I have the ultimate solution for your "victimhood" problem: No one has a right of return: Arabs who left in '48 and '67 have no right to return to Israel; Jews who left in '48 have no right of return to Arab lands. This should end all this mess. Yet you would not agree to that. Why?

This is my question to you. Yet I doubt that you can respond, because if you do, it will prove the double standard you were raised in. So, you still bicker and foam at the mouth. Nothing will make you happy.

Ramzi: *I see checkpoints everyday!*

Walid: *Again, only racists would see the problems done to them without seeing what they have done to others. Palestinians are smuggling bombs and you want Israel to open checkpoints?*

Let's look at the log in our Arab eye before we look at the spec in our Jewish cousins.

Ramzi: *I live the occupation every day!*

Walid: *You think Israel was bad? Wait till Hamas takes full control and Islamists would rule over you, then don't complain to me about victimhood.*

We declared a war on Israel in 1967, we lost, and now you are crying about an occupation?

What about the Jordanian occupation? Jordan took that land illegally, yet you NEVER ONCE objected and cried for liberty. Why? Why have you never called it a Jordanian occupation? Why is it only an Israeli occupation?

Could it be that the answer is simpler then you think? While the world keeps saying that the problem is complicated. It's not. The problem is simple – WE WERE RACISTS. WE HATED JEWS.

This is the only reason why we never objected to a Jordanian occupation, yet we screamed victimhood when Israel won the war that WE declared.

Ramzi: *I feel it everyday! I get yelled at everyday by Israeli occupational forces! I see people dying everyday because Israel doesn't allow us to have our basic needs!*

Walid: *Nonsense. Stop bombing buses, start singing songs of peace, demonstrate all over for peace, then see how Jews will fall backwards for you.*

Yet what did you do instead:

- You elected Hamas and proved to the world that you are racists.

- You severed your ties with Israel, then later complained about Israel keeping you out.

- You kept carrying olive branches in one hand, while you carried a bomb in the other.

Ramzi: *I would love to see you waiting in a line at a checkpoint to go from your home to your work and then being turned back by someone 20 years younger than you!*

Walid: *I lived there for 18 years. I had to carry my I.D, I had to go through checkpoints all the time, but don't forget, when the checkpoints relaxed a litte, I also carried a bomb to blow up an Israeli infrastructure.*

Yet I saw what I did wrong. I saw why Israelis set up checkpoints. I changed my heart and my mind. I stopped playing the victim. I moved on with my life. And when I did, I wasn't allowed to go back home.

You already expressed your view that we should not be allowed to go home. What about my land? Who stold my land, Ramzi? Was it Israel? Or was it Palestinians? Who is the land-thief?

Ramzi: *I would love to see you begging for a permit in order to live!*

Walid: *I can go to Israel any time, walk anywhere, and even pray as I wish whether Muslim or Christian.*

Yet I can't go home to your "Palestine," why? Why can I go to Israel but not to Palestine? Why when truth hits you directly in the face do you reject it? Why when facts are so obvious do you reject them? The answer is simple, it's a state of heart. It has nothing to do with education, victimhood, poverty…it's a racist mind.

Ramzi: *I would love to see you crying for the loss of your child who got shot without having anything to do with any conflict! Just for the fact of standing next to a window in front of a sniper, this was the case of my friend Moussa Abu Eid from Beit Jala!*

Walid: *Wait a second, I lost several from my family. My cousin was killed by Israeli bullets. Yes, Jews killed my cousin, yet my cousin was on his way to Ben Yehuda Street to plant a bomb.*

How come we complained about his death, and forgot his crime?

The answer is simple – again, only a racist would see what people do to them, while they forget what they do to others of a different race.

I also lost two women from my family when Israelis hit Muhammad Abayat with a missile. They were innocent. Yet you gave refuge to people like Abayat. You allowed him to live in your midst fully knowing what he did. You approved of his actions. Yet when he decided to live amongst civilians to kill civilians, and when you knew what you were doing, and when the Israelis had to kill him for killing innocent Jews, and when only Arab civilians died, you objected. Yet you never objected when Abayat killed innocent Israelis. Why?

Yes, innocent people die on both sides. But peace can only come when we look into our own actions, and not only to our enemies reactions.

You seem to forget that you are from Beit Jala, and when terrorists occupied Christian homes to shoot civilians in Gilo, you never objected. You only object at what the Israelis do! Again, you are 100% racist.

It would be impossible for me to make you see that. It has to be your inner soul that needs to see it.

Ramzi: *I would love to see you humiliated by an Israeli soldier, these people that you admire so much!*

Walid: *Again, you forget that I was in prison in Jerusalem. Prison is humiliating for anyone. What else do you want Israel to do with terrorists? Give them apartments? They already gave them guns – 40,000 to be exact, given to the P.A. Police. What did the P.A. Police do? They stood by while Joseph's Tomb was burned by our people. Every Jewish holy place was desecrated. Shame on you for being so silent on this.*

I however have nothing to be ashamed of. I got rid of my bigotry, racism, and hatred. I am free at last, free at last, free at last!

Jesus came to give us peace, love, and freedom. This is something you never experienced. And because you never experienced this, you yourself are a victim – not a victim of the Israelis, but a victim to slavery – the slavery of hatred, the slavery of racism, the slavery of a system imposed on you by Arab imperialism.

Yes, Palestinians need to be free. Yes we have an occupation – an occupation of the mind and not land.

When Jesus came, they thought that He came to get rid His people of the occupation by the Romans. Instead, He stunned everyone, because He came to rid us from the occupation and slavery of our own sins.

Yet look at reality, Jews never occupied anything, they simply liberated the land from the Jordanian occupiers, and when they did, and only because they were JEWS, you screamed in pain and agony.

Ramzi: *I would love to see your house demolished because you are suspected of knowing an activist in this or that organization! I* *would love to see you walking above road blocks in order to try to pass from your house to your neighbors house!*

Walid: *Is there anything else you can offer besides whining?*

You never objected to all the bomb factories, the suicide belts, the dead Palestinian brainwashed kids...

Can you imagine what the world would be like if judges were all like you? You can't balance truth from fiction, right from wrong...

Ramzi: *I would love to see you living a Palestinian life for just 1 hour!*

Walid: *Again, you keep forgetting who you are talking to here. I lived there for 18 years. Let me turn this around so you can see how I feel. I would love to see you lose your land, to have it taken by your own relatives for the simple reason of becoming Christian. I would love to see you get a letter from your Jerusalem-Christian-Arab lawyer which states "You cannot come home to Palestine, not only you will lose your land if you come home, but you will lose your son since he was born Muslim."*

Have you put yourself in my shoes? Probably not, since you don't care about anyone else except your party line. I would love to see you convert from Islam to Christianity, then go to Saudi Arabia and declare that in public.

I would love to see you as a Christian Sudanese, then move to Sudan and see how you get treated. Yet you elected the very system that persecuted anyone who was not Muslim.

Governments are always elected to fit the state of the people's hearts. When Germans elected Nazism, they had only themselves to blame and no one else.

I would also wonder how your wife and kids would be treated in an Arab society that would hate you and would kill you for converting from Islam.

Ramzi: *By the way, after sending this email, I will contact a few local authorities to see if you really are from Bethlehem, which I doubt! I even doubt your very own existence, or at least, the past you are talking about!*

Walid: *Ok, you have made a bet with me. I will take you on. I will prove that I am from there, and prove I lived there for 18 years. The payment for this bet is, if I prove this to you, you will agree to carry*

*a sign in Gaza which will say "down with Hamas terror." You would
only have to do that for ONE HOUR. Then you will understand what
it feels like to live in a true occupation – the occupation of Hamas.
Do we have a deal?*

Ramzi: *With Regards, Ramzi*

This exchange with Ramzi is typical. It shows that the Jihadist mind
simply writes off your suffering and builds it's case on perceived Muslim
suffering. They ignore their enemy's suffering and never look at the log
in their eye.

Ramzi never took on the bet. He would never carry such a sign, only the
signs that call for ending the so-called apartheid wall. An Italian man,
Angelo Frammartino, 25, espoused the typical anti-Israel views of a far-
leftist, as he expressed in a letter to the newspaper in 2006:

*We must face the fact that a situation of no violence is a luxury in
many parts of the world, but we do not seek to avoid legitimate acts
of defense…I never dreamed of condemning resistance, the blood of
the Vietnamese, the blood of the people who were under colonialist
occupation or the blood of the young Palestinians from the first
intifada.*

Sadly ironic, on August 10, during a terrorist assault at Sultan Suleiman
Street, near Herod's Gate in Jerusalem, he was stabbed – twice in the
back and once in the neck. He died shortly after. Palestinians thought he
was a Jew. It didn't matter what his ideas were. To them, he was a Jew
and deserved to die.

The lesson is – don't be like Angelo.

Chapter 10
They Use Reverse Logic

REVERSALISM is another term I have coined. Reversalism explains the phenomena that exists in the culture of death, by which logic is turned upside down and there is much play on words. The reality is that if we reverse the typical Muslim accusations to reflect on them, we would get the truth. When one examines all the supposed conspiracies, one finds that only the terrorist conspiracy is real. Jihadism has one main conspiracy – the destruction of modern secular society and the establishment of Islamic hegemony.

In this reversalist mentality, Zionists are Nazis, liberating Iraq from Saddam is an occupation, death is life, sorrow is joy, conspirators are victims, and victims are terrorists. It's quite amazing. So much of this reversalist mindset is a result of trusting conjecture. Conjecture is always the tool of bigoted scholarship, if one can indeed call it scholarship.

Reversalism has unfortunately crept into our politically-correct culture. The Jewish Diaspora, then returning home, became the Israeli occupation. Jewish refugees, 850,000 of them forced to leave Muslim lands, are no longer considered to be one of the worst refugee problem in history. In reversalist fashion, our politically-correct culture has taken that title away from the Jews and given it to the Palestinians. I explain this subject in detail, in my previous book, *Why I Left Jihad: The Root of Terrorism and the Return of Radical Islam.*

This reversalism occurred as a result of Arab pressure, the United Nations, and plain anti-Semitism. One can almost ascertain the true facts if one reverses the statements made by jihadists, their supporters, or those who do not adhere to the facts of history but make excuses for them.

After examining the jihadist mindset, Westerners can solve the puzzle that is the Middle East. For centuries, the jihadist mindset has been conditioned to think in certain patterns, in order to label the opposition and discount anyone who brings critical thinking to the table. These "plugs" to conscious thinking need to be examined and understood in order to comprehend the jihadist epidemic. One would almost have to write a dictionary with new definitions to explain this.

For example, Palestinian journalists are in the habit of comparing Israel's actions in the territories with those of the Nazis. In anti-Semitic publications, Israeli leaders are portrayed as oppressors. Benjamin Netanyahu, while serving as Prime Minister, was portrayed as a Nazi and described as "a Zionist terrorist who is worse than Hitler."

It is quite amazing to hear such gross exaggerations permeate the Muslim world, especially when they use the Nazi-style propaganda to accuse others of Nazism.

The notion that *Zionism is Nazism* has been fostered by the reversalist mentality, which goes much deeper than is often realized. The goal of reversalist ideology seeks to deprive the Jew of an equal place in the world, even the right to exist. It implies that the Jews have no claim to be free and independent like other people.

The Palestinians are currently engaged in rewriting their history. Professor Rafi Yisraeli of Hebrew University stated: "While constructing their national myths, they are erasing Jewish history, dispossessing the Jews from their status as a people, determining that the Jews are tribes and not a people and, therefore, do not deserve the land and that those who do are the Arabs who, in their opinion, are the descendants of the Canaanites." The Palestinian media is full of fabrications of this type. The TV studios host Muslim historians who exchange views and answer viewers' phone-in questions. "We are the most ancient people, and the most ancient culture is the culture of Palestine," historian Professor Azzam Sisalam explains to the viewers. "The Hebrews are an Arab tribe. The land belongs to us and to our Christian brethren. As a historian I challenge any of their historians who claim that the ruins belong to them."

With this reversalist mentality, what is Jewish now becomes Muslim. These false historians wipe out the days of the First and Second Temples, and determine that the Western Wall was built by Arabs. "All the excavations did not prove the location of the holy place that they invented," said Arafat in an interview on Palestinian Television in 1998. "For over thirty years they occupied the land, and they did not succeed in bringing one shred of proof with regard to the site of the temple."

They would cite sources that do not exist and present them as the absolute truth, and they conceal archeological findings. They reiterate their claim over and over again until it becomes a "fact." (Professor Rafi Yisraeli of Hebrew University, Article by Amos Nevo, "Yediot Ahronot," March 10, 2000) So in essence, even the ownership of Jewish holy places like the Western Wall which is known throughout the ages as Jewish have become Muslim. These analogies are not simply allegoric. Muslim mobs burned and destroyed Joseph's tomb, a historically known synagogue were the tomb on Joseph, a biblical patriarch to Israel was buried, then danced in celebration, painted the dome green, and converted it to a mosque. Over sixteen synagogues were desecrated on the West Bank, literally *all the* synagogues in Judea.

DEATH MEANS LIFE

Real life is death, and death is life. "My son was not destroyed; he is not dead; he is living a happier life than I am," said Muhammad Farhat's mother. Umm Nidal was referring to the Qur'an: "And say not of those who are slain in the way of Allah: 'They are dead.' Nay, they are living, though ye perceive (it) not" (Sura 2:154). Umm Nidal continued: "Because I love my son, I encouraged him to die a martyr's death for the sake of Allah...Jihad is a religious obligation incumbent upon us, and we must carry it out. I sacrificed Muhammad as part of my obligation. This is an easy thing. There is no disagreement [among scholars] on such matters." (MEMRI.ORG, Special Dispatch Series – No. 391)

FUNERALS ARE WEDDINGS

As my aunt Fatima did when Raed my cousin was killed in his terror attempt to bomb Ben Yehuda street, the family had conducted a wedding celebration. The death announcements of the shaheeds are often more like announcements for a wedding, rather than a funeral. One newspaper ad read: "Congratulations will be accepted immediately after the burial 10 P.M. at the home of the martyr's uncle." (Al Ayam, Palestinian Authority, October 4, 2001).

JOY IS SADNESS

Recently in Gaza, thugs broke up a gathering of singers and their fans, issuing a snippy statement that Palestinians were in need of resistance fighters, "not singers, corruption mongers, and advocates of immorality."

Abu Musab al-Zarqawi's tribe in Jordan, the Al-Khalayleh, claimed in November 2005 that they had disowned Zarqawi, who had sown havoc in Iraq. Al-Khalayleh made that public declaration in the aftermath of Zarqawi's attack on three Amman hotels. The day of the attack, November 9, 2005, was dubbed the Jordanian 9/11. But blood has its claims, and in truth, Zarqawi had been a man of high standing in Jordan and in other Arab lands. After his death, the regime in Amman may have announced that his corpse would not "stain Jordan's soil," but his clan held a "Martyr's Wedding" for him, and four members of Jordan's parliament turned up at that funeral ceremony. (Fouad Ajami, Wall Street Journal, June 22, 2006)

LOSSES ARE VICTORIES

Abdulrahim Ali Modei, the Islamists' information minister, conceded at a recent news conference that many Islamist troops had been killed, but he did not sound discouraged. "These are victories," he said. "Our soldiers are in paradise now." (New York Times, December 25, 2006, *Ethiopia Bombs Airport in Somali Capital*)

VIOLENCE IS PEACE EXPRESSED BY VIOLENCE

The jihadists' convoluted logic is amazing, but the Western response is more amazing. The Pope said that religion should not be spread by violence and that jihad violence is against God's nature. Muslims view such an opinion as an insult and call the Pope a liar. Muslims respond to the Pope's insult by becoming enraged and committing more acts of jihad violence. So, is the Pope a liar? Of course not. The liars are the jihadists. They deny that jihad is violent, then they set about expressing their opinion with violence. Does this make any sense?

If this type of thinking was made into a flowchart, it would appear as an endless coil. Muslims felt insulted. The result was an even more insulting display of Muslim protests, flag burning, effigy of the Pope (who is holy to Catholics worldwide), anti-Western and anti-Semitic cartoons, and pro-jihad propaganda.

In the U.S., the History Channel airs programs which aim to prove that Jesus had love interests, and yet, Christians don't riot. Christians seem able to tolerate controversial topics such as the DaVinci Code, The Life of Brian, and an array of archeology that questions the authenticity of the Bible. What is the difference between Westerners and Middle Easterners?

I believe it's our Judeo-Christian heritage.

Even with all of the evidence, many will dismiss my logic as being demonization of Islam. Many will never see the truth until it's too late, yet they are not the ones who will pay the price – we all will.

THEY BLAME INTERNATIONAL ZIONISM

Arab anti-Semitism has adopted many of Europe's classic anti-Semitic myths, even those that Western anti-Semites have discarded as being too primitive. Yet, these anti-Semitic lies are accepted by scholars and presidents throughout the Middle East. Many in the West argue that the issue with the Middle East is a lack of education. But anti-Semitism in the Middle East has nothing to do with education only, but rather, a state of mind and consciousness.

However, before we talk about international Zionism, we must mention *The Protocols of the Elders of Zion.*

Arab Voice has been serializing an Arabic-language version of *The Protocols of the Elders of Zion* on its website (www.arabvoice.com). *The Protocols* is no ordinary book. It purports to be the secret transcription of a Zionist Congress, which met in Switzerland in 1897, recorded by a tsarist spy and first published in St. Petersburg in 1903. At the meeting, Jewish leaders allegedly discussed their plans to establish Jewish "sovereignty over all the world." *The Protocols* includes their boasts of being "invincible" and describes plans to establish a "Super-Government Administration" which will "subdue all the nations." In reality, *The Protocols* is a fabrication, forged by the tsarist secret police, the Okhrana, around 1898-99. This pseudo-document had limited impact until twenty years later, after World War I and the Russian Revolution, when its message about a Jewish conspiracy to dominate the world was well received. *The Protocols* quickly became a best-seller, appearing in German translation in January 1920. The former German royal family helped defray publication costs, and deposed Kaiser Wilhelm II had portions of the book read out loud to dinner guests. Translations into other languages quickly followed. Henry Ford endorsed the book, as did *The London Times.* Although the book's forged nature was established by 1921, somewhat reducing its appeal and outreach (the Times and Ford both retracted their endorsements), it remained a powerful force. (Daniel Pipes, New York Post, November 5, 2002)

In Egypt, the book made its first appearance in 1951. It was prefaced by Abbas Mahmud al-Aqqad, one of Egypt's most famous and respected writers and one of my favorites when I attended school in the Middle East. In his foreword, al-Aqqad voiced his surprise that this amazing book waited so long to be published in Egypt in its integral version, whereas all Arab countries should be fully aware of its contents, being as they are the victims of the Balfour Declaration and of the foundation of the Jewish State on Palestinian territory. (Hadassah Ben-Itto, *The Lie that Wouldn't Die,* p. 334)

The book has been publicly recommended not only by our scholars but Presidents Nasser and Sadat in Egypt, President Arif of Iraq, King Faisal of Saudi Arabia, Colonel Qaddafi in Libya, and various other monarchs, presidents, prime ministers, and other political and intellectual leaders. (Bernard Lewis, *Semites and Anti-Semites,* pp. 208-220)

In March 1970, a Lebanese newspaper placed *The Protocols* first on its list of non-fiction bestsellers. Besides the growing number of Arabic translations and editions, there is a rapidly developing body of original anti-Semitic literature in Arabic, much of it based directly or indirectly on *The Protocols,* which is extensively cited as authoritative. (Bernard Lewis, *Semites and Anti-Semites,* pp. 210)

PATRIOTS ARE TRAITORS AND INTERNATIONAL ZIONISTS

There is an array of media samples aired in the Middle East that I will mention in this book to help Westerners understand the Middle East mindset and how this fabrication is used:

The following excerpts are from an interview with Samir 'Ubeid, an Iraqi researcher living in Europe, which aired on Al-Jazeera TV on October 31, 2006:

> **Samir:** *I don't call it the Nobel prize – I call it the "Hubal" [idol] prize.*
>
> **Interviewer:** *Hubal? [Hubal is a pre-Arabian pagan diety]*
>
> **Samir:** *Yes, because it often encourages heresy. It encourages attacks against the heritage, and encourages those who scorn their people and their culture. The proof is that it was awarded recently to Pamuk, who had encouraged civil strife, which might preoccupy Turkey and the Muslims in general. He held Turkey responsible for what the Ottoman state did, when he referred to the massacre of the Armenians.*
>
> **Interviewer:** *In other words, if you are a traitor to your country, you deserve this prize.*
>
> **Samir:** *If you are a traitor to your country, and a heretic, who curses his Prophet, you deserve a Nobel Prize.*
>
> *Why has the prize been awarded to 167 Jews, and to only four Arabs out of 380 million Arabs – and all four are considered traitors? For*

example, Al-Sadat got the prize during the normalization process, and as a price for Camp David, together with Begin, who carried out the Deir Yassin massacre, and who was in the "Haganah" gangs. Later, the prize was awarded to [Ahmad] Al-Zewail, in order to buy his invention, and Al-Zewail has disappeared since.

Interviewer: *You mean the Egyptian Ahmad Al-Zewail?*

Samir: *Yes, the Egyptian chemist. The prize was also awarded to Mohamed ElBaradei, and in this case, it is soaked in the blood of the Iraqi children and people. Mother Teresa was brought, along with a group of people like her...*

Interviewer: *Some say the prize was awarded to her for her missionary activity in Africa, India, and so on...*

Samir: *Let's assume she was righteous, according to the logic of the media, which is now controlled by the Jews and Hollywood. When they awarded the prize to Teresa, they were trying to award an "artificial hymen" or "artificial honor" to this prize. My colleague said that there is democracy. What democracy is there, if out of 1.5 billion Chinese, only two or three were awarded the Nobel? If you examine the Russian scientists and writers, who shook the world with their literature and their knowledge...What about Sakharov, what about Tolstoy? In addition...*

Interviewer: *But Sakharov was awarded the Nobel prize.*

Samir: *I meant Chekhov. Chekhov! Chekhov!*

Are we Arabs not included in the transfer of the scientific genetic code? We, the descendants of Al-Khawarizmi, Al-Jahez, Al-Razi, Avicenna, and Ibn Al-Haytham – are we all born idiots? Is there not a single scientist among us? Are we not included in the genetic code? Is intelligence not transferred down among us Arabs?

Interviewer: *Scientific creativity occurs in freedom and democracy, brother.*

Samir: *Democracy does not explain how it was awarded to 167 Jews, from among those 15 million scattered around the world, while abandoning 1.5 billion Chinese, a billion Indians, and 380 million Arabs. This is racism.*

The [Grameen] bank for the poor won the prize because some of its shareholders are giants like Haliburton and others.

They infiltrated this bank, which became in the pocket of the Freemasons. This prize stems from the core of the Protocols of the Elders of Zion.

THE HOLOCAUST IS A JEWISH RITUAL NOT NAZI

To show how upside down some of the analogies in the Middle East are, I would like to provide the following excerpt, from an interview with former PLO ambassador to Vienna, Ghazi Hussein, which aired on New TV on June 21, 2006:

Ghazi Hussein: *"Holocaust" means burning a human being alive. This was originally a Jewish religious term, which means a "sacrificial offering" to God, burned completely at the altar. Thus, the Holocaust is considered the most sacred rite of the Jews, and it is denoted in Hebrew by the word "Shoah," which means "fire." Describing the annihilation of the Jews in Nazi Germany as a "Shoah" is intended to portray it as sacred...*

Nazism began with the persecution of assimilated Jews, in close cooperation with the Zionist movement. The Nazis signed an agreement with the Zionist movement, which was represented by the Jewish Agency in Palestine. This agreement called "Haavara," was an official agreement between Nazi Germany and the Zionist movement. According to this agreement, German Jews were permitted to immigrate only to Palestine...

Hitler wanted to cleanse Germany of the Jews. The Zionist movement wanted to cleanse Germany of the Jews. The Nazi interests coincided with those of the Zionist movement – to cleanse Germany and the areas occupied by the German forces of the Jews, and to make them immigrate to Palestine alone...

If we take the number of Jews in the world in 1939, when World War II broke out, and compare it with the number of Jews in the world in 1945, considering the increase in the number of Jews every decade, divided by five, the result is that the number of Jews decreased from 600 to 800,000 [sic]...

They exaggerated this figure, in order to exert economic and political pressure, to extort, and to fight whoever dares to criticize the Israeli Holocaust against the Palestinian people...

Judaism divides the world into Jews and non-Jews. Judaism is hostile towards Christianity and Islam. In accordance with the resolution of the Zionist Congress conventions, including the secret resolutions of the first Zionist Congress, which some call "the Protocols of the Elders of Zion," they want to spread internal strife in all countries, and to generate disorder and unrest, so that ultimately, they will rule the world.

So, in their reversed arguments, it was Hitler who laid the cornerstone for the establishment of Israel, and not Chaim Weizmann. Christians, too, divide the world – into Christian and non-Christian. What is crucial though, is how we view these divisions. Judeo-Christianity does not take away any entitlement from Muslims to live as equals in their culture. Yet, with Islamism this is not the case. Non-Muslims are either Kuffar or Dhimmi and have no rights whatsoever.

The following excerpts are from an interview with the president of the Middle East Center for Studies and Public Relations, Dr. Hisham Jaber, which aired on Al-Manar TV on July 11, 2005:

__Jaber:__ I have some doubts about the September (2001) events – and some articles and books share my opinion. I believe the events of 9/11 were not planned, prepared, or perpetrated by al-Qaeda alone. Absolutely not. A force greater than al-Qaeda was behind these events. Whenever an ordinary crime takes place, the question is: "who benefits?" – let alone when the crime is of such huge proportions. What happened in Britain, and why Britain of all places?

The perpetrator believes that he carried out an operation in retaliation for the oppression afflicted upon the world's wretched people by Western policies, and especially by the U.S. and Britain. This is what he believes. In addition, I say that the actual perpetrator – the person who actually commits a suicide operation – is not a mercenary, but he may have been tricked into it. So who is the planner? The planner who is behind him is the one who benefits from what happens. We all know that after 9/11 the persecution of Muslims began in the U.S. and Europe, but later subsided to a certain extent. For three or four years, we have been concerned – in the wake of these painful events – about the possibility of some sort of annihilation, or perhaps an unbalanced civil war in Europe and the U.S.

between Muslims and non-Muslims, or let's say, the Westerners. It is global Zionism that stands to gain the most from this.

Regardless of the logic of conspiracy, I would like to say something. We read history, and we know that since the Protocols of the Elders of Zion, Zionism has forged the New Testament – and by now, 60 million in the U.S. alone have left Christianity to become believers in the Torah. Global Zionism has tried to forge the holy Quran, and has printed many copies of this forgery. It was discovered that many extremist movements were backed by (global Zionism).

The following excerpts are from an interview with Nabil Shaker Al-Taleqani a Muslim cleric from Denmark:

Nabil Shaker Al-Taleqani: *(The Europeans) have a materialistic theory, a man-made theory. This theory is prone to mistakes. On the other hand, the theory that descended from the heavens is a complete theory that retains the spiritual aspect. When I look at people living here (in Europe), they are empty. Statistics show that eighty percent of the patients in their hospitals are mentally ill and depressed. Why? Because they are detached from spirituality. What is more honorable, spirit or matter? Spirit. This is why they need Islam and the Muslims.*

The first terrorist organization in history was the Sicarii, formed by a group of extremist Jews of the zealot sect, and the brothers know this.

Moderator: *This is further proof that the Jews carried out terrorist attacks and so on, but they were able to conceal and bury it and make Islam look like terrorism.*

Nabil Shaker Al-Taleqani: *There is a fundamental point, Mr. 'Issam. There is a fundamental point. Go back to the book* <u>The Protocols of the Elders of Zion</u>. *We must return to the twenty-four protocols, to these secret documents. When we turn the pages of these protocols, we see there are some people who pretend to be Muslims, but are actually Jews, and they are the ones who began to distort Islam. These people are behind this media, which is entirely against Islam and the Muslims.*

The following excerpts are from an interview with Dr. Hossein Mozaffar, member of the Iranian Association for the Defense of the Palestinians, which aired on the Iranian TV Quran Channel on October 20, 2006. In their view, Herzl collaborated with Hitler to finish the Jews. There was no mention in the Middle East of the involvement of Haj Amin Al-Husseini, the supreme Muslim Council. Further, the Holocaust was not a result from Hitler's genocide, but typhus which infected Muslims, Christians, and Jews.

> **Dr. Hossein Mozaffar:** In 1987 [sic], Herzl, the founder of International Zionism, organized a conference in Basel, Switzerland. Speeches were delivered there. They collected the main themes of these speeches, and called each chapter a "protocol." These protocols were collated into a booklet, which was secret in the beginning. Later, as a result of natural disasters and floods, it was exposed and became available to the public.

> Following World War II, [the Zionists] tried to penetrate the Middle East and the Islamic countries. Back then, Hitler and Herzl collaborated in this matter. Then England and America joined forces to support this cause. England agreed to support the emigration of the Jews, on condition that Palestine be placed under British mandate.

> [...]

> Due to their Protocols and their principal ideas, the Zionists are influential in all the centers of power in England, America, as well as the global powers. It is also true with regard to the media. They control eighty percent of the international media. It is all part of their plan. If I had the book here with me, I would read to you from their Protocols, and show you that controlling the media, the economic centers, and the financial resources is among their main objectives.

> **Interviewer:** Every economic company you hear of...

> **Dr. Hossein Mozaffar:** has Jewish roots.

> [...]

> The typhus disease infected the entire population during the war, and [the Germans] had no choice but to burn their clothes and their bodies. There were Muslims, Christians, and Jews ~ 600,000 altogether. Then, the [Jews] turned the 600,000 into six million. Then they set up exhibitions and built crematoria. All this was their own handiwork, in order to prove that they were oppressed, and to claim that they have a right to the land, because they were refugees.

[...]

Interviewer: *One of my friends...I call him a "friend" because we served together in the army. He was a Jew, but had Zionist thoughts. He used to say very interesting, and even demagogic, things. He would say: "Look, this is why we say we are the Chosen People – although we are very few, look how much money we have. Look how much wealth we have, while you Muslims are so poor."*

Participant: *But the Muslims are much more numerous...*

Interviewer: *"You have oil and everything, but you are still poor."*

Dr. Hossein Mozaffar: *True, because they believe in their superiority, they consider the killing of non-Jews to be permitted. In their schools, they teach how to commit genocide of Muslims. They consider themselves to be the Chosen People. The words they use are very degrading. Excuse me for saying so, but they even believe that non-Jews are inferior to dogs, because dogs should be fed, but it is forbidden to feed non-Jews.* (MEMRI.ORG)

It's interesting, if one takes this Jihadist claim above:

"they [the Jews] believe in their superiority, they consider the killing of non-Jews to be permitted."

and reverses it:

"they, the Jihadists, believe in their superiority, they consider the killing of non-Muslims to be permitted."

Now the statement would be accurate. This is classic reversalism.

It's the classic reveralist mentality were aggressors are victims, and victims are aggressors.

THE ART OF DENIAL – THE HOLOCAUST

Ahmedinijad:

It was a good day for the Jews, when the Nazi Hitler began his campaign of persecution against them," writes Sif Ali Algeruan in Al-Hayat Al-Jedida, a Palestinian newspaper: "They began to disseminate, in a terrifying manner, pictures of mass shootings directed at them, and to invent the shocking story about the gas ovens in which, according to them, Hitler used to burn them. The newspapers are filled with pictures of Jews who were mowed down by Hitler's machine guns, and of Jews being led to the gas ovens. In these pictures they concentrated on women, babies and old people, and they took advantage of it, in order to elicit sympathy towards them, when they demand financial reparations, contributions and grants from all over the world. The truth is that the persecution of the Jews is a myth, that the Jews dubbed 'the tragedy of the Holocaust' and took advantage of, in order to elicit sympathy towards them...Even the crossword puzzles that appeared in the newspapers contain definitions such as "a Jewish center for commemorating the Holocaust and the lie," as a clue for Yad Vashem. "Some of them go hand in glove with the Holocaust deniers," says Esti Vebman, researcher of anti-Semitism. "It is true that there have been of late intellectual circles that are willing to agree that such a historical incident, like the Holocaust, did indeed happen, but from the deniers' point of view there were no gas chambers and no six million who died." (MEMRI.ORG)

THE ART OF DENIAL – THE HAVOC IN FRANCE

Even after the mass hysteria during the ten days of Muslim rioting and arson in France, the Union of French Islamic Organization chairman, Lhaj Thami Breze, cast doubt over the parties behind the accelerating violence.

He accused several parties, including far-rightists and Zionist lobby, of fishing in the troubled water to "smear the image of Muslims and Arabs." The Muslim leader said many of the incidents involving the burning of public properties remain ambiguous.

"The rioting, which started as a spontaneous reaction, is not like that anymore. Some parties are feeding these incidents," Breze charged.

"The perpetrators of such actions can never be Muslims," he declared.

So why does chairman Lhaj blame it on Jews? He knows very well that Anti-Semitism is alive and well in Muslim countries, and the crimes committed in France can be justified, and the guilty party has a way to transfer the guilt to someone else – The Jews.

Chapter 11
The Metamorphsis

THE TERRORISTS MAKE UP NAZI SIMILARITIES

I have chosen to fight anti-Semitism. Why? Because, defenders of Jews in Nazi Germany were viewed by their neighbors as traitors, but after the evil ended, these "traitors" were recognized as righteous gentiles. So, why did the majority of Germans choose to live through the nightmare instead of stopping it?

The Middle East and the Islamic world in general are bent on destroying Israel. Why don't we stop the repetition of history and save so much human suffering? Not only will Jews suffer, but Arabs will suffer as well. Israel's right to exist saves Palestinian lives. Israelis don't want to kill Palestinians. However, the Palestinian dogma will cause civil war and strife, and in the end, Israel will be blamed for it.

There is a rift between Hamas and the P.A., a rift between Shia and Sunni in Iraq, a rift between Christians and Muslims in Lebanon, a rift between Arabs and non-Arab Muslims in Darfur. None of these conflicts were created by Israel or the West. Why are we, as Arabs, not paying attention to the real issues? Hundreds of thousands die, but instead of focusing on solutions, we play the blame game.

Keep in mind that there is no freedom of speech, thought, or religion in any Arab or Muslim nation. These nations, once fully taken over by Islam, would be no different than Communist Russia or Nazi Germany. Like Communism and Nazism, Islamism has the same inclination to export its radical ideas. Islamism does not respect national borders, and the end justifies the means.

We are all capable of bigotry. No one is immune. In Nazi Germany, the majority of once normal Germans supported Hitler, and the Arab masses stood behind Hitler's great friend, the Mufti Haj Al-Ameen Al-Husseni, President of the Supreme Muslim Council, who called for the death of every Jew, civilian or soldier. Yet, instead of confessing what we do, as many Germans did, our Muslim leaders continue to espouse a barrage of denials. Even the Pope made amends with the state of Israel for the mistakes of the Catholic Church. Ikrima Sabri, the Mufti of Jerusalem has stated: "[the Holocaust] is not my problem. Muslims didn't do anything on this issue. It's the doing of Hitler who hated the Jews." (Associated Press.)

The thriving relationship between the Arab/Muslim world and Nazi Germany has been well documented. Sabri's predecessor, the Grand Mufti of Jerusalem, Haj Amin el-Husseni, recruited Hitler's Bosnian-Muslim troops – a unit of the Hanjar (dagger) Division of the Waffen SS, one of eight Nazi divisions.

Haj Muhammad Effendi Amin el Husseini oversaw the extermination of Orthodox Serbs in Bosnia and in Kosovo. Husseini never stood trial for the genocide of thousands of Orthodox Serbs.

You might ask yourself why the Middle East has no Holocaust memorials, books that fight anti-Semitism, or confession regarding anti-Semitism. The reason is simple – the founders of Islam instituted oppressive edicts and committed considerable genocide.

Haj Amin was not the only Muslim leader who instituted harsh measures towards the "heathen" Jews. Umar bin Al-Khattab, the Apostle of Muhammad, the founder of Islam, the second Caliph of Islam, and one of the ten promised by the Prophet of Islam to enter paradise, was the original anti-semite.

In many Arab and Islamic countries, Jews were forced to obey Umar's rule and wear distinctive clothing and a yellow badge of shame on their shoulders. (Sound familiar?) In the ninth century, for example, Baghdad's Caliph Al-Mutawakkil designated a yellow badge for Jews, setting a precedent that would be repeated centuries later in Nazi Germany.

Jews were ordered by decree to wear yellow markers during the rule of Harun Al-Rashid in 807, Al-Hakim the Fatimid Caliph in 1005, and Emir Ismael Abu-Al-Walid in Granada from 1315-1326.

It is amazing that during today's demonstrations, Islamists and the extreme liberal left wave the slogan "Zionism = Nazism," yet a comparison between Nazi law concerning Jews and Dhimmi Law (aimed at Jews and other citizens with no rights) in the Omar Charter reveals striking similarities:

Nazism: *Jews need to wear a mark on their clothing to identify them as Jews. The Star of David for identification with the word (Jude) (must be) on the chest. A yellow banner is to be fixed around the shoulder or arm, as to be recognized as a Jew. They must live in the Jewish Ghettos.*

Islam: *Dhimmis (Jews & Christians) must wear identifiable clothing and live in a clearly marked house. For Jews, a yellow banner is to be fixed around the shoulder or arm, as to be recognized as a Jew.*

Nazism: *Jews are not permitted to serve in the army or navy. They are not allowed to bear arms.*

Islam: *He must not ride a horse or bear arms. He must yield the right-of-way to Muslims.*

Nazism: *Jews cannot hold public offices, whether national, state, or municipal, salaried or honorary, (they) are closed to Jews. Jews cannot be judges in criminal and disciplinary cases. Jews cannot serve on juries.*

Islam: *Dhimmis cannot be a witness in a legal court except in matters relating to other "Dhimmis" or be a judge in a Muslim court.*

Nazism: *As compensation for the protection that Jews enjoy as aliens, they must pay double the taxes the Germans pay.*

Islam: *As compensation for the protection that Dhimmis enjoy, they must pay "Jizzieh," a special tax to be imposed on Dhimmis only.*

Nazism: Marriage to Jews is prohibited. Adoption of Jews and by Jews is prohibited.

Islam: A Jew cannot be the guardian of a Muslim child, or the owner of a Muslim slave.

Nazism: Jews must live in Ghettos.

Islam: They may not build their houses in the neighborhood of Muslims. (Faqeeh Al-Muluk, *Omar Charter,* Vol. 2, pp. 124-136.)

You might argue that Westerners have committed the same types of attrocities, yet in the West, we confess our faults, and move on. Why is it so different in the Middle East?

THE SOURCE OF UMAR'S DECLARATION

The Omar Pact was not extracted from Omar Ibin Al-Khattab. Rather, his covenant was derived from the highest of Islamic sources:

1. The killing of converts (after their three-day warning), came from Muhammad, the prophet of Islam – "Whoever changes his Islamic religion, kill him."

2. The Quran, 9:29, orders that non-Muslims must be fought until they believe in Islam or pay the Al-Jizzieh Tax:

   Fight against such of those who have been given the Scripture as believe not in Allah nor the Last Day, and forbid not that which Allah hath forbidden by His messenger, and follow not the Religion of Truth, until they pay the tribute readily, being brought low.

3. Muhammad ordered:

   Allah's Apostle said, "I have been ordered to fight with the people till they say, 'None has the right to be worshiped but Allah,' and whoever says, 'None has the right to be worshiped but Allah,' his life and property will be saved by me except for Islamic law, and his accounts will be with Allah, (either to punish him or to forgive him.)" (Sahih Al-Bukhari, 9:57)

4. Muhammad ordered that in a Muslim society, if a Muslim kills a non-Muslim, then the Muslim is not put to death:

No Muslim should be killed for killing a Kafir (infidel). (Sahih Al-Bukhari, 9:50)

5. However, a Muslim who kills a Muslim and a non-Muslim who kills a Muslim, are both to be killed:

O ye who believe! the law of equality is prescribed to you in cases of murder: the free for the free, the slave for the slave, the woman for the woman. But if any remission is made by the brother of the slain, then grant any reasonable demand, and compensate him with handsome gratitude, this is a concession and a Mercy from your Lord. After this whoever exceeds the limits shall be in grave penalty. (Q 2:178)

Yahya related to me from Malik that he heard that Umar ibn Abd al-Aziz gave a decision that when a Jew or Christian was killed, his blood-money was half the blood-money of a free Muslim. (Malik, Book 43, No. 43.15.8b)

6. Mohammad practiced and ordered ethnic cleansing by removing all Jews, Christians and pagans from the Arabian Peninsula. In fact, just before his death, he stated:

While we were in the Mosque, the Prophet came out and said, "Let us go to the Jews." We went out till we reached Bait-ul-Midras. He said to them, "If you embrace Islam, you will be safe. You should know that the earth belongs to Allah and His Apostle, and I want to expel you from this land. So, if anyone amongst you owns some property, he is permitted to sell it, otherwise you should know that the Earth belongs to Allah and His Apostle." (Al-Bukhari 4:392)

7. Muslims are ordered to push the non-Muslims to the narrowest part of the road when meeting them:

Do not initiate the greeting of salaam to a Jew or Christian, and if you meet them in the street, push them to the narrowest part of the road. (Narrated by a Muslim, 2167)

In summary, Muslims are ordered by the highest levels of authority in Islam – the Quran, Muhammad, and His apostles – that Christians and Jews:

a. Cannot build any new houses of worship in their neighborhoods, and can't repair the ones that fall into ruin;

b. Cannot evangelize and cannot forbid their kin from becoming Muslims;

c. Cannot wear clothes that make them look like Muslims, and they must wear distinguishing clothes;

d. Cannot engrave Arabic inscription on their seals;

e. Cannot do anything publicly pertaining to their religion (show their crosses or stars, be heard worshipping, etc.);

f. Cannot take slaves who have been allotted to Muslims (the reverse is possible);

g. Cannot build houses overtopping the houses of the Muslims.

HATRED HAS A LONG HISTORY

The Mufti of Jerusalem, Haj Amin AlHusseni, the good friend of Adolf Hitler, was not original when he publicly stated, "I declare a holy war, my Muslim brothers! Murder the Jews! Murder them all!" (Leonard J. Davis, and M. Decter, *Myths and Facts*)

Neither was he simply a hijacker of the faith. Neither did he see much difference between Islamist goals and Nazi goals. He was always in close contact with the Nazi Party. He had communications with Heinrich Himmler, a good friend of Adolf Hitler, with whom he coordinated the final solution for the Jews on November 21, 1941.

Today, Hitler is one of the heroes of the Palestinian youth, as shown by an international study on the perceptions of democracy among young people in the world, conducted by researchers from the University of Hamburg. Booksellers in the Middle East report that Hitler's book, *Mein Kampf*, is one of their best sellers. The book is distributed by Al-Shurouq, a Ramallah-based company, to East Jerusalem and the territories controlled by the Palestinian Authority.

According to Agence France Presse, the book, previously banned by Israel, was allowed by the Palestinian Authority. Bisan publishers in Lebanon first published this edition in 1963 and again in 1995. The book costs about $10. The cover shows a picture of Hitler, a swastika, and the title, in both German and Arabic.

The translator of *Mein Kampf*, Luis Al-Haj, wrote the following as part of his introduction to the book:

> *Hitler the soldier left behind not only a legend stained by tragedy itself; the tragedy of a state whose dreams were shattered, a regime whose pillars were torn down, and a political party that was crushed.*
>
> *Hitler was a man of ideology who bequeathed an ideological heritage whose decay is inconceivable. This ideological heritage includes politics, society, science, culture, and war as science and culture.*
>
> *The National Socialism that Hitler preached for and whose characteristics were presented in his book My Struggle, and whose principles he explained in his speeches before he took power, as well as during the 13 years he spent at the head of the German nation – this National Socialism did not die with the death of its herald. Rather, its seeds multiplied under each star.*
>
> *We cannot really understand the efforts of this man without examining the principles enclosed in his book My Struggle that the Nazis turned into the "Gospel of National Socialism."*
>
> *This translation of the book My Struggle has never been presented to Arab speakers. It is taken from the original text of the author, Adolf Hitler. The text as untouched by the censor. We made a point to deliver Hitler's opinions and theories on nationalism, regimes, and ethnicity without any changes because they are not yet outmoded and because we, in the Arab world, still proceed haphazardly in all three fields. (Arabic translation of the introduction to Adolf Hitler's* <u>Mein Kampf</u>, *distributed by Al-Shurouq, a Ramallah-based book distributor, in East Jerusalem and territories controlled by the Palestinian Authority.)*

Nazism never died. It simply cloaked itself with a religious twist. It gets repackaged and resold, not to the uneducated but to the spiritually empty.

Chapter 12
Spiritual Recruitment

ARROGANCE, LIES, AND DENIALS

I believe racism is the reason for denial of the Holocaust, denial of factual history, denial of the right for Jewish existence, and denial of the obvious historic Jewish connections to Israel. In *Why I Left Jihad,* I have documented much of the missing links that do not exist in the Arab history textbooks.

EXPLANING DEFEAT WITH ARROGANCE

For years after the Six Day War erupted, the question on everyone's mind was – "How did Israel win against us?" Of course, many Arab leaders resorted to lying, and the masses bought it. The most common lie that circulated was that Americans were piloting the Israeli planes and that the weapons used by Arab armies malfunctioned. After all, how could the Arab leaders explain that historically subservient Jews won against all of the massive armies of Egypt, Iraq, Syria, and Jordan?

The Arab mindset would tend to exaggerate and claim that the Arabs were not, in reality, fighting Jews but American air forces with American pilots.

Lies like these are conceived out of a sense of arrogance. The masses buy into the lies, and people reject the facts because of the same arrogance. Arab and Muslim arrogance is killing us. Most of the hate mail I get comes from an attitude of arrogance and pride. "How dare you say what you say?" is a typical comment I receive. Rarely do I get an email offering serious discussion. For ten years, I attempted to argue with their arrogance, which produced very few results. The Middle East would do well to develop an attitude of humility, confession, and reconciliation. Something that is lacking. What we need is "The meek shall inherit the earth," (Bible, Psalm 37:11) and not "you were the best of all people." (Quran, Al Imran: 110)

One of Muhammad's daughters, Umm Kalthoum, testified that she had never heard the Apostle of Allah condone lying, except in these three situations:

1. For reconciliation among people.

2. In war.

3. Amongst spouses, to keep peace in the family. (*Ehiaa Ulum al-Din*, by the famous Islamic scholar al-Ghazali, Vol. 3: pp. 284-287, Ahmad, 6.459. H)

The second point of interest deals with Jihad war. The goal of jihad is well defined in the Quran:

They seek to extinguish the light of Allah by their mouths. But Allah refuses save to perfect His light, even if the Disbelievers are averse. It is He who has sent His messenger with the guidance and the true religion, in order that He may make it prevail over all religions, even if the pagans are averse. (Quran, 9:32-33)

In the Muslim world, everyone knows the term Al-Harbu Khid'a – war is deception.

Again, I believe that the reason there is so much denial and deception in the Muslim world is a combination of arrogance and racism, more than the desire to lie.

RECRUITMENT FORUMS – SPIRITUAL

Most Westerners think that recruitment merely occurs in recruitment centers and through messengers who seek out available and willing souls.

In reality, the recruitment centers are already visited daily, when Muslims voluntarily visit the local mosque, especially on Fridays.

The local mosque has been the best place to recruit. Simply change the preacher into a fiery, Jihadist, and the rest is history. The mosques are the preparation centers and facilitate the spiritual and mental preparedness process. All that is left are the technicalities. Just as the Gospel message states – "the harvest is plenty, but the reapers are few," it can be said in the Middle East, the willing souls are plenty, but the explosives are few.

For more than a decade, Quranic verses have been chanted in the mosques and sermons glorifying self-sacrifices as a consecration of oneself to God have been mixed with prayers. Flyers with poems have been distributed to Palestinian mothers and fathers to encourage their children to kill themselves for the love of Allah and for their country. (The Voice of Palestine radio, May 25, 2001, from *Terror Suicide: How Is It Possible?* Israel Orbach, Department of Psychology, Bar-Ilan University, Ramat-Gan, Israel).

Palestinian Minister of Religious Endowment, Sheik Yousef Jum'a Salamah, aired on Palestinian Authority TV on March 10, 2006:

> *Many mothers have sacrificed their husbands in defense of the religion and the homeland. Many mothers have lost their children, who were martyred in defense of this blessed land.*
>
> *Who is Al-Khansaa, who has become a role model? When her brother Sakhr died, before the advent of Islam, she was overwrought. All day long she recited poetry: "The sunrise reminds me of Sakhr, and I remember him at every sunset. If not for the many people around me weeping for their brothers, I would have killed myself." Just one brother – yet she couldn't bear it.*
>
> *But when Allah opened her heart to the faith, and she became a Muslim, she sent her four sons to the Battle of Al-Qadissiya, where they were martyred. When the surviving soldiers returned victorious from the battlefield and informed her that her four children had been martyred – did she cry? Did she recite poetry? Did she rip her clothes, and uncover her hair? No. She said: "Praise be to Allah, who honored me with their deaths, and I pray to Allah that He*

reunite us under His mercy." Brothers, victory lies there. Victory lies there, not in this world.

[...]

There, the Palestinian, Arab, and Muslim woman will hold her head high, Allah willing, due to all her sacrifices for her religion and homeland - good sons, devoted husbands, relatives, and so on and so forth. That's how a woman should be.

Mecca, in Saudi Arabia, is the holiest place of Islam. Here, jihad sermons abound. Imam Sudayyis at the Al-Haram Mosque in Mecca presented a Friday sermon entitled, <u>Either Victory or Martyrdom.</u> In his sermon he discussed Jewish history and modern jihad. The following excerpts are from that sermon which was broadcast live on Channel 1 of Saudi TV:

The history of the (Jewish) people is written in black ink, and has included a series of murders of the prophets, the Mujaheedin, and righteous people. This, although the book descended upon Moses, is all mercy. Allah has said (and this is preceded by the Book of Moses which was a guide and a mercy for people before him): "So where is this mercy in all this barbarity, devoid of moral and human values? But maybe it is the beginning of their end."

Oh Brothers in the land of missions and the cradle of valor, Oh Sons of the brave Mujaheedin, Oh descendants of conquering heroes, you have revived the hopes of this nation through your blessed jihad. By Allah, be patient until, with Allah's help, one of two good things will be awarded you: either victory or martyrdom. Our hearts are with you; our prayers are dedicated to you. The Islamic nation will not spare money or effort in support of your cause, which is the supreme Muslim cause, until the promise made by Allah, who never breaks a promise, is fulfilled. (MEMRI.ORG)

Time and again, Palestinian TV features parades of endless rows of newly enlisted suicide volunteers, ready for the call, dressed in military uniforms and masks covering their faces, marching with determination and yelling out mantras and war slogans in an ecstatic trance. Such an atmosphere is like the "Pied Piper of Hamlin" – electrifying, enchanting, and mesmerizing to the youngsters. During the last two years, the admired leader Yasser Arafat repeatedly appeared on TV and solemnly declared that he was going to lead a march of a million shaheeds to

Jerusalem. Such tactics and atmosphere can heighten the suggestibility of youngsters to an almost complete submission, especially when coupled with the promises of psychological and materialistic incentives and rewards. (The Voice of Palestine radio, May 25, 2001, from *Terror Suicide: How Is It Possible?* Israel Orbach, Department of Psychology, Bar-Ilan University, Ramat-Gan, Israel).

MARTYR GLORIFICATION

Each terror attack brings in a new wave of volunteers, especially after the enthusiastic report of a "successful" attack, glorifying the attack and the attacker. The reports are always accompanied by a video clip of the suicide bomber, recorded before the act, who, donned in uniform and holding a gun, declares his or her determination to kill himself or herself for the Palestinian people and for Allah.

One might choose to volunteer by actively seeking out a terrorist organization. One might even be approached by a mediator after making a statement, sometimes quite innocently, showing an interest in becoming a shaheed. Terrorist organizations sometimes choose to approach a family member of a shaheed or a victim of Israeli action, offering an opportunity to avenge his/her relative's death. Arin Ahmad, a bomber who backed out at the last minute, is a nineteen-year-old girl whose boyfriend was either killed by the Israeli army (according to the Palestinians) or killed in an accident while preparing a bomb (according to the Israelis). In the company of her friends, she felt a sudden urge to avenge her boyfriend's death and uttered that she would like to become a shaheed. Arin claims that a few days after her remark, she was approached by a terrorist organization operator; and following a preliminary, confidential investigation and a brief interview, she was drafted (Ha'aretz, Israel, June 21, 2002).

Usually, at this point in the recruitment procedure, a secret meeting is arranged with a high-ranking official or a noted religious personality, in which the volunteer is told that he or she was chosen for the holy mission, promoting his or her beliefs in the exclusivity of being inducted, as a shaheed, into the prestigious and holy fraternity.

The volunteer then receives a new name – Al Shaheed Al Hai – the (still) living martyr. From then on, the suicide attacker-to-be is required to keep the bombing plans totally secret. Yet, many of them do convey the secret to family members. Satiti, another youngster who volunteered, told in his inquiry that his parents tried to prevent him from killing himself, but he was determined because what he had heard in the mosques was much more important (Ha'aretz, Israel, June 21, 2002). There is repeated emphasis that the Shaheed Al Hai is part of a selected group of an organization with a strong group affiliation and commitment. There is a total compartmentalization of information, and the volunteer gets to know only his operator.

SECLUSION, INDOCTRINATION, AND RITUALS

After the initiation, the volunteer is kept in seclusion (although not total isolation) for about a month, in a training site or a mosque. The exact nature of the training that they go through is not clear. Part of the training includes sessions of direct religious and political indoctrination. Satiti disclosed that he spent a month in a mosque, where he learned how important it is to be a shaheed, that it is the noblest purpose of all, that this is the most important goal for the Palestinian people from a nationalistic and religious standpoint, that this is a holy war, that only the worthy and the best can become shaheeds. In the mosque, Satiti also learned about all the rewards for which he and his family would be eligible, including the black-eyed virgins and financial assistance. He also learned to believe that this world is only a corridor to the hereafter and that he should constantly think about heaven, the waiting virgins, the holy commandment that he is about to perform, and the great source of pride he will be for the Palestinian people and his family (see Ha'aretz, Israel, June 21, 2002).

The training and education culminate in a video ritual. It is staged as a scene of commitment, of no return. The Shaheed Al Hai appears in uniform, bearing arms and holding the Quran. In the background appear the canonized symbols. In a short speech, he or she consecrates himself or herself to total self-sacrifice for god and the Palestinian people. This video is presented in the media after the suicide attack. On the day of the attack, the Shaheed Al Chai is instructed to bathe, to clean and purify himself or herself, to pray, and to dress in his or her best clothes. Then, he or she is accompanied to the site of the attack and given last instructions.

However, not all suicide bombers go through this lengthy process. In some cases, especially with women, the procedure is hasty and abrupt. Arin Ahmad, the nineteen-year-old girl, was approached just a few days after she expressed her desire to become a shaheed. She was very surprised, as she expected to be called on only after a few months and after preparation. The operator called her and gave her instructions about the meeting place and about what she would wear. "They did not give me time to think," Ahmad recalled. She did not carry out the mission. Apparently, the preparatory period was missing.

CONFESSIONS

It is difficult to tell the difference between teachers who truly speak of peace and those who are saying it due to government pressure or for Western consumption. Yet, certain confessions from Al-Jazeera do come out. Lebanese political analyst Adib Farha, on Al-Jazeera TV on July 16, 2005, stated:

> The problem seems to be that we have two types of discourse: One for external consumption, and another for internal purposes. The leaders of the ethnic groups and the great imams condemn these terrorist operations. However, I have lived in an Arab Muslim country, which I shall not name, and there, in Friday sermons, you regularly hear the Imam calling to kill the enemies of Arabs and Muslims: "Kill them and take revenge upon them. Destroy their hopes and their lives," and so on. This is incitement. True, we do have enemies. But we should not ask god to take revenge upon them. This is not how you conduct political matters.

Yet, not all mosques preach hatred. Moderate Friday sermons usually come from the United Arab Emirates, which is considered moderate by the U.S. The following excerpts are from a Friday sermon in the UAE by Sheik Mubarak Lamhiri, which aired on UAE TV on July 29, 2005:

Dear brothers, this ongoing series of crimes and incidents, which are shaking the Islamic nation - whether directed at Muslims or non-Muslims - are harmful to this great nation, and to Islam and Muslims in the East and West, in Muslim and non-Muslim countries alike.

[...]

Dear brothers, our disaster is not caused by people of other religions. This matter is clear, dear brothers. Our disaster is caused by people of our own religion, who commit acts that distort the image of Islam and cause it to be hated. By Allah, if a Muslim preaches to a non-Muslim and talks to him about the tolerance of Islam, what will the latter tell him? The non-Muslim will say, "We watch on TV day and night what Muslims do." This is distorting the image of Islam. By Allah, whoever contemplates the image of Islam today finds no reason to join it.

[...]

Dear brothers, what happened in Sharm Al-Sheik, and even what happened in Western countries, in London, harms Islam. It harms the pure image of Islam. How odd it is that those who call upon others to support Islam are harming Islamic and distorting its pure image. Dear brothers, these people belong to the enemies of Islam. People who distort the image of Islam belong to the enemies, who tarnish the good name of this religion with every bad deed. What saddens me, dear brothers, is that among us Muslims there are people who raise doubts. They say, "No, no. They did not do this." There are Muslims who say such things. How is this possible, while they boast and compete among themselves in issuing communiques attributing these crimes to themselves? Praise Allah, there are many...

Is there a criminal who says, "I am a criminal?" Have you ever heard of a thief who says, "I am a thief?" The criminals of these times are indeed strange – they kill innocent people and boast about their killings on TV, as you all can see. And what is their pretext? The victory of Islam. By Allah, Islam will not be victorious through such barbaric and abhorrent actions, which harm Islam.

[...]

One of them was driving a fuel truck, which he rigged with explosives, and then he blew it up among innocent people – innocent people who were not involved. And what was his pretext? He wanted to get to Paradise. He wanted to hug the black-eyed virgins. Is this how we reach Paradise? Is this how a Muslim gets to hug the black-eyed virgins – by killing people and spilling blood? What about Allah's wrath over such actions? What about the religious rulings that forbid such barbaric actions?

[...]

Dear brothers, whoever justifies such actions, wherever they are committed, is an accomplice. Whoever permits them and sympathizes with them - such a person, dear brothers, is an accomplice. (MEMRI.ORG)

The following excerpts are from a Friday sermon, which aired on Al-Shariqa TV on July 15, 2005:

How is Islam supported by spilling the blood of civilians throughout the world – In Afghanistan and Iraq, New York and Madrid, Casablanca and Algeria, Saudi Arabia and Qatar, and recently in London, by these criminals who have left the community of Muslims, and who falsely pretend to belong to Islam? How is Islam supported by kidnapping journalists and workers, truck drivers and medical staff, and display them in the media as they are butchered like sheep? Did Islam command this? Absolutely not. Therefore, we must condemn such evil and sinful deeds. We must condemn the killing of innocents, the destruction of cultures and annihilation of civilizations, and the spreading of fear among peaceful souls, especially, brothers, when it is done in the name of Islam, and in defense of Muslims' causes. What image do they want Islam to have?

Chapter 13
Facing the Moment of Death

CREATING THE DISSOCIATIVE TRANCE

Facing the moment of death is a must in every suicide. Indeed, it is evident that preparation for facing death is an important part of the entire process. This was documented for suicide attackers in the September 11, 2001 events in the U.S., as well as in Israel. The aim of part of this process is to give death a new meaning; to increase suggestibility; to install tranquility and peace of mind; to reduce fear; to increase enthusiasm; to mobilize the anger and aggression toward the target; and, at the same time, to keep the mind clear to focus on the mission, and to pay attention to the smallest details. Such a state of mind, habituating contradictory experiences of excitement and calmness at the same time, is characteristic of some dissociative processes (Kahan, 1995). The techniques employed in creating such a state of mind can be learned from the letters of instructions to the suicide attackers, left in the care of Muhammad Atta. The preparation instructions come from an important authority, and the death mission is related as a dramatic, unusual moment of transcendental fusion with god or as the culmination of self-actualization in the service of the nation's existence.

The Palestinian suicide attackers are also instructed to part from their families, friends, and neighbors, in a good mood (not disclosing their mission); to prepare for the meeting with god; to consider the fact that they are going to a better life, that passage to the other life will be smooth with no pain, that it will be like a bird's flight, and that they are eagerly awaited in heaven. They are asked to focus on the purpose of their action, the purification; and how the post-self will witness the dramatic victory. They are instructed to be calm, to have peace of mind, to be confident in their mission, to smile, and to encourage themselves. The days and minutes before the action are very structured; and they are persuaded to pray that God will receive the sacrifice, to fast, and to repeat mantras. They should wash and clean their body and dress in their best garments for the great moment (Al Istiqlal, March 26, 1999).

The last days take on the characteristics of a long, holy ritual. They are even instructed about small details like how to wear their clothes. The calming tone, the repetitions, the mantras, and the reassurances create a hypnotizing atmosphere. Such an atmosphere causes a dissociative split between the inner state of mind and the reality of life. Life disappears into the background, while they experience the inner elation and determination to carry out the mission (see also, Stein, 2002).

This dissociative split is reflected in the words of Satiti. When he was asked about his feelings when he saw, on the site, the innocent men, women, and children whom he was going to kill, he said, "I did not see them at all. We don't see them at all; what was in front of our eyes was the shaheed. Everything is for the commandment. The shaheed is of the highest level. I wanted to take part in the freedom of my people, to carry out the holy commandment, to give pride to my people and friends." Later he added, "They told me to think only about the commandment and the reward waiting in paradise with the virgins, and all the honor that I will receive." (Ha'aretz, Israel, June 21, 2002) This is very similar to what Shneidman (1980) has described as tunnel vision and what Orbach (1994) has described as the dissociative state of mind before the suicidal act is carried out.

Arin Ahmad, who was not prepared for the suicide, remained in touch with herself and with the reality of the situation. She realized that, contrary to the information she was given, the site she was about to attack was not a military base full of armed soldiers. She said in the inquiry, "I got out of the car. The place was not what I saw on the map. I saw many people, mothers and children, boys and girls. I remembered an Israeli girl with whom I used to have contact. Suddenly, I realized the meaning of what I was about to do. I said to myself, 'How am I going to do such a thing?' I changed my mind." (Ha'aretz, Israel, June 21, 2002). Arin remained intact and did not experience tunnel vision or dissociative splits and, thus, could not carry out the suicide attack, in spite of her personal distress and longing for her deceased boyfriend.

LAST MINUTE PRESSURES

Sometimes, the suicide attack is carried out as a result of last-minute pressure. In the case of Arin, the operators who accompanied her tried to pressure her. They said to her, "You are going to be in the highest status…You will be a real hero. This is in the memory of Jared [the dead boyfriend]. You will join him in heaven. You will be with him in paradise." Arin believes that they said that because she had already made all the preparations to complete the mission. When Arin made up her mind to back out, they yelled at her, "You have disappointed us, you are behaving like a little girl. You have lost your chance to be in heaven…Your boyfriend is waiting for you." (Yediot Aharonot, June 21, 2002).

They told her that they would be back when they found a more appropriate target for her, but then, she and her operators were all arrested. Arin was supposed to carry out her mission with another youngster, Badir Ahmed, who also tried to back out at the last minute and asked to go home. The operators talked to him and pressured him in the same way they had done with Arin. They eventually convinced him to complete his mission, and he blew himself up. (Yediot Aharonot, Israel, June 21, 2002).

PREPARATION TO KILL

Beheading

"And I saw thrones, and they sat upon them, and judgment was given unto them: and [I saw] the souls of them that were **beheaded** for the witness of Jesus, and for the word of God, and which had not worshipped the beast, neither his image, neither had received [his] mark upon their foreheads, or in their hands; and they lived and reigned with Christ a thousand years." (Rev 20:4)

How is it possible that a call to behead people could convince all those who were demonstrating in the photo below?

The answer for this is simple – they receive a heavy dose of recitation and memorization from the Middle Ages. All Islamic history in the Middle East covers poetry, the Quran, Hadith, and songs that have beheadings in them:

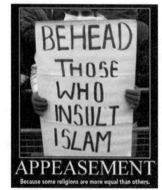

We are those who built our forts

Out of the skulls

Which we brought from the land of the tyrant

By force and on top of the booty

Our Messenger is the one who made us

Noble builders of glory

Our Messenger is the sun of truth

Who lit the face of the world

"What Sharon is doing now is not strange. What the Zionist Entity state is doing to our people in Rafah is not strange. They are avenging the deaths of their cowardly soldiers who were torn to shreds, here in the southern entrance of Gaza, in the Zaytoun neighborhood. They saw our children playing soccer with the heads and body parts of their soldiers. Our children do not fear body parts or blood, nor do our women or youth…" (Sheikh Ibrahim Mudeiris, P.A. cleric, from a Friday sermon at a mosque in Gaza; aired on P.A.TV, May 21, 2004)

Talk of beheading is not unusual in class discussions or even casual conversations in Muslim circles. One could find hundreds of examples of beheadings in Muslim writing, which are currently used in school textbooks, news media, poetry, and even street graffiti. One example from Islamic history goes as follows, Abu Musa said:

I came to the Prophet along with two men of Ash'ariyin, one on my right and the other on my left, while Allah's Apostle was brushing his teeth. Both men asked him for employment. The Prophet said,

*"O Abu Musa!" ("O Abdullah bin Qais!"). I said, "By Him Who sent
you with the Truth, these two men did not tell me what was in their
hearts and I did not feel (realize) that they were seeking employment." As if I were looking now at his Siwak (tooth brush) being
drawn to a corner under his lips, he said, "We never appoint for our
affairs anyone who seeks to be employed. But O Abu Musa, go to
Yemen." The Prophet then sent Mu'adh bin Jabal after him and when
Mu'adh reached him, he spread out a cushion for him and requested
him to get down (and sit on the cushion). Behold, there was a
fettered man beside Abu Musa. Mu'adh asked, "Who is this (man)?"
Abu Musa said, "He was a Jew and became a Muslim, and then
reverted back to Judaism." Then Abu Musa requested Mu'adh to sit
down, but Mu'adh said, "I will not sit down till he has been killed."
This is the judgment of Allah and His Apostle [for such cases] and
he repeated it three times. Then Abu Musa ordered that the man be
killed, and he was killed. Abu Musa added that they discussed the
night prayers and one of them said, "I pray and sleep, and I hope
that Allah will reward me for my sleep as well as for my prayers."*

The historic event of the fettered Jew is meant to make believers callous.
After beheading the Jew, the two men sat and had a silly discussion
about prayers and sleep. Usually, and in most acts of jihad killing, one
would see the jihadists smirk and smile to give the sense of joy and
pleasure to the process of killing.

Beheadings are a commandment in the Quran:

*"Strike terror (into the hearts of) the enemies of Allah and your
enemies." (Sura 8:60) "Fight (kill) them (non-Muslims), and Allah
will punish (torment) them by your hands, cover them with shame."
(Sura 9:14) "I will instill terror into the hearts of the unbelievers,
smite ye above their necks and smite all their finger-tips off them.
It is not ye who slew them; it was Allah." (Sura 8:12, 17) "When ye
encounter the infidels, strike off their heads till ye have made a
great slaughter among them." (Sura 47:3)*

Yet, Muslim apologists will claim that jihad is self-defense. On the
contrary, one could find an array of Islamic Hadith in which jihad is
nothing more than raids and massacres:

*A raiding party led by Zayd set out against Umm in the holy month
of Ramadan. During the raid, Umm suffered a cruel death. Zyad
tied her legs with rope and then tied her between two camels until
they split her in two. She was a very old woman."* (Tabari VIII:96)
*"Make war upon such of those (Christians and Jews) to whom the
scriptures have been given as believe not in god and his apostle
have forbidden, and profess not the professor of truth, until they
pay tribute out of hand, and they be humbled."* (Sura 9:29) *"Kill
the disbelievers wherever we find them."* (2:191)

One would wonder why Islam, beginning from the Quran and Hadith,
openly admits such edicts. Why wouldn't Muslims remove these issues
from their history? To answer it simply, they were not ashamed of this
history. Rather, they were proud of it and still are. For Israel to show
Muslims footage on the Holocaust would not deter anti-Semitism, since
to watch such footage either brought denial or a sense of pleasure to
watch Jews die.

Even in history not directly associated with Islamic writers, much of this
type of genocide by beheading is well documented. For centuries, from
the Iberian peninsula to the Indian subcontinent, jihad campaigns
waged by Muslim armies against infidel Jews, Christians, Zoroastrians,
Buddhists and Hindus, were punctuated by massacres, including mass
throat slittings and beheadings. During the period of "enlightened"
Muslim rule, the Christians of Iberian Toledo, who had first submitted to
their Arab Muslim invaders in 711 or 712, revolted in 713. In the harsh
Muslim reprisal that ensued, Toledo was pillaged, and all of the
Christian notables had their throats cut. On the Indian subcontinent,
Babur (1483-1530), the founder of the Mughal Empire, was revered as a
paragon of Muslim tolerance by modern revisionist historians. He
recorded the following in his autobiography "Baburnama," about infidel
prisoners of a jihad campaign:

> *Those who were brought in alive (having surrendered) were ordered
> beheaded, after which <u>a tower of skulls was erected in the camp.</u>
> (The Baburnama – Memoirs of Babur, Prince and Emperor,* trans-
> lated and edited by Wheeler M. Thacktson, Oxford University
> Press,1996, p. 188. Emphasis added.)

Recent jihad-inspired decapitations of infidels by Muslims have occurred across the globe – Christians in Indonesia, the Philippines, and Nigeria; Hindu priests and "unveiled" Hindu women in Kashmir; Wall Street Journal reporter, and Jew, Daniel Pearl. We should not be surprised that these contemporary paroxysms of jihad violence are accompanied by ritualized beheadings. Such gruesome acts are in fact, sanctioned by core Islamic sacred texts and classical Muslim jurisprudence. Empty claims that jihad decapitations are somehow "alien to true Islam," however well-intentioned, undermine serious efforts to reform Islamic doctrine. (*The Sacred Muslim Practice of Beheading,* Andrew Sullivan, May 13, 2004)

BEHEADING IS TAUGHT IN SCHOOL

Americans complain about violence in schools. Consider the Muslim education. One Palestinian school textbook teaches:

> *...This noble [Quranic] Sura [Surat Muhammad]...deals with questions, of which the most important are as follows: Encouraging the faithful to perform jihad in god's cause, to behead the infidels, take them prisoner, break their power, and make their souls humble – all that in a style which contains the highest examples of urging to fight. You see that in His words: 'When you meet the unbelievers in the battlefield, strike off their heads,' and, 'when you have laid them low, bind your captives firmly. Then grant them their freedom or take a ransom from them, until war shall lay down its burdens.'* (*Studies in Theology: Tradition and Morals,* Palestinian textbook, Grade 11, 2001 pp. 291-92)

> *...When you meet them in order to fight [them], do not be seized by compassion [towards them] but strike the [their] necks powerfully...Striking the neck means fighting, because killing a person is often done by striking off his head. Thus, it has become an expression for killing even if the fighter strikes him elsewhere. This expression contains a harshness and emphasis that are not found in the word 'kill,' because it describes killing in the ugliest manner, i.e., cutting the neck and making the organ – the head of the body – fly off (the body).* (Commentary on the Surahs of Muhammad, Al-Fath, Al-Hujurat and Qaf, Grade 11, [2002] p. 9)

Chapter 14
How Did Jihad Begin?

There is a label that many in academia circles like to use in order to dismiss anyone who equates jihadism with terrorism. They always attempt to write one off by stating, "you are not an expert on Islam."

Do Muslims become Muslim as a result of being experts on Islam? Or do Christians become Christian as a result of being experts on Christianity?

And for the sake of argument, even if we accept that jihad in true Islam is void of terrorism, there is no difference in our research since we are interested in observing how Muslims interpret jihad from their holy writ. This is the crux of the matter. Does it take an expert on Islam to observe how the Muslim on the streets understands what jihad is?

Yet, Westerners must weed out the "experts" who speak differently to Arabs than they do to Americans. But we can do better than that. Americans can understand fully by ignoring both Muslim apologists and Islamophobes like myself. Simply go to every mosque in the Middle East, and record the sermons, which are delivered in Arabic or Persian. Once Americans observe what is said in the Muslims' own language, he will fully understand how jihad is interpreted.

Academics usually don't strap on explosives and blow up others. Yet, academics in the Middle East are calling on other Muslims to become suicide bombers.

If these pro-terror academics are wrong in their interpretation of Islam, then why are their critics not fighting them? Instead, the critics are busy fighting us, the "Islamophobes."

They simply counter that this madness is small in number. How many Sudanese Christians must die for us to realize how big their number really is? How many "Irans" must evolve before we wake up? How many 9/11s must be repeated until we've had enough? How many Hamas- or Hezbollah-style governments must be established before we comprehend the threat?

The games that are played back and forth in academic circles are based on the notion that Islam did not begin with violence – that the early chapters of the Quran are an invitation to the true, original faith, and a call to correct the Christian message that God has a Son. "Say: He is Allah, the only one, Allah, the everlasting. He did not beget and is not begotten, and none is his equal." (Quran 112).

This invitation came without compulsion.

> There is no compulsion in religion. Truth stands out clear from error: whoever rejects evil and believes in god has grasped the most trustworthy handhold that never breaks. And god hears and knows all things. (Quran 2:256)

Muhammad's message was not palatable to the Meccans at first, and his adherents, small in number, found themselves increasingly persecuted for their beliefs by the elite of the Quraysh because he had called for one god and denounced the multitudes of gods worshipped in the Ka'ba.

So, Muhammad proselytized among the tribesmen of the oasis of Yathrib, about 150 miles to the north of Mecca, who accepted his message.

It is this volume of Islamic history that apologists use to defend the peaceful side of Islam. It is these references that are used to paint Islam as peaceful to the West.

After suffering so much persecution at the hands of the Meccans, Muhammad decided to immigrate to Yathrib (Medina) in 622. This is called "Al-Hijrah" (The Immigration).

This immigration is when the Islamic calendar begins, but it is not when Islam was founded. This is crucial, since the advent of Islam is not marked by the time the Quran was revealed but when Islam began to take a different stage in history – the proclamation of Islam to the whole world began in this era.

Medina, which was a collection of small villages and forts spread over the oasis, was divided politically among two pagan Arab tribes – the Aws and the Khazraj – and three smaller Jewish tribes – the Banu Qaynuqa, the Banu al-Nadir, and the Banu Qurayza. Muhammad and the Muslims based their community within Medina, and over a period of five years, they converted the Arab tribesmen that occupied the territory.

It was in this context that jihad arose, and the campaigns to gain adherents and control territory constituted the focus of the community's activity during the last nine years of the Prophet's life. Muhammad is recorded as having participated in at least twenty-seven campaigns and deputized some fifty-nine others – an average of no fewer than nine campaigns annually.*

These campaigns can be divided into four groups:

The five "thematic" battles of Badr (624), Uhud (625), Khandaq (627), Mecca (630), and Hunayn (630), were undertaken with the goal of dominating the three principal settled areas of the Hijaz: Mecca, Medina, and al-Taif.

---

* David Cook, *Understanding Jihad,* See al-Waqidi, *Maghazi* (Beirut, 1984 repr.), I, p. 27;

Muslim, *Sahih* (Beirut, n.d.), V, pp. 199–200;

Abd al-Razzaq, *Musannaf* (Beirut, 1983), V, pp. 294–95 (Nos. 9659–60);

The full list in Ibn al-Nahhas al-Dumyati, Mashari al-ashwaq (Beirut, 2002), II, pp. 896–908;

The clarification of J. M. B. Jones, "The Chronology of the Maghazi – A Textual Survey," *Bulletin of the School of Oriental and African Studies* 19 (1957), pp. 245–80 (detailing a total of eighty-six).

Raids against the Bedouin were undertaken to force local tribesmen to support – or at least allow – the Muslims attacks against Jewish tribes in order to secure the oases in which they resided. Two raids against the Byzantines, at al-Muta (629) and Tabuk (631), and the campaign led by Usama b. Zayd (632) against Syria, though less than successful at best, heralded the direction of Muslim conquests during the years following the Prophet's death in 632.

This evidence categorically demonstrates the importance of jihad to the early Muslim community. It is no coincidence that a number of the Prophet Muhammad's early biographers refer to the last ten years of his life as al-maghazi (the raids). (David Cook, *Understanding Jihad*, al-Waqidi; Ibn Hisham)

The Quran documents the injunction to wage Jihad:

> *Permission is given to those who fight because they are wronged. Surely Allah is capable of giving them victory. Those who were driven out of their homes unjustly, merely for their saying: "Our Lord is Allah." Had Allah not repelled some people by others, surely monasteries, churches, synagogues and mosques, wherein the name of Allah is mentioned frequently, would have been demolished. Indeed, Allah will support whoever supports Him. Allah is surely Strong and Mighty. (22:39–40)*

The Muslims sought recompense for their losses due to leaving everything behind in Mecca. So, they attacked the Quraysh caravans, which constituted the first serious battle for the Muslims, the battle of Badr, in which the Muslims were victorious and were given booty and the spoils of war. In fact, a chapter was dedicated in the Quran called the Spoils (chapter 8).

According to *Sura* 8, it was god who induced the believers to march forward (8:5), compelled the Muslims to attack the Meccan reinforcements instead of the caravan (8:6), and supplied angels to assist the Muslims (8:9):

> *It was not you [the Muslims] who slew them, but Allah; and when you threw it was actually Allah who threw, so that he might gener-*

ously reward the believers. Allah is hearing, knowing. (8:17) (David Cook, David Cook Pub., *Understanding Jihad*)

Later on, Sura 9 was sent with the main subject of revocation of the immunity granted by god and Muhammad to those tribes which had not converted to Islam. After the lifting of the immunity, the Muslims must fight all unbelievers:

> *Then, when the sacred months are over, kill the idolaters wherever you find them, take them [captive], besiege them, and lie in wait for them at every point of observation. If they repent afterwards, perform the prayer and pay the alms, then release them. Allah is truly All-Forgiving, Merciful.* (Sura 9:5)

So, how does one deal with this? At first, Islam came with a proclamation of peace, no compulsion. Then Islam came with an injunction of raids, wars, and Jihad, not only for booty, but to convert non-Muslims by force.

Despite references in the Quran that call for tolerance, Sura 9 verse 73, Islam's highest jurisprudence, abrogates (cancels) them all. In Surah Al-Tawbah, the most famous verse on jihad is the "verse of the sword." This verse abrogates over one hundred other verses in the Quran. It made most of the Quranic verses calling for tolerance, forgiveness and peace towards nonbelievers null and void.

The Law of Abrogation (Al-Nasekh Wal-Mansookh) was given by Allah in the Quran:

> *Whichever verse we relinquish or cause to be forgotten we replace it with its equal or with that which is greater, did you not know that god is capable of all things?* (2:106)

Verses from the Quran were abrogated (Mansookh) by newer ones (Nasekh) many times. From Al-Tawbah 9:5 and 9:29, the verse of the sword says the following:

> *When the sacred months are passed, kill those who join other gods with Allah wherever ye shall find them, besiege them, and lay wait for them with every kind of ambush. And in 9:29 Make war upon such of those whom the Scriptures have been given as they believe*

*not in Allah, or the last day, and forbid not that which Allah and His
apostle have forbidden...*

The question should not even be whether Islam condones or accepts
the idea of abrogation. If Muslims would condemn abrogation, then
we could move towards positive results. The problem is that almost
all Muslim jurisprudence accepts this, especially since the Quran
mentions it.

In his book, *How to Perfect the Science of the Quran* (Al-Itqan), Al-Syoti,
in Vol. 2 p. 37, writes:

> *The Verse of the Sword has abrogated (annulled) one hundred and
> twenty four Quranic verses and all what came in the Quran on
> matters of forgiving and ignoring, unbelievers have been replaced
> (Mansookh), by the verse of the sword.*

For further examples on the acceptance of the principle of abrogation
in Islam, refer to the following highly-respected teachers of Islam: Kitab
Al-Nasekh Wal-Mansookh by Al-Neesaburi, Al-Hafeth Ibnu Katheer Ibin
Abas, Al-Tasheel Lulum Al-Tanzeel, Al-Husain Ibn Fadl, Abu Abdullah
Muhammad Ibn Hazm, Al-Muhaqiq Abu Al-Qasim Hibatullah Ibn Sala-
meh, Al-Sudy Wa-Al-Dahak, Muhammad Abdulsalam Faraj.

Yet, what we need to be asking ourselves is this – does the Muslim on
the street believe in this abrogation?

Every Muslim does at different levels.

For if abrogation is condoned, then Muslims would permit drinking:

> *O ye who believe! Approach not prayers while drunk, until ye can
> understand all that ye say.* (Al-Quran 4:43)

Because of this verse, every Muslim believes that the forbidding of
alcohol came later:

> *"O ye who believe! Intoxicants and gambling, (dedication of) stones,
> and (divination by) arrows, are an abomination of satan's handi-
> work; eschew such (abomination), that ye may prosper."* (Al-Quran
> 5:90)

The Quran was revealed over a period of twenty-two and one-half years.
Many reforms that were brought about in the society were gradual, in

order to facilitate the adoption of new laws by the people. An abrupt change in society always leads to rebellion and anarchy.

If, indeed, Muslims do not believe in abrogation, then many of them would worship in the direction of Jerusalem as Muhammad did. This custom was later abrogated to direct all worship towards Mecca's Black Stone:

> The fools among the people will say, "what has turned them from the direction they were facing in their prayers aforetime?" Say, "To god belong the East and the West. He guides whomsoever he will to a straight path."

> We have seen thee (Muhammad) turning thy face about in the heaven; now we surely turn thee to a direction that shall satisfy Thee (Muhammad).

> Turn thy face towards the Holy Mosque (Kaaba); and wherever you are, turn your faces towards it." (The Cow, II: 135-40)

Yet, most Muslims believe in the laws of abrogation, to the point that even the Quran supersedes the Bible:

> And We have sent down to you the book with truth, authenticating what is present of the book and supersede it. So judge between them by what GOD has sent down and do not follow their desires from what has come to you of the truth…(5:48)

This is the reason why Muslims rarely or never study the Bible. If you ask all Muslims why they don't believe in the Bible, the common answer is always that it has been corrupted.

Islam, like any other religion, cannot be vaccinated from critical scrutiny. The Bible has endured archeological, historical, and scientific reviews from the academic circles, as well as accusations of corruption by people in the highest levels of Islamic jurisprudence.

Biblical archeological review did not come about to give bias for the Bible, but to critique it. Yet, we do not find Quranic archeological reviews. Why?

Well, when I compared the two manuscripts, the Quran and the Bible, there was little to review from a historical or archeological perspective. Understandably, both manuscripts were not written in order to preserve archeology, but man's origin and destiny. I would expect that the Quran would say volumes on our origin. But what details can we find on the history of mankind? The Quran is simply a collection of summarized events that few historians would use as reference.

Muslims freely deny some aspects of the historical Jesus. They deny the crucifixion event and the integrity of the Bible. A Judeo-Christian culture respects and fights for the rights of all to express their views.

Yet, in the Islamic world, the measuring stick is very different when examining the Quran and Hadith. Indeed, if freedom of religion is why Muslims fight, then where does the freedom to disagree with Islam exist in fifty-five Muslim states?

Look at Sura 5:32 in context:

> ...whoever kills a soul, not in retaliation for a soul or corruption in the land, is like one who has killed the whole of mankind; and whoever saves a life is like one who saves the lives of all mankind. Our messengers came to them with the clear proof; but afterwards many of them continued to commit excesses in the land.

The catch, seldom quoted, is "corruption in the land." Although Muslims, in general, are angered when the Quran is misquoted, no one objects to the corruption of the text by politicians as long as it serves certain goals. The next verse, Q5:34, continues:

> Indeed, the punishment of those who fight Allah and His Messenger and go around corrupting the land is to be killed, crucified, have their hands and feet cut off on opposite sides, or to be banished from the land. That is a disgrace for them in this life, and in the life to come theirs will be a terrible punishment.

The tribe of Ukl faced such a fate for simply changing their minds and denouncing Islam. Sahih Al-Bukhari, Vol. 8, put it graphically:

> **Narrated Anas:** Some people from the tribe of 'Ukl came to the Prophet and embraced Islam. The climate of Medina did not suit them, so the Prophet ordered them to go to the (herd of milch) camels of charity and to drink, their milk and urine (as a medicine). They did so, and after they had recovered from their ailment (became healthy) they turned renegades (reverted from Islam) and

killed the shepherd of the camels and took the camels away. The Prophet sent (some people) in their pursuit and so they were (caught and) brought, and the Prophet ordered that their hands and legs should be cut off and that their eyes should be branded with heated pieces of iron, and that their cut hands and legs should not be cauterized, till they die.

The Quran teaches its followers to respect the sanctity of the lives of other Muslims, except those who *"fight Allah and his Messenger"* and are guilty of *"corruption in the land."* These people must be killed, mutilated, or banished.

In Q2:216:

Warfare is ordained for you, though it is hateful unto you; but it may happen that you hate a thing which is good for you and it may happen that you love a thing which is bad for you.

Believers, do not make friends with any but your own people. They [i.e. non-Muslims] will not fail to corrupt you. They long for your ruin. Hatred has already shown itself out of their mouths, but more grievous is what their breasts conceal.

In this context of Q3:118, non-Muslims seek to "corrupt" Muslims.

The evidence of the abrogation of the verses that call for tolerance and patience cannot be refuted. People in the West must not ignore what is taught in the East, that is, *"Islam to the West."* The banners held high at Islamic rallies and demonstrations go beyond even this – *"Islam to the World."*

Chapter 15
Analyzing Jihadists

ARE MUSLIM TERRORISTS CRAZY?

If they are, then the Chairman of the Arab Psychiatric Association is crazy as well. Adel Sadeq, Chairman of the Arab Psychiatric Association, was quoted as saying:

"When the martyr dies a martyr's death, he attains the height of bliss...As a psychiatrist, I say that the height of bliss comes with the end of the countdown: ten, nine, eight, seven, six, five, four, three, two, one. And then, you press the button to blow yourself up. When the martyr reaches 'one,' and then 'boom,' he explodes, and senses himself flying because he knows for certain that he is not dead...It is a transition to another, more beautiful world, because he knows very well that within seconds he will see the light of the creator. He will be at the closest possible point to Allah..." (Hadith Al Madina, Egypt, April 23, 2002, as cited in *Al Quds Al Arabi,* London, April 23, 2002)

Similarly, Dr. Adele Sadeq, an Egyptian psychiatrist, instead of explaining the psychological process of the suicide martyr, comments:

> We Arabs must know that this war will not end. The conflict will continue. This is not a conflict over land alone...This war will not end, and anyone who deludes himself that there will be peace must understand that Israel did not come to this region to love the Arabs or to normalize relations with them. Anyone who thinks that peace will come either now or in the future has limited histor-

ical vision. Either we will exist or we will not exist. (Interview in Hadith Al Madina, Egypt, as cited in *Al Quds Al Arabi* [London], April 23, 2002)

We have examined some of the misconceptions by Western psychologists. We are not dealing with psychology, per se, but with a theocratic system that has been with us for over a millennia. Muslim terrorists are not crazy, but they adhere to an ideology that wants to gulp up the world.

ARE TERRORISTS THE UNDERDOGS

Allow me to tell you, and we use the Palestinian terrorists as an example – it's a myth that the Palestinians are the underdogs in this conflict. It's not an Israeli-Palestinian war, but an Israeli-Islamonazi war. The issue is not land or a Palestinian state. The hypocrisy is striking. Where are the accusations when it comes to true aggression? The world is basically silent when more than a million Sudanese are dead from starvation and mass execution, silent when Christians die in Indonesia, silent when Turks kill Cypriots.

The West is blind to the unprovoked stoning of the minority Jews by Palestinians in Hebron or the slaughter of nearly an entire Jewish family – a pregnant mother and her four children, out on a shopping trip.

I cannot imagine what that father has gone through. But there was no worldwide outcry for this family. The world simply concludes that the Jews must have done something to deserve this.

MAKE IT SAY THE OPPOSITE

Play on words is always a Muslim tactic. An exchange between myself and the Muslim reformer Khaleel Muhammad of San Diego University can shed some light.

> **Argument:** *"word for war, as Mr. Shoebat ought to know, is Harb, and NOT Jihad."*
>
> **Response:** *Interestingly, Dr. Khaleel knows Jihad very well, not the "self struggle" type. In a previous statement it seemed that he knew*

quite well what it meant [he said]: "I see no reason for Muslims to apologize for Jihad."

To denounce that, will bring Khaleel under Jihad.

It is a fallacy that jihad represents an inner struggle; Jihad means the kind of genocidal slaughter of infidels for which Osama bin Laden calls for.

Inner struggle? There are over one hundred quotes by Muhammad referring to jihad by the sword, by killing, by taking no prisoners, by forced conversion, or by enslavement – with only one quote referring to an internal struggle – called for by Mohammad, after the complete conquest and occupation of Arabia.

Public claims of pacifism are typical of the Islamic leadership, and the West eagerly devours them, refusing to believe that a major world religion poses such a danger to humanity. Of course, there are Muslims who reject many of the classical sources and truly focus on the peaceful verses of the Quran, seeking to re-interpret the verses because they truly do not want to engage in violence. These "liberal" Muslims seem to "re-write" Islam rather than correctly interpret it. They are peaceful despite Islam, not because of it.

In one dialogue, Khaleel Muhammad, Assistant Professor at the Department of Religious Studies at San Diego State University, quoted Abu Hamid al-Ghazali, 12th century jurist and theologian, ignoring that when Ghazali was asked a question regarding living in foreign non-Muslim countries, Ghazali responded:

"Muslims could live under non-Muslim rule as long as they do not forget that they are Allah's missionaries and, if needed, His soldiers." (Abu Hamaid al-Ghazali, FrontPageMag.com, conversation with Kamal Nawash, Walid Shoebat and Professsor Khaleel Muhammad, Asst. Prof. Dept. Relig. Studies at San Diego state Univ., Aug. 13, 2004.)

I suppose that Dr. Khaleel Muhammad might have another meaning of "soldiers." He also pointed to Khalid Abou el Fadl, whose argument is that "only fringe elements among Muslims consider that [jihad is] war" and that "the Quran refers to jihad only in terms of intellectual effort to apply divine revelation in promoting peace through justice." Abou el Fadl also was quoted as saying, "There is no such thing as Islamic terrorism, but there have always been Muslim terrorists."(Ibid)

I have heard of Hamza Yusuf, Tariq Ramadan, Fazlur Rahman, and Amina Wadud who have all said the same thing, yet, on the other hand, their advocacy consists of "extreme" denial of the facts regarding the meaning of jihad according to Islam.

Take Tariq Ramadan for example. I was prevented by the Canadian government to speak at an invitation by the Simon Wiesenthal Center in Ottawa. The sad part about this trip is that the Simon Wiesenthal Center did not want to publicize it to the media; they wanted the speaking engagement kept quiet. The typical fear to stand up and fight, apparent in most Jewish organizations, is alarming.

Yet, Mr. Ramadan is allowed into Canada without question. He is considered Islamist royalty – in 1928, his maternal grandfather, Hasan al-Banna, in Egypt, founded the Muslim Brotherhood (Al-Ikhwan-ul-Muslimeen), probably the single most powerful Islamist institution of the twentieth century. Tariq is a Swiss citizen because his father, Sa'id Ramadan, also a leading Islamist, fled from Egypt in 1954, following a crackdown on the brotherhood. He has praised the brutal Islamist policies of the Sudanese politician Hassan Al-Turabi. Mr. Turabi in turn called Mr. Ramadan the "future of Islam." Mr. Ramadan was banned from entering France in 1996 on suspicion of having links with an Algerian Islamist who had recently initiated a terrorist campaign in Paris. Ahmed Brahim, an Algerian indicted for al-Qaeda activities, had "routine contacts" with Mr. Ramadan, according to a Spanish judge (Baltasar Garzón) in 1999.

Djamel Beghal, leader of a group accused of planning to attack the American embassy in Paris, stated in his 2001 trial that he had studied with Mr. Ramadan.

Along with nearly all Islamists, Mr. Ramadan has denied that there is "any certain proof" that bin Laden was behind 9/11.

He publicly refers to the Islamist atrocities of 9/11, Bali, and Madrid as "interventions," minimizing them to the point of near-endorsement.

And there is other incriminating evidence dug up by Jean-Charles Brisard, a former French intelligence officer doing work for some of the 9/11 families, as reported in Le Parisien:

> *Intelligence agencies suspect that Mr. Ramadan (along with his brother Hani) coordinated a meeting at the Hôtel Penta in Geneva for Ayman al-Zawahiri, deputy head of al-Qaeda, and Omar Abdel Rahman, the blind sheikh, now in a Minnesota prison. Mr. Ramadan's address appears in a register of Al Taqwa Bank, an organization the State Department accuses of supporting Islamist terrorism.* (Daniel Pipes, New York Sun, August 27, 2004)

Chapter 16
Moderate Imposters

HOW TO IDENTIFY THEM

When one questions a supposed moderate, it's always important to ask the right questions – Did Muhammad kill the Jews of Arabia? Yes or No?

It's a double edged sword. If a Muslim denies it, then he denies Islamic history and much of the text written in Al-Sera Al-Nabawiyeh (The Hadith), where the collection of the deeds and works of the Prophet are documented. It's like rejecting the New Testament for a Christian. Unless he is liberal, he is cornered with the fact. Denying it shows a liberal attitude towards his faith, yet accepting it corners the respondent to either justify it or condemn it.

At a speaking engagement in Los Angeles on Yom Kippur in 2006, a moderate Muslim finished his speech to a Jewish audience, and I asked him the question, "Did Muhammad kill the Jews?" To which he answered, "Yes, but they had a fair trial."

This, out of the mouth of a moderate? This, in a day and age when even the Pope made mends of old holocausts? Yet from a Muslim it would be difficult. Why?

Because killing the Jews was committed by the founders themselves – Muhammad, Omar his disciple, Ali his nephew, and the rest of the Calpihs whether Umayyads, Abbasids...

Similarly, Dr. Khaleel Muhammad, the professor of San Diego University and member of the board of Center for Islamic Pluralism, will never denounce the Khaibar massacre of Jews. No apology for Muhammad killing the Jews of Arabia. Interestingly, the Christian Reformation started when followers went to the text and to the founders of the faith, who clearly prohibited genocide and murder. As we see in Luke 6:27-28: "But I tell you who hear me: Love your enemies, do good to those who hate you, bless those who curse you, pray for those who mistreat you. If one strikes you on one cheek, turn to him the other also."

Yet Muslims cannot do the same. Not a single verse exists in the Quran with "love your enemies," since the founders themselves, Muhammad, the prophet of Islam, the Sahaba (companions), and the Caliphs, all participated in jihad by killing infidels and anyone who opposed the Islamic system.

THE PURPOSE FOR "MODERATES"

Jihad has been classified either as *al-jihad al-akbar* (the greater jihad), the struggle against one's soul (*nafs*), or *al-jih d al-asghar* (the lesser jihad), the external, physical effort, often implying fighting. Muslim scholars explained there are five kinds of *jihad fi sabilillah* (struggle in the cause of God):

Jihad of the heart/soul *(jihad bin nafs/qalb) is an inner struggle of good against evil in the mind, through concepts such as tawheed.*

Jihad by the tongue *(jihad bil lisan) is a struggle of good against evil waged by writing and speech, such as in the form of da'wa (proselytizing), Khutbas (sermons). It is one weapon in the jihadi arsenal.*

Jihad by the pen and knowledge *(jihad bil qalam/ilm) is a struggle for good against evil through scholarly study of Islam, ijtihad (legal reasoning), and through sciences (such as medical sciences).*

Jihad by the hand *(jihad bil yad) refers to a struggle of good against evil waged by actions or with one's wealth, such as going on the Haj pilgrimage (seen as the best jihad for women), taking* *care of elderly parents, providing funding for jihad, political activity for furthering the cause of Islam, stopping evil by force, espionage and the penetration of Western universities by salafi Islamic ideology, in numerous Middle East Studies departments funded by Saudi Arabia.*

Jihad by the sword *(jihad bis saif) refers to qital fi sabilillah (armed fighting in the way of God, or holy war), the most common usage by Salafi Muslims and offshoots of the Muslim brotherhood.* (Wikipedia.com)

Although the Jihad struggle from the Muslim point of view is not complex, Islamists have evolved the struggle into modern concepts. Walid Phares, a Middle East analyst breaks down this political Jihad into:

1. Economic jihad or oil as a weapon

2. Ideological jihad through the co-optation [takeover] of the entire U.S.-Middle Eastern studies establishment, funded by the Saudis

3. Political jihad or mollification of the public

4. Intelligence jihad, infiltrating not just American neighborhoods, but providing the translators and interpreters that the FBI, CIA, and DIA rely on

Note the black flag of jihad flying over the White House.

5. Subversive jihad within the country, using groups like CAIR, which they fund and the ACLU, to silence and disable critics.

6. Diplomatic jihad, controlling U.S. foreign policy and in particular using Saudi influence to dissuade the administrations from taking action against Wahabi interests. (Walid Phares, *Future Jihad*)

I would like to stress points 2 and 3, since these fall under the guise of moderate Islam to start a political Jihad in the U.S.

Although one can find liberal Muslims, rarely would we find moderate movements that call for reformation, except in the U.S. and other Western countries.

According to Khaleel Mohammad, professor at San Diego State University, a major obstacle that stops the reformation of Islam is "the status forced on Muslims by non-Muslim powers so that Muslims, instead of trying to genuinely reform their religion, are instead forced to defend against horrendous lies."

In other words, Khaleel must be busy fighting the "Islamophobes," instead of reforming.

One such organization which fights Islamophobes is CAIR. The true purpose of CAIR is to legitimize the activities of Islamic militants and to neutralize opposition to Islamic extremism. They serve as perception management, in support of fundamentalist Muslim terrorists, and/or al-Qaeda, and/or the International Islamic Front for the Jihad Against Jews and Crusaders. (Aug. 15, 2005 update: plaintiffs in Estate of John P. O'Neill, Sr., et. al. v. Al Baraka, et. al. p. 12)

A recent civil suit filed by the estate of 9/11 victim, and former high-ranking FBI counter-terrorism agent, John O'Neill, Sr. may have best described CAIR's true agenda: "their goal is to create as much self-doubt, hesitation, fear of name-calling, and litigation within police departments and intelligence agencies as possible so as to render such authorities ineffective in pursuing international and domestic terrorist entities." (FrontPageMagazine.com March 10, 2005)

CAIR was born from the IAP, which was an active organization during the early 80s.

Read the words of Omar Ahmad, Co-Founder of the Council on American-Islamic Relations: "Islam isn't in America to be equal to any other faiths, but to become dominant. The Koran, the Muslim book of scripture, should be the highest authority in America, and Islam the only accepted religion on Earth." (http://www.anti-cair-net.org)

Executive Director Nihad Awad is former Public Relations Director for the Islamic Association of Palestine (IAP). Nihad is a Palestinian, born in

Jordan, and is now a U.S. citizen. Nihad once stated, "I am in support of the Hamas movement." (http://www.anti-cair-net.org)

Yet, Hamas, which Nihad Awad supports, has a vision that "Israel will exist and will continue to exist until Islam will obliterate it, just as it obliterated others before it." (Hamas Charter)

Ibrahim Hooper, CAIR's spokesperson, stated, "I wouldn't want to create the impression that I wouldn't like the government of the United States to be Islamic sometime in the future...But I'm not going to do anything violent to promote that. I'm going to do it through education."

Randall "Ismail" Royer, the CAIR-National Civil Rights Coordinator & Communications Specialist, on January 16, 2004, pleaded guilty to charges of using and discharging a firearm during, and in relation to, a crime of violence; and with carrying an explosive during commission of a felony. Mr. Royer faces a mandatory minimum sentence of twenty years in prison. (Mr. Royer also uses the first name of "Ismail.")

At the time Mr. Royer committed those crimes, he was in a leadership position at the Council on American Islamic Relations (CAIR), a Washington D.C. based organization which claims to protect the civil rights of Muslims in the United States and Canada. (It should be noted that years earlier, as a student, Royer worked a short period with CAIR before he joined Bosnian Forces fighting Serbs in 1994.)

Also, on April 13, 2005, Ghassan Elashi, founder of the Council on American-Islamic Relations – Texas (CAIR – Texas), long-time associate of CAIR's top leadership, and beneficiary of CAIR fund-raising support, was convicted on Islamic terrorism related charges in Dallas, Texas.

According to the federal indictment, Elashi was laundering money for Islamic terrorist organizations from 11/95 through 4/01.

Dating back to the early 1990s, Elashi had close ties to CAIR's leaders. Elashi founded the CAIR Texas chapter sometime before October 2000 (CAIR Texas first appeared as an affiliate on the CAIR National website in October 2000).

The other major purpose of CAIR is to expose Islamophobes. The Council on American-Islamic Relations (CAIR) described Daniel Pipes,

Director of the Middle East Forum (a think tank based in Center City), as "the nation's leading 'Islamophobe' and an advocate for Israeli interests." Pipes runs the Institute of Peace, a Washington-based federal institution, funded entirely by Congress, whose mandate is to promote "peaceful resolutions of international conflicts." CAIR complains that "Pipes' nomination sends entirely the wrong message as America seeks to convince Muslims worldwide that the war on terrorism and the war against Iraq are not attacks on Islam."

Islamists activists have only one goal, to Islamize the West, as described by Daniel Pipes on how Islamists are gaining momentum:

> **Siraj Wahaj,** *the first imam to deliver a Muslim prayer for the U.S. House of Representatives, holds that if Muslims unite, they could elect their own leader as president; "take my word, if 6-8 million Muslims unite in America, the country will come to us."*

> **Isma'il Al-Faruqi,** *the first academic theorist of a United States-made-fundamentalist-Muslim, argued in 1983 that "Nothing could be greater than this youthful, vigorous, and rich continent [of North America] turning away from its past evil and marching forward under the banner of Allahu Akbar [G-d is great]."*

> **Zaid Shakir,** *formerly the Muslim chaplain at Yale University, believes the Koran "pushes us in the exact opposite direction as the forces...at work in the American political spectrum" and from this argues that Muslims cannot accept the legitimacy of the existing order.*

> **Masudul Alam Choudhury,** *a Canadian professor of business, matter-of-factly advocates the "Islamization agenda in North America."*

> **Ahmad Nawfal,** *Jordanian who spoke often at American rallies a few years ago, says that if fundamentalist Muslims stand up, "it will be very easy for us to preside over this world once again."*

> **Shamim A. Siddiqi** *wrote a book on establishing "Islamic rule" in the United States, with the goal of Muslims creating "a strong lobby in Washington for the promotion of Islam...in this country as well as elsewhere in the world."*

Some organizations also express a hope that one day Muslims will take over in the United States. The International Institute of Islamic Thought in Herndon, Virginia, aims for nothing less than "the Islamization of the humanities and the social sciences." Just one month after the September 11 atrocities, a delegate at the San Jose convention of the American Muslim Alliance, a militant Islamic group, announced: "By the year 2020, we should have an American Muslim president of the United States."

While there is no reason to suppose that the aspiration to replace the Constitution with Islamic law will succeed, the fact that this goal can be found among fundamentalist Muslims does have a major implication. (Daniel Pipes, New York Post, November 12, 2001)

It means that the existing order – religious freedom, secularism, women's rights – can no longer be taken for granted. It now needs to be fought for.

ONLY THEY SUFFER

Mouin Rabbani, Director of the Palestinian American Research Center in Ramallah, stated that the common thread among all suicide bombers is the:

> bitter experience of what they see as Israeli state terror. Without exception, the suicide bombers have lived their lives on the receiving end of a system designed to trample their rights and crush every hope of a brighter future…Confronted by a seemingly endless combination of death, destruction, restriction, harassment and humiliation, they conclude that ending life as a bomb – rather than having it ended by a bullet – endows them, even if only in their final moments, with a semblance of purpose and control previously unknown. (MEMRI, December 16, 2003)

When Westerners read this, they must imagine some sort of a holocaust in which Jews are massively targeting Arabs for destruction. The fact is that you rarely ever hear of Jews going into Arab neighborhoods to plant bombs, and you never hear of Jews crashing planes into buildings full of civilians.

Long before the existence of the state of Israel, the Jews of Hebron were exterminated. The Muslims cut off the Jewish men's testicles, raped the women and chopped off their breasts, and slashed the babies to death. The massacre was ordered by the Grand Mufti, Haj Amin Al-Husseni, who instigated the riots and called on the masses to "kill them wherever you find them, and rape their women." Al-Husseini collaborated with Adolf Hitler to rid the Muslim world of Jews and even organized an SS Hanjar ("dagger") Muslim division for the service of Hitler that was literally Islamo-Nazi. You will never hear of Jews carrying out such atrocities. The two cultures are quite different in that they share no universal language of ethics or morality to allow for any true détente.

There is no moral equivalency in the Palestinian-Israeli conflict. The West not only refuses to see this, it makes the murderers sympathetic characters. We never hear about the Hebron massacre, but everyone talks of Deir Yassin.

Jenin was the same story, repeated recently, accusing Israel of being an aggressor and forgetting that many Israeli soldiers were killed in their attempt to dismantle bomb factories created in former houses. They do not understand that they are looking at wolves in sheep's clothing. But even some wolves can be transformed into sheep. Nothing is impossible in my view. After all, I myself was once a wolf.

Both stories of Deir Yassin and Jenin are well documented. Yet, the news media released stories of so-called massacres. Then when the investigations were over, it was too late – no massacres had actually been committed, but the word was out that Israel was the villain.

Chapter 17
Intent –
The Missing Element

INTENT DOES NOT COUNT

Viewing the way things are reasoned in Muslim countries is interesting, especially when the intent is taken out of the equation. Imagine living in a society where involuntary man-slaughter is viewed as murder in the first degree.

My life in the U.S. has taught me differently, especially when I first served jury duty. I learned that intent is everything. To judge without prejudice is extremely crucial to reaching justice.

I started to ask myself why I hated Israel and the West, and I started to document all my findings, which I explained in detail in my previous book, *Why I Left Jihad*. My conclusion is that many of the puzzle pieces were left out. Israelis did not intend to kill civilians when they attacked Qana or Jenin. Rather, they sought to dismantle major terrorist infrastructures.

Qana gets over a million hits on the internet, with references to holocausts and displays of dead bodies and mangled children and infants, so as to entice the world's psyche on the horrors of Israel. However, one important ingredient is missing – intent.

Without intent, we would have a world of chaos. Intent is missing from all of the arguments that propagate hatred against Israel. Without intent, Dresden and the bombing of Nazis is a world crime. Without intent, we can justify putting Patton on trial instead of Hitler's henchmen. Without intent, we can see dead German civilians as innocent victims. We can suppose that they did not salute the Fuehrer with joy, staring at him in public squares with glossy eyes, fixated on Hitler as if he was a god. Intent is everything.

Conclusions were made regarding Qana before any evidence had been considered to determine precisely what had occurred, that Hezbollah deliberately embedded military forces, arms caches, and missile batteries among civilians. Hezbollah is known to position missile launchers in residential apartments and directly next door to apartment blocks. Yet, instead of condemning Hezbollah's war crime, many in the world choose to blame Israel for the consequences of Hezbollah's actions.

Jenin suffered similar judgment from a world that cares less about intent yet is quick to count casualties.

Jonathan Foreman, in an article entitled "Media Miss Israeli Restraint" (New York Post 4/17/02), wrote:

> The tactics chosen by the Israeli army – sending infantrymen from house to house – simply make no sense unless the avoidance of civilian casualties was a priority.

In other words, had Israel intended to kill civilians, they would have sent the air force and bombed everything, a tactic they had to resort to with Hezbollah.

Yet, Arabs ignore what Syria's then-President Assad did at Hama in 1982 – where he crushed the Muslim Brotherhood at the cost of at least 10,000 lives. Arabs ignored the hundreds of thousands killed by Saddam Hussein, especially when the intent in both cases was to eradicate civilians.

In order to give the world the impression of an Israeli massacre in Jenin, the number of Arab dead was estimated at 200 or more. The actual number was much lower.

Inconvenient facts did not deter Palestinians from creating a propaganda film on Jenin. The film mentions a mass gravesite that IDF soldiers dug for the Palestinian dead. *Every international organization which investigated the matter concurs that there were 52 Palestinian dead in Jenin* and that all the bodies were returned to the Palestinians for burial. Yet, Dr. Abu Riali, director of the hospital in Jenin, spoke of, "thousands of victims," when he was interviewed on Al-Jazeera television. (IMRA, independent Media Review Analyst, *Seven Lies About Jenin,* Provided by Israel Press Government Office)

This history of lies keeps repeating itself. The old story of Deir Yassin is similar to the Jenin story. Beir Zeit, a Palestinian University student who interviewed every Arab survivor, admitted that the number of deaths was 110. The story has been exaggerated, and conflicting testimonies cloud the facts, but the best study on this issue is *The History of the 1948 War* by Professor Uri Milstein, one of Israel's most distinguished military historians. It's meticulous, detailed, and accurate.

(Sharif Kanani and Nihad Zitawi, Deir Yassin, Monograph No.4, Destroyed Palestinian Villages Documentation Project (Beir Zeit: Documentation Center of Beir Zeit University, 1987, p. 6)

In 1952, a hearing was conducted by Israel, during which Israeli judges heard eyewitness testimony on the events at Deir Yassin, then issued a ruling that has had important implications for understanding what happened in that battle. Dear reader, how often have the Arabs issued any ruling, from any court, or held any hearing for the countless massacres of Jews in any Arab country?

Long before Deir Yassin, Arab and Jewish armies were already battling. An "Arab Liberation Army," sponsored by the Arab League and manned by volunteers from various Arab countries, had always attacked civilian Jewish communities in Palestine prior to 1948. My own father witnessed Arab villagers, along with Arab soldiers, raid Jewish communities. The Muslim leader, Haj Al-Ameen El-Husseni, who collaborated with Hitler, had SS trained graduates battle the Jews; some of their bodies, lying alongside the corpses of dead Palestinian fighters, were found with their SS identifications. The fact is that every Arab village in Israel participated in attacking Jewish settlements in order to destroy the Jews. The Arab attackers faced the consequences of their actions; raids on civilians will always have repercussions. (See Milstein, p.263 [interview with Zalivensky], Also ZOA)

Deir Yassin was a heavily armed nest of terrorists who, in 1947-1948, had been attacking nearby Jewish neighborhoods and traffic on the Jerusalem – Tel Aviv highway. Mordechai Ra'anan, leader of the Jewish soldiers who fought in Deir Yassin, deliberately exaggerated the number of deaths as 254 in order to undermine the morale of the Arab forces. No body count was conducted to tally the dead. (Milstein, pp. 264-265, interviews with Ezra Yachin, Mordechai Ra'anan, Benzion Cohen and Yehuda Lapidot; Testimonies of Mordechai Ra'anan, Benzion Cohen, and Yehuda Lapidot)

Despite Ra'anan's clear admission of the lie, the figure, 254, was circulated by Palestinian Arab leader Hussein Khalidi and was the basis for a widely re-printed article in the New York Times, which became the permanent reference for the story from then on.

A tally of Jewish losses revealed 42 Israeli wounded and 6 dead, out of an attacking force of 132 soldiers. One of the commanders of the Jewish forces, Ben Zion Cohen, says, "(The Arabs were) shooting from every house."

While the Jewish soldiers with loud speakers warned in advance to "Lay down your arms! Run for your lives," the Arabs fired at the vehicle, and the battle erupted. The claims of rape and other atrocities were fabricated to incite Arab violence against Israel. Arab eyewitnesses, interviewed in a PBS documentary, revealed that they were told by Dr. Hussein Khalidi to fabricate claims of atrocities at Deir Yassin in order to encourage Arab regimes to invade the Jewish state-to-be.

Deir Yassin resident Abu Mahmoud recalls, "Jerusalem at the Hebron Gate. We checked who was missing, and who we had gathered in survived. Then the [Palestinian] leaders arrived, including Dr. Khalidi."

In 1948, Hazem Nusseibeh, an editor of the Palestine Broadcasting Service's Arabic news and a member of one of Jerusalem's most prominent Arab families, admitted that he too was told by Hussein Khalidi, the originator of the massacre story, to fabricate claims of atrocities in order to encourage Arab regimes to invade the Jewish land. The following is a Jerusalem Report detailing Nusseibeh's account of a meeting at the Jaffa Gate of Jerusalem's Old City with survivors from Deir Yassin and Palestinian leaders, including Hussein Khalidi: "I asked Dr. Khalidi how we should cover the story," recalled Nusseibeh. "He said, 'We must make the most of this.' So we wrote a press release stating that at Deir Yassin children were murdered, pregnant women were raped. All sorts of atrocities." (Hazem Nusseibeh, an editor of the Palestine Broadcasting Service's Arabic news in 1948, was interviewed for the BBC television series *"Israel and the Arabs: the 50-year conflict."*)

Abu Mahmud, a survivor, declared, "We said there was no rape. [Khalidi] said we have to say this [that there was rape], so the Arab armies will come to liberate Palestine from the Jews." The PBS narrator added, "Arab radio stations passed on the false reports, ignoring the protests of the witnesses." The famed syndicated columnist Sid Zion, whose articles originate in the New York Daily News, wrote on March 23, 1998, calling the "massacre" claims "one of the great hoaxes of the 20th century." (Ibid)

Deir Yassin has ever since been the rallying call for Arabs and the enemies of Israel. Arafat compares it to Auschwitz. It is one of the great hoaxes of the 20th century; comparable to the libel that Jews drank Christian blood...The fight for Deir Yassin was part of the war and a necessary battle for Jewish survival. The Irgun, under Menachem Begin, warned the Arabs and asked them to evacuate their women and children. Hundreds left, but hundreds stayed. A pitched battle ensued, and when the smoke cleared, 120 Arabs were killed, 40 Jews were seriously injured, and 4 Jews were dead...The Israeli government and every other historical study have long since discredited the "massacre" claim. But like all libels, it stands, negating truth and proof.

Civilians always die in any war. The same goes for Lebanon – Israel never attacked Lebanon for the sole purpose of killing Arabs but to destroy Hezbollah, which was lobbing missiles at Israel. Arab media captured all the damage done by Israel, yet the media failed to show the other side of the story.

The Middle East is plagued by an unbalanced media, and if you review the supposed atrocities committed by Israel or the Americans in Iraq, you would find the reason why the Middle East is a hotbed for terrorism. Yet, for all of my life, I rejected the Western press because I always listened to Arab media and always believed the inflated numbers of civilian casualties. The Arab media used to inflate the Jewish civilian casualties, since more civilian Jews dead would boost our moral. The Arab media is more careful these days now that they understand that Western media sympathizes with the under dog.

Don't forget the story of the accident on my way to school in Bethlehem, when a Jew accidentally struck an Arab girl which sparked an Intifada. Or consider the child in Gaza who was struck by an Israeli jeep, which sparked a major Intifada outbreak. Without consideration of the intent, such incidents will certainly cause uprisings.

The erosion of the standards of crime prosecution, with respect to the Western media's coverage of the Middle East is alarming. Why do we swallow this misinformation and leave the intent out of the picture?

I can only answer this question by digging deep into my past heart, which was filled with racism. Racism is a blinder. Racism builds scales that cover our eyes and hearts. Racism caused us to lie to such a degree that entire communities would fabricate funerals of martyrdom.

An Israeli production showed an interesting segment that documented how Palestinian film crews produce staged incidents. For instance, after the Jenin "massacre," a "funeral" in Jenin was caught on video by Israel and shows that the casket falls, the body rolls out, gets up and climbs back in the casket. The segment also shows staged rock-throwing scenes where there are no Israelis involved, and how injuries are faked by Palestinian actors. (Paliwood, Jenin, April 2002)

Yet, these clips are not shown in our media. Why?

Indeed, we can collectively act like savages, and in the 21st century, although we are more educated, we act like educated savages. It's ironic that entire communities will participate in the staging or even in the killing. Westerners have no clue about the magnitude of deception carried out in the Middle East. They believe that the world there is like the U.S. Yet, they are ready to buy into supposed atrocities, massacres, and intentional killings. Westerners need to stop comparing themselves to Middle Easterners. They live on opposite sides of the planet.

Yet, the West keeps thinking that they can moderate Islam. Sheik Yousuf Al-Qaradawi, whose sermons in the U.S. I have watched, was invited by the IAP Islamic Association of Palestine, a branch of Hamas terrorist organization, to speak. He clearly talked about Jihad and martyrdom as being the same in terms of fanaticism, as Osama bin Laden. Yet the European Union invites him as an official to hand out fatwas in Europe. The only way Qaradawi will denounce the killing of innocent people is if the West agrees to support all policies invoked by his Islamist agenda. There is a way the West can have peace with Islam. They can either submit or convert to Islam. That is the only peace Islamists understand. Just as Israel negotiated for peace after winning every battle with the Arabs, the Arabs negotiated for total surrender. It's really quite amazing.

Qatar TV aired this sermon on March 23, 2005 by Sheik Yousef Qaradawi:

> Some may say that the attack targeted the British who are fighting us...But, brothers, it is unjust to blame all the British or even all the Americans for the crimes of their governments. Millions marched in countries that participated in the war in Iraq, in Britain, Spain, and Italy. Their governments went to war, but the peoples protested against this in the millions.
>
> Am I allowed to kill theses people? Am I allowed to kill the mayor of London, who came to the defense of the Palestinian cause and of the Islamic preachers...Are we allowed to kill these people? We want [the attackers] to understand the religion and to know what is forbidden. They have a flaw in their understanding of Jihad. They believe that Jihad means fighting the entire world. Who has said such a thing? (MEMRI.ORG)

This type of thinking should make Westerners wonder how Muslims feel about those in America who don't protest the war in Iraq. As a Westerner, you must read between the lines.

Chapter 18
Myth vs. Fact

MYTH – WE ARE FIGHTING TERROR ORGANIZATIONS

Dr. Mary Habeck, a professor at Johns Hopkins University, author of the book, *Knowing the Enemy: Jihadist Ideology and the War on Terror*, claims to be an expert and gives lectures to Yale graduates at Culver Academies. Habeck supposedly offers a rare look into the minds of terrorists. The jihadists, she explains, represent less than 1 percent of Muslims who have a "fanatical" interpretation of Islamic law. Habeck presented an optimistic view for the eventual suppression, if not defeat, of the radical movement, due in part to the fact that it remains a very unpopular ideology, even among other Muslims. She points out that al-Qaeda, the only jihadist group to openly attack the United States, has not been able to mount another successful attack against the American homeland. (South Bend Tribune, by Adam Jackson, 2-4, 2006) As if our war is with only al-Qaeda? Such a narrow view on the subject hardly gives Westerners an accurate insight into this movement.

If we review the threat in a much larger picture, neither Hezbollah, Hamas, nor Iran are terror organizations. Hezbollah is part of the Lebanese government and infrastructure. Hezbollah is a Shia sect. Sunnis will morally support them, as we witnessed during the last Israeli-Lebanese war – Hamas carrying both Hezbollah's yellow flag alongside the green Hamas flag. Hamas honored Hezbollah by doing the same. Yes, Shia and Sunni will always hate each other, but when it comes to Israel, they unite – temporarily.

Shia and Sunni hate each other passionately. In Iraq, they kill each other without mercy. In the end, this will be the downfall of the Islamic invasion against Israel, in which *every man's sword shall be against his brother.*

Islamic fundamentalism is not a mere cult. It has the potential to go beyond small groups to become fully complete societies. Again, the Iranian Revolution, Hamas, and Hezbollah are prime examples.

This Islamic Revolution has the potential to engulf all of the Muslim world. It's much bigger than the West thinks. CAIR, for example, and other Muslim groups, accuse the estimates made by one expert, Daniel Pipes of being inflammatory assertions about Islam, including his estimate that from ten to fifteen percent of Muslims are militant Islamists. Yet, this number is in no way an exaggeration. If anything, it is a gross under-estimate. Pipes, whom many Muslim apologists complain about, is really moderate on his estimates. If one counts the moral support for Islamic fundamentalism in the Middle East, instead of listening to so-called experts like Mary Habeck, one can get a better picture of the estimates coming from Middle Eastern agencies.

A MOST CRUCIAL SURVEY

In November 2004, Al-Arabia Network surveyed some 113,000 individuals throughout the Arab world. *73.2% of respondents said they wanted a Hamas official to replace the recently deceased Yasser Arafat as the Palestinian leader.* (www.inthebullpen.com/archives/2004/11/27/poll-palestinians-support-hamas)

This speaks volumes – that over seventy-three percent of Arabs want Islamic fundamentalism.

The majority of Muslims in Nigeria (fifty-six percent) say that many or most Muslims there support al-Qaeda.

This by no means indicates that those who replied "no" to al-Qaeda would not support other forms of Islamic fundamentalism. Let me give you an example. While having lunch at an Arab-owned restaurant, I was sitting with a pastor and a Jew. The Jewish man complimented the restaurant by saying he had been dining there for years and could testify that these are peaceful people. When the Arab waiter came to the table, I spoke in Arabic and identified myself as Palestinian. I asked him for his view on eradicating Jews, to which he said he doesn't approve. I quoted the famous Hadith (trees and stones), to which he responded, "yes, but the time is not yet, we must first establish the Khilafa." So, if this same question were asked in a survey, many would outwardly answer "no" but their inward answer would be, "no – not yet."

Khilafa is an Arabic word which means a Muslim state government, of which the Khalifa is the head, or vicar, considered to be the successor of the prophet Muhammed on earth. Both Khilafa and Khalifa are major terms Westerners should know and study – carefully. Had someone like this waiter participated in a survey, he would probably say that he is against the radical Muslim movement. But, most Muslims I know would support the notion of having a Khilafa, at least some day, since it is an essential part of Islamic dogma that all Muslims study and accept. There is a high percentage of "moderate" Muslims (as Westerners would call them) who don't agree with accomplishing Khilafa through terrorism. However, if Islam would ever gain power on a state level, these same "moderate" Muslims would believe the Caliph must head the Muslim Umma (nation), and then he would be entitled to declare Jihad against the infidel. Sheikh Yusuf al-Qaradawi, the world-renown Muslim scholar, explains the necessity to await a Khalifa (Caliph) before carrying out the full extent of Sharia Islamic Law. "If a sane person who has reached puberty voluntarily apostatizes from Islam, he deserves to be punished. In such a case, it is obligatory for the caliph (or his representative) to ask him to repent and return to Islam. If he does, it is accepted from him, but if he refuses, he is immediately killed." So if this scenario took place and Qaradawi would ask a Muslim to kill the apostate, or if someone asked Qaradawi to carry out the punishment, the response would most likely be "wait for the Khilafa to be established first." This was always the common response to all our questions and request for fatwas by local imams.

Yet, even without the establishment of Khilafa first, the number of fundamentalist radicals in Pakistan is alarming – about thirty-five percent of Pakistanis say such extremist groups have the support of most or many of the people in that country, and according to a PEW Research Group survey in 2004, sixty-five percent support Osama bin Laden. Pakistan already has nuclear weapons. In Turkey, as many as thirty-one percent say that suicide attacks against Americans and other Westerners in Iraq are justifiable.

In Jordan, fifty-five percent support Osama bin Laden, and in Morocco, forty-five percent.

Sixteen percent of Indonesian Muslims (almost thirty million people) supported bombings, while a further twenty-five percent declined to offer an opinion. More recently, the highly regarded PEW Research Group, in its PEW Global Attitudes Project, showed a reduction from sixteen percent of Indonesian Muslims to "only" ten percent (eighteen million people). (Quadrant Magazine, Australia August 2006 – Volume L, Number 9)

The same survey, however, showed that sixty-five percent of Indonesia's Muslims today do not believe that the September 11 attacks on the United States were carried out by Arabs! (Quadrant Magazine, Australia August 2006 - Volume L Number 9)

Westerners don't read between the lines. After the bombing of hotels in Jordan by the order of al-Zarqawi, interviews on CNN with Jordanians show that the support stops when Arabs are killed, not Americans. One interviewee said "We supported Zarqawi, but after this we don't."

This whole thing is alarming, yet when I warn Westerners, I will be labeled an alarmist and a bigot. If Islamic terrorism is restricted to certain groups or cults, as thought by many Westerners, then how do we explain these major statistics? Instead, Western experts seem to numb their people into believing that all is fine, and it's all about the economy!

We have the potential for a rise of several Nazi Germanies, with a religious twist that says fight, not because the Fuhrer said so but because God Almighty ordered it. Do not worry about killing or dying because the end is paradise. Yet, the world in the West continues in a deep sleep.

I had a painful experience when I worked with Ibrahim Abdallah, an ex-terrorist living in America who appeared with me in the media. He received over four hundred threats from his "friends" and neighbors for appearing on TV and radio interviews, speaking against terrorism. In one community event he attended with over 130 people, he stated that only a small handful of friends and relatives approved of him speaking out against terrorism. The rest, he said, put him down and reprimanded him. Finally, Ibrahim decided to quit due to all the pressure he received from his family and community. He was eventually coerced to release a tape reversing his previous statements. Coercion worked!

MYTH – TERRORISM IS CAUSED BY HOPELESSNESS

Charles Krauthammer, in his column in the Washington Post (6/20/02), wrote:

> *Whenever a massacre occurs in Israel, Palestinian spokesmen rush out to say: "Yes, this is terrible, but this is what happens when you have a people with no hope for an end to the occupation." Apologists in the West invariably echo this explanation.*
>
> *Of all the mendacity that pollutes Middle Eastern discourse, this is the worst. It assumes that the listener is not only stupid but suffers from amnesia. Two years ago at the Camp David summit, in the presence of the President of the United States, the Palestinians were offered an end to the occupation – a total end, a final end – by the Prime Minister of Israel. They said no. They said no, because in return, they were asked to make peace.*

The following paragraph from Israel National News (Wed. June 19, 2002) addresses the desperate and depressed Palestinian theory:

> *Are suicide terrorists "depressed?" – British Foreign Secretary Jack Straw said today, "We can all feel a degree of compassion for those youngsters" who kill themselves and others, but added, "they must be so misguided and depressed to do" what he called "despicable" attacks. His remarks came a day after Cherie Blair, wife of the British Prime Minister, implied that the terrorists' despair and "lack of hope" was what drove them to commit murder. Interestingly, Muhammad al-Ghoul, a 22-year-old in the first semester of a*

master's degree program in Islamic studies at A-Najah University,
did not quite fit the above characterization when he flipped the
switch yesterday that killed himself and 19 others in the bus from
Gilo. "I am happy that my body will be the response for the attacks
conducted by the Israelis and that my body will turn into an explo-
sive shred-mill against the Israelis," his father quoted al-Ghoul's
suicide note as saying. "How beautiful it is to make my bomb
shrapnel kill the enemy. How beautiful it is to kill and to be
killed...for the lives of the coming generation."

Similarly, the mother of Muhammad Farhat, who murdered five Israeli
boys in the Atzmonah pre-military academy in March 2006, did not
speak of sadness or despair in an interview with a London Arabic-
language newspaper. She did say,

Because I love my son, I encouraged him to die a martyr's death for
the sake of Allah...Muhammad was seven when the martyr 'Imad
'Aql lived with us at home, [and] despite his young age, he was [an]
assistant to 'Imad 'Aql...'Imad lived with us for 14 months, and he
had a room in our house from which he would plan the operations.
The mujahideen would come to him and plan and sketch everything
out, and little Muhammad would be with them, thinking and plan-
ning. This was the source of Muhammad's love of martyrdom. This
is the atmosphere in which the love of martyrdom developed in
Muhammad's soul. I, as a mother, naturally encouraged the love of
Jihad in the soul of Muhammad and in the souls of all my sons, all
of whom belong to the Al-Qassam Brigades. My eldest son, Nidal
(31), is wanted now by the Israelis. My second son set out on a
martyrdom operation, but was discovered, arrested, and sentenced
to 11 years' imprisonment. I have another son who is the escort of
Sheikh Ahmed Yassin. The atmosphere to which Muhammad was
exposed was full of faith and love of martyrdom...He would bran-
dish his weapon and tell me: "Mom, this is my bride." He loved his
gun so much. (Extensive excerpts from the above interview,
translated by MEMRI)

MYTH – ISRAEL INTRODUCED TERRORISM

Jews were victims of Arab terror long before the Irgun blew up the
King David Hotel. Perhaps the first recorded instance of Arab terror

against the Jews was when the Meccan army exterminated the Jewish tribe of Quraiza ordered by the founder of Islam, Muhammad. In Syria, the infamous blood libel of 1840 brought about the death, torture, and pillage of countless Jews, falsely accused of murdering a priest and his servant to collect the blood for Passover matzos! Arab terrorism was rampant during a wave of anti-Jewish riots in 1920-21 (which was characterized by the brutal murder in Jaffa of the prominent Jewish author Y. Brenner) and during the "Disturbances" of 1929 (which included the massacre of the Jewish community in Hebron). In his book, *Days of Our Years,* Dutch-Canadian journalist Pierre Van Passen described the violence ruthlessly incited by the Mufti of Jerusalem, Haj Amin al-Husseini – an ally of Hitler and his agents, as well as the media bias of the time:

> *The Arab Higher Committee, the Mufti's political creation, sent out its bands of terrorists to ravage the land. This campaign of organized violence and destruction, which started in 1936, and which went on almost uninterruptedly for two years, was declared to be a spontaneous emanation of an exasperated Arabic national sentiment. Murderers and bandits who threw bombs into Jewish hospitals and orphan asylums, who killed from ambush and tore up young orange plantations in the night, were elevated to the rank of national heroes.* (Andrea Levin is Executive Director of CAMERA, **www.camera.org**, IMRA *Independent Media Review and Analysis*)

The Palestinian terrorism campaign was stepped-up on the eve of the U.N. Partition Resolution of November 1947 and led to the joint Arab invasion of 1948-49, which delineated the boundaries of the newly established State of Israel.

After the War of Independence, Arab terrorism expanded in scope. In 1952, when "fedayeen" terrorist border incursions reached their height, there were about 3,000 incidents of cross-border violence, extending from the malicious destruction of property to the brutal murder of civilians. In the years 1951-1955, 503 Israelis were killed by Arab terrorists infiltrating from Jordan. 358 were killed in attacks from Egypt, and 61 were killed in attacks originating from Syria and Lebanon. This anti-Israeli violence encompassed both frontier settlements and population centers, and was perpetrated, for the most part, against innocent civilians. In March 2002, the Israeli Foreign Ministry issued a list of the major terror attacks occurring prior to Israel's possession of the disputed territories.

Arabs claim that Jews are guilty of terrorism too, since the Irgun blew up the King David Hotel. Why did the Irgun blow up the King David Hotel? The British restricted immigration by Jews to their ancient homeland during World War II, cutting off the escape route of European Jewry. This led to Jewish resistance organizations fighting the British. The King David Hotel was the site of the British military command and the British Criminal Investigation Division. British troops invaded the Jewish Agency on June 29, 1946, and confiscated large quantities of documents. The information about Jewish Agency operations, including intelligence activities in Arab countries, was taken to the King David Hotel. At about the same time, more than 2,500 Jews from all over Palestine were placed under arrest.

The documents seized by the British had to be destroyed. In order to prevent casualties, three telephone calls were placed, one to the hotel, another to the French Consulate, and a third to the Palestine Post, warning that explosives in the King David Hotel would soon be detonated. The British apparently did not believe the warnings.

Perhaps a more disturbing question than "why did the Irgun blow up the King David Hotel" is the question, "Why did the British locate their military headquarters and investigation division in a civilian building?"

MYTH – TERRORISM IS A FORM OF RESISTANCE

Steve Plaut wrote about how the media uses the word "resistance" to describe one of the clearest signs of the growing nazification of so much of the world's media. The increasing trend is to label Palestinian atrocities, such as the exploding of a bus full of children in Haifa, as "Palestinian resistance." The PLO and its amen choruses routinely explain away such mass murders of Jewish children and other civilians as "Palestinian resistance," as do the BBC and many other establishment media outfits. Of course, describing Palestinian behavior as "resistance" makes precisely as much sense as describing as "resistance" the campaign of the Wehrmacht and Gestapo in the 1940s against the various anti-German partisan forces. In other words, it is yet another Orwellian inversion. The Palestinians are not the forces that resist evil, but rather, they are the savages. The Jews are those who are resisting savagery. Resistance against fascism and barbarism is what Israel does when it assassinates terrorists and blows up their homes. The trendy use of the term "resistance" for Palestinian violence is a rather naked attempt by anti-Semites to justify those atrocities, exactly as would be an attempt to label 1944 German anti-partisan activity as "resistance." It is entirely consistent with the long insistence by the press on referring to Palestinian mass murderers as "activists" and "militants," as if they are marchers in a gay pride parade or save-the-whales march, rather than terrorists and mass murderers of children. (Steven Plaut, *Arab Terror,* FrontPageMag.com March 11, 2003)

MYTH – TERRORISTS ARE OPPRESSED

Efraim Karsh, in his article "What Occupation?" (Commentary July-August 2002), addressed this slander, and excerpts of some of his points follow:

> It should be recalled, first of all, that this occupation did not come about as a consequence of some grand expansionist design, but rather was incidental to Israel's success against a pan-Arab attempt to destroy it...In the wake of the war, the only objective adopted by then-Minister of Defense Moshe Dayan was to preserve normalcy in the territories through a mixture of economic inducements and a minimum of Israeli intervention. The idea was that the local populace would be given the freedom to administer itself as it wished...In sharp contrast with, for example, the U.S. occupation of postwar Japan, which saw a general censorship of all Japanese media and a comprehensive revision of school curricula, **Israel** made no attempt to reshape Palestinain culture. It limited its oversight of the Arabic press in the territories to military and security matters, and allowed the continued use in local schools of Jordanian textbooks filled with vile anti-Semitic and anti-**Israel** propaganda. Israel's restraint in this sphere – which turned out to be desperately misguided – is only part of the story. The larger part, still untold in

all its detail, is of the astounding social and economic progress made by the Palestinian Arabs under Israeli "oppression." At the inception of the occupation, conditions in the territories were quite dire. Life expectancy was low; malnutrition, infectious diseases, and child mortality were rife; and the level of education was very poor. Prior to the 1967 war, fewer than sixty percent of all male adults had been employed, with unemployment among refugees running as high as eighty-three percent. Within a brief period after the war, Israeli occupation had led to dramatic improvements in general well-being, placing the population of the territories ahead of most of their Arab neighbors...During the 1970's, the West Bank and Gaza constituted the fourth fastest growing economy in the world – ahead of such "wonders" as Singapore, Hong Kong, and Korea, and substantially ahead of Israel itself...Under Israeli rule, the Palestinians also made vast progress in social welfare. Perhaps most significantly, mortality rates in the West Bank and Gaza fell by more than two thirds between 1970 and 1990, while life expectancy rose from 48 years in 1967 to 72 years in 2000...The Palestinian economy is not doing as well at present. Efraim Karsh explains:

Between 1994 and 1996, the Rabin and Peres governments had imposed repeated closures on the territories in order to stem the tidal wave of terrorism in the wake of the Oslo accords. This had led to a steep drop in the Palestinian economy. With workers unable to get into Israel, unemployment rose sharply, reaching as high as fifty percent in Gaza.

Efraim Karsh points out that the Israelis have withdrawn from most areas populated by Palestinian Arabs, so there is no longer even a benevolent occupation left. He wrote:

Since the beginning of 1996, and certainly following the completion of the redeployment from Hebron in January 1997, ninety-nine percent of the Palestinian population of the West Bank and the Gaza Strip have not lived under Israeli occupation. By no conceivable stretching of words can the anti-Israel violence emanating from the territories during these years be made to qualify as resistance to foreign occupation. In these years there has been no such occupation.

MYTH – ISLAM MEANS PEACE

Despite the efforts of the media and academia at political correctness, Islam means *"submission,"* not *"peace"* – submission to the complete will of Allah (Islamic god) and the duties laid out in the Quran for his followers, and this includes jihad. The Hans Wehr Dictionary of Modern Written Arabic defines *"Islam"* as *"submission, resignation."*

Other forms of the word, "Aslim Taslam" are seen in letters sent by Muhammad and his followers after him during the Muslim conquests from North Africa to South East Asia. This invited them to surrender to Islam's authority and to believe in Muhammad as the messenger of Allah. The words "Aslim," (submit) and "Taslam" (and get peace) are known by every Muslim to mean π"surrender and you will be safe," or in other words, "surrender or face death." The root word "Islama" "istislam," means "handling over, submission, surrender, capitulation, unreckoning approval, resignation."

There is no connection in meaning between *salam* (peace) and *islam* (submission).

MYTH – JIHAD MEANS INNER-STRUGGLE

Jihad is not merely a struggle with the temptations in life but the struggle to wage war against the infidels, to protect the nation of Islam from the heathens and to convert them to Islam. This is Islam's definition of peace. Muhammad explained in one of the Hadiths:

> *Allah's apostle was asked, "What is the best deed?" He replied, "To believe in Allah and his Apostle." The questioner then asked, "What is the next?" He replied, "To participate in Jihad (war) in Allah's cause."* (Narrated by Abu Huraira. Vol. 1, Book 2, No. 25.)

The definition of jihad, according to scholars such as Ibn Qudamah Al-Maqdisi, Ibn Taymiyyah and Ibn Aabideen, is:

> *Exhausting the utmost effort fighting for the sake of Allah, directly by your body or by assisting by money or by your saying or by recruiting Mujahideen (Islamic fighters) or by any other means to help fighting.*

According to Maliki Fiqh Imam Ibn Arafa, Jihad is: "a Muslim to fight the infidel without a treaty, for the sake of Allah, to make his name the highest through his presence." (Transmitted by Sheikh Khalil in Mukhtasar Al-Khalil)

Shaafi stated, Jihad is: "to fight the (Infidels) for the sake of Allah by your body or money or tongue or by recruiting the people." (Fiqh Imam Shirazi in Al-Muhazab Fil Fiqh Al-Shaafi)

It was stated to Hanbali, Jihad means: "to start to fight the (Infidels) whether as a Fard Kifayah (acquired knowledge) or Fard Ayn (revealed knowledge) i.e. both are mandatory one for the community of Muslims and one for the individual Muslim, protecting the believers from the Infidels or guarding the border or frontier and to fight in the front line is the pillar." (Fiqh Imam Ibn Qudama Al-Maqdisi)

All four major Islamic schools of thought agree that jihad is not merely a personal struggle, but a call to wage war on the infidels by all means possible: giving money, recruiting and training people – these are also means of jihad.

The highest authority is the prophet of Islam:

> When you meet the unbelievers in jihad, chop off their heads. And when you have brought them low, bind your prisoners rigorously. Then set them free or take ransom from them until the war is ended. Sura 47.4

> Muhammad is Allah's apostle. Those who follow him are ruthless to the unbelievers but merciful to one another. Sura 48.29

> Those that make war against Allah and His apostle and spread disorder in the land shall be slain or crucified or have their hands and feet cut off on alternate sides, or be banished from the land. They shall be held up to shame in this world and sternly punished in the hereafter. Sura 5.33-34

> Allah revealed His will to the angels, saying: 'I shall be with you. Give courage to the believers. I shall cast terror into the hearts of the infidels. Strike off their heads, strike off the very tips of their fingers!' That was because they defied Allah and His apostle. He

that defies Allah and his apostle shall be sternly punished by Allah.
Sura 8.12-13

In order that Allah may separate the pure from the impure, put all the impure ones [i.e. non-Muslims] one on top of another in a heap and cast them into hell. They will have been the ones to have lost.
Sura 8.37

Muster against them [i.e. non-Muslims] all the men and cavalry at your command, so that you may strike terror into the enemy of Allah and your enemy, and others besides them who are unknown to you but known to Allah. Sura 8.60

Prophet, make war on the unbelievers and the hypocrites, and deal harshly with them. Hell shall be their home: an evil fate. Sura 9.73

When We resolve to raze a city, We first give warning to those of its people who live in comfort. If they persist in sin, judgment is irrevocably passed, and We destroy it utterly. Sura 17.16-17

We have destroyed many a sinful nation and replaced them by other men. And when they felt Our Might they took to their heels and fled. They were told: 'Do not run away. Return to your comforts and to your dwellings. You shall be questioned all.' 'Woe betide us, we have done wrong' was their reply. And this they kept repeating until We mowed them down and put out their light. Sura 21.11-15

MYTH – WAHABI SECT OF ISLAM IS TO BLAME

The problem with the experts in our government agencies is that they seek to define the principles with which we are at war, in combination with the organization with whom we are currently at war (al-Qaeda Wahabi) or the state that seeks war with us (Iran's Khomenism). However, there is no official definition that identifies the basic doctrine of what this enemy truly believes or the source of these problems. We are dealing with an ancient religious idology that has been at war with the West, and is totally incompatible with it.

If Wahabi Islam is the source of all the troubles, then where did the Muslim Brotherhood, Tablighis, Islamic Jihad, Jema'a Islamiya, and an array of other terror groups come from? Did Wahabism come up with these?

Similar to Islam's definition of the two houses of Islam or Kufr, we in the West seem to have broken down their world into the house of Wahabism and house of moderate Islam.

If there is such a thing as moderate Islam, then what are their books and reference manuals? What conflicts arose between the two? Where are the exchanges and debates on ideology over the decades?

The only two houses within Islam are the Shia and Sunni, similar to the Christian faith where we have Catholics and Protestants. Yet we can define the differences, internal struggles...

When we view Evangelical Christianity, we do not define it as a stand alone and separate from Protestantism.

In America, Baptists, Presbyterians, or Methodists can visit each other and worship within the same church. Evangelicals, at times, might point to Catholics as infidels and out of the faith. Similarly, Sunni, at times, point to Shia as infidels and out of the faith. Yet, not all do so, as some Evangelicals look at Catholics as within the fold, and so do Sunni.

Yet, in the Middle East, we never differentiated between the four sects of Sunnis (Maliki, Hanball, Shafi'i, and Hanafi). We were all Muslim, and all of us believed in Jihad against Israel and the West.

I grew up in the Middle East, and I never addressed any Muslim as Salafi or Wahabi. To us, there were Shia or Sunni, and even that distinction ended as I watch my people rally for Hezbollah carrying both the flags of Hamas and Hezbollah.

This Western analogy seems to suggest that we are fighting a cult which sprouted out of Islam, similar to fighting David Koresh and the Branch Davidians as a corrupted form of Protestant Christianity. Not so. Jihad is well-defined in all four main branches of Sunni Islam as a global takeover. The West should not be blinded by how some liberal Muslims define jihad. Rather than defending liberal Islam, we must defend our very own existence.

Yet, in almost every publication I read where Westerners attempt to pinpoint the blame, they always choose the term "Wahabi Islam," a form of Islam that came out of Saudi Arabia.

Between 1950 – 1970, in response to colonial occupation and imperialist exploitation, the Middle East adopted a secularist, nationalist reponse in what is called Pan-Arab movements. Nasser in Egypt, Ben Bella in Algeria, Bourguiba in Tunisia all pushed through social reforms, some of which directly undermined imperialist economic and political interests in the region.

In the 1950s, 1960s and 1970s, there were strong left-wing currents across the Muslim world. In Syria, South Yemen, Iraq, Somalia, Libya and Ethiopia, there were left-wing coups and the creation of state capitalist regimes. In other countries there were strong waves of mass movements which threw up left-leaning populist leaders, such as Nasser. Modernization, it seemed, could (and was about to) annul Islam as a political force.

However, in the early seventies, especially after the death of King Faisal of Saudi Arabia, the Muslim Brotherhood became very active in the Middle East.

Before that, the World Muslim League, founded in Mecca in 1962, distributed books and cassettes by Hassan al-Banna, Qutb and other foreign luminaries.

Saudi Arabia successfully courted academics at al-Azhar University and invited Muslim fundamentalists to teach at Saudi universities. During these times, the Middle East was not too interested in Islam's Sharia governing every aspect of life.

Then, in the late 1950s and the 1960s, the Middle East was gripped by a struggle between the traditional monarchies and the secular pan-Arab radicals, led by Nasser's Egypt, with the pan-Islamist Salafis an important third force. (Abdullah M Sindhi, King Faisal and Pan-Islamism)

By embracing pan-Islamism, Faisal countered the idea of pan-Arab loyalty centered in Egypt with a larger transnational loyalty centered in Saudi Arabia. During the 1960s, members of the Egyptian Muslim Brotherhood and its offshoots, many of them teachers, were given sanctuary in Saudi Arabia, in a move that undermined Nasser, who was allied with Communist Russia, while also relieving the Saudi education crisis. (Madawi al-Rasheed, p.144)

So, in reality, the web of Islamic fundamentalism is old and intertwined. The Salafis, who simply called for the return to Islam, originated as an intellectual movement at al-Azhar University in Egypt, led by Muhammad Abduh (1849-1905), Jamal al-Din al-Afghani (1839-1897), and Rashid Rida (1865-1935).

The early Salafis did not object to Western industrialization but thought that their own society would be better off by adapting Islamic law, and following the Prophet Muhammad's way of governance and life.

The name Salafi comes from Al-salaf al-saliheen, which simply means the "pious predecessors" of the early Muslim community.

The reality is that no matter how we look at it, the war is between Islam and non-Muslims.

One could argue that there have been battles between al-Qaeda and Arab governments. The reality is that these governments are not moderate in the Western sense – they do not want to lose their dictatorial seats. They would follow Islamic laws in many aspects, but when it comes to their seat of power, that's when the buck ends. Are these moderates? Hardly.

In Afghanistan, for example, it doesn't matter whether Muslims there follow the Taliban or the Northern Alliance – you would find the majority of either camp would decide that a convert from Islam is to be killed. What's so moderate about that?

So, in essence, we decided that the moderate is the one who will aid us against an immediate enemy. Then, we decided not to offend Muslims and declared the war on Wahabism and the Shia Revolution in Iran.

When Abdul Rahman, an Afghan Christian convert was arrested in Kabul, the U.S. and many other governments in the West responded to the fundamentalist Chief Justice Mullah Fazal Hadi Shinwari and the other mullahs surrounding him. American troops fought to remove the Taliban from power, but unfortunately, this did not bring freedom and democracy to the people of Afghanistan. The American government simply replaced the Taliban with many Islamic fundamentalist factions from the Northern Alliance.

There are many people in Afghanistan suffering to establish a secular democracy. Instead, we allowed another Islamic fundamentalist regime to arise in Kabul. So, now the Northern Alliance members, representatives of the Taliban, Parchamists, and Khalqis are filling the seats in the Afghan parliament, which robs aid money designated to help the poor in Afghanistan.

The Northern Alliance is simply composed of Muslim fundamentalists. By their hands, thousands of Hindus and Sikh compatriots were looted, raped, and expelled from Afghanistan. The Northern Alliance bands of Qanooni, Rabbani, Sayyaf, Massoud, Khalili, Dostum, and Mohaqiq slaughtered thousands of Kabul residents between 1992 and 1996.

Yet this thinking is dangerous because, in the Middle East, my friend today is my enemy in the future.

The war should be identified as: a war with fundamental Islam; and peace with liberal Islam, where women have the freedom to choose to marry whomever they want, which also includes the right to choose a non-Muslim man.

If we do this, Westerners would discover the reality of how many true friends they have in the Muslim world – very few. Yet, we want to delude ourselves by believing we have Muslim partners in our efforts to establish liberty, freedom, and democracy for all. We don't. Let me repeat, our ways and their ways come from different sides of the planet.

I shall give an example of the mistake Westerners make by simply identifying Wahabism as the enemy. Freedom House, a Washington-based organization founded by Eleanor Roosevelt and now chaired by former CIA Director, James Woolsey, conducted a survey of literature found in America's leading mosques. They came to three conclusions, two of which were accurate. The Saudi government and the royal family are the primary purveyors of Islamic religious materials in America and worldwide. The overwhelming majority of the Islamic literature printed by the

Saudi government and distributed in American mosques and Islamic schools is uncivilized, hateful, violent, and treasonous. (New report on Saudi government publications, Freedom House, Published by the Center for Religious Freedom)

But then they claimed, without evidence or reason, that such materials were reflective of Wahabi extremism, and were, therefore, a corruption of Islam.

Yet all of these books and pamphlets match those used throughout the whole Muslim world:

- the teachings of Ibn Ishaq's Sira (the only biographical account of Muhammad written within 200 years of his death),

- Tabari (Islam's earliest and most authentic history of Muhammad and his formation of Islam),

- Bukhari's collections of Hadith (Islam's most revered collection of Muhammad's words and deeds),

- The Quran which is devoid of context and chronology and thus dependent upon the above as the prime sources.

It is good that Freedom House conducted this survey, translated these documents, and made the incriminating evidence available to everyone for free.

Yet, the very survival of the civilized world is dependent upon an understanding that fundamental Islam is also mainstream Islam, i.e., that the vast majority of Muslims subscribe to the above doctrine.

MYTH – PALESTINE IS A STATE

The honest, non-politically correct definition of Palestine is – an Arab fiction, a psychoses of death and destruction. We can see this from all of the media coverage on Palestine. Arabs only wanted a Palestinian state after their loss in the Six Day War in 1967.

Yet, the Arabs, with all their battle cries and after using the oil embargo initiated in 1973 called on Western governments to support the establishment of a Palestinian state. This became a successful political strategy. So now, the territorial tug-of-war distracts Western attention from the real issue, the destruction of the Jews, in which Arabs play the underdog and Israel is an occupier.

This fantasy that consumes the fanatics is the main argument to pressure the world against Israel. Yet, it's nothing more than a religious holy war. We do not have a demand for a viable state, but an Islamist state. We have seen this from the Palestinian elections, as well as the consensus from all of the polls. It's in the culture, the tradition, the religion, the music, and in every other aspect of the Arab life – destroy the Jews. This was Arafat's game plan, and he was a chip off the same block as Saddam Hussein, Osama bin Laden, and Ahmed Yassin – different names, same goals.

After all, it was Mustafa Azzam, a Palestinian from Jenin, who was Osama bin Laden's mentor and the inspiration for al-Qaeda. Islamic jihad is all interconnected. In reality, it's not International Zionism that is threatening the world, but Islamic jihad. What they accuse the West of doing, they need to apply to themselves. The Arabs never searched for the log in their own eye before they pointed at the spec in Israel's eye. And why should they look at themselves? Their religious traditions do not adhere to this analogy; only to the principle that they are the best of nations.

What the world must acknowledge is that Arafat never wanted a Palestinian state because he never wanted the conflict to end. If he did, he would have accepted the Barak agreement that gave him everything he claimed he wanted. He rejected this offer and all offers. What does a nation do when it agrees to give their enemy nearly everything that was demanded, but the enemy rejects the offer anyway? What then did Arafat want? Obviously, there is no other answer but the destruction of Israel and the Jews. If this reality cannot be fathomed, then examine Nazi Germany and the Holocaust. The difference between Nazis and Muslim fundamentalists is that they don't need to establish concentration centers, the center is already there – Israel. The dream of the fulfillment of the prophecy "The trees and stones will cry out…" is at hand.

Blaming Israel for the plight of the Palestinians, as Arafat and other Arab leaders have done, is essentially turning reality upside down. Israel has done more for the Palestinians than the Arab leaders ever did. Israel built, for the Palestinian people, schools, hospitals, and apartments. Jordan and Egypt don't want the Palestinians back and neither does any other Arab country.

The Palestinians have lived in poverty for one reason: Arafat stole their money and kept the masses under his control. Millions in financial aid came flowing in, but he and his cabinet, who called the Jews thieves, pocketed much of the money donated by American tax dollars and by the United Nations. Again, what they accuse others of, they are guilty of themselves.

As for the Palestinian Authority's treasury, almost all of it has been stolen or dribbled away. Their own auditors reported that nearly forty percent of the annual budget – $323 million – was wasted, looted, or misused. In President Arafat's regime, bribery was prevalent, services were nil, connections were everything, and might was the only right.

Still, the cry today is to aid the Palestinians. We see it from a variety of positions, including a book by ex-president Carter, "Peace, not Apartheid." Yet, these books ignore the real reason for Palestinian poverty:

1. Arafat stole millions from his own people

2. He would never come to any agreement with Israel and

3. Other Arab leaders have a stake in filtering money to the Palestinians to keep the conflict going and, therefore, keep the face of Israel as the villain on the world's billboard.

We've seen this kind of madness before. The Nobel Committee awarded this murderer and long-time terrorist a peace prize, even though Arafat stated regarding Oslo: "No...no. Allah's messenger Mohammed accepted the al-Hudaibiya peace treaty, and Salah a-Din accepted the peace agreement with Richard the Lion-Hearted."

Now, we have Hamas. I predicted its victory in my previous book, *Why I Left Jihad,* long before Palestinian elections commenced:

Depending on the outcome of the peace process, if the PLO does not deliver the land to the Palestinians, Hamas is the likely candidate to take over Palestinian leadership. (Walid Shoebat, *Why I Left Jihad, The Root of Terrorism,* and *The Return of Radical Islam*)

The fact is, prior to the Six Day War in 1967, there was never a demand by Arabs to create a Palestinian state. The Palestinian Charter never included Judea, which was in Jordan, as part of Palestine. The "Palestinian nation" is a fiction of the Arab Jihadist mind.

Westerners are increasingly secular, materialistic, and ignorant of the past. We see all causes as material, all behavior as the result of the physical environment or of psychological forces that also have their origins in immediate material or environmental conditions. Islamic terrorism, thus, is explained as a response to ignorance and poverty, or to wounded nationalist self-esteem, or to autocratic tyranny, or to postcolonial and post-imperial fallout. The proposed solutions are likewise material: increase development aid to reduce poverty and the despair it breeds; compel Israel to weaken itself in order to remove the constant irritant to Arab nationalist and ethnic esteem; promote democratic institutions to subvert tyranny; and provide rhetorical and fiscal reparations to compensate for colonial and imperial guilt.

Such analyses of the roots of terrorism, of course, reduce the Islamist to Western materialist categories. It either completely ignores, or considerably discounts, the historical, spiritual, and cultural dimensions of his motives, reducing those to mere epiphenomena of some deeper material cause. *It also begs the question of why other peoples, more poor and more oppressed than those in the Middle East, do not resort to terrorism.* As a way of getting to the roots of Islamist terrorism, these material-based analyses obscure more than they enlighten, particularly since, for years, the enemy has become adept at manipulating these Western assumptions, which they also see as weaknesses and symptoms of spiritual bankruptcy and cultural inferiority. (Bat Ye'or, *Eurabia, The Euro-Arab Axis,* Fairleigh Dickinson University Press)

The retreat was confirmed by the deep humiliation of the Ottoman Empire's dismemberment after World War I. Any hopes that *Islam could regain its lost glory militarily were dashed when a tiny Israel three times defeated Arab armies.* These further defeats confirmed that jihad could not be pursued with military force and that other means would have to be pursued. King Hassan II of Morocco said as much at the meeting of the Islamic Conference of Foreign Ministers in 1980. The summary of his remarks states, "The significance of Jihad in Islam did not lie in religious wars or crusades. Rather, it was strategic political and military action, and psychological warfare, which, if employed by the Islamic Umma [the worldwide Islamic community], would ensure victory over the enemy." (Bat Ye'or, *Eurabia, The Euro-Arab Axis,* Fairleigh Dickinson University Press)

"Palestinianism" becomes the vehicle for pursuing the struggle with the West, one that exploits hatred of Jews under the guise of anti-Zionism, thus giving cover to a traditional anti-Semitism, driven underground by the Holocaust. Palestinianism also expresses various cultural pathologies of Western societies, such as Western self-loathing, the idealization of the non-Western "other," the glamour of guerilla resistance, refugee pathos, and a sentimentalized post-colonial guilt. The ultimate goal, however, is not the establishment of a Palestinian state but the prosecution of jihad against the West: "The Arab-Israeli conflict, deliberately blown out of all proportion by the Euro-Arab associative diplomacy, is just one arena of an incessant global jihad that targets the entire West. PLO practices of airplane piracy since 1968, random killings, hostage takings, and Islamikaze bombings have been adopted worldwide as effective jihadist tactics against Western and other civilians, including Muslims." (Bat Ye'or, *Eurabia, The Euro-Arab Axis,* Fairleigh Dickinson University Press)

So, now we have the Arab outcry – only by Islam can we win.

MYTH – ISLAM WAS HIJACKED

When I spoke at Boeing in 2005, I stated, "When Muslim terrorists hijacked Boeing aircrafts and slammed them into the Twin Towers, I turned on the TV, and when all the mayhem was over, they told us that Islam was hijacked."

Osama bin Laden surely does not consider himself a hijacker of Islam.

The Taliban in Afghanistan, Mujahideen Khalq Iran, Hamas, Muslim Brothehood in Egypt, The Abu Sayyaf Group, Palestinian Al-Aqsa Martyrs Brigade, al-Qaeda, Kurdish Ansar al-Islam, Hezbollah of Lebanon, The Janjaweed of Sudan, Jemaah Islamiyah, from Malaysia, Lashkar-e-Tayyiba in Pakistan, The Mahdi Amy in Iraq, and Palestinian Islamic Jihad, are hardly abductors of Islam. They are a global front to establish an Islamic Umma (Nation) worldwide. If Islam has been hijacked, then why haven't the rest of the Muslims, who must, therefore, also be victims, declared war on these hijackers? Why is the war predominately between the U.S. and these countries.

Was it hijacked when the Sudan killed millions? When Turkey killed millions? When Muhammad declared war on the Jews and killed them? When Ahmadenedjad threatened to wipe Israel off the map?

If Islam was indeed hijacked, why were there celebrations in Cairo on 9/11, with people invited to special celebratory feasts in Saudi Arabia, the West Bank, Pakistan, and in Muslim sites everywhere, including a hospital room at the Mass. General, and by Muslims throughout this country?

Are we inventing all the verses in the Quran? The Hadith? The biography of Muhammad? All the Muslim websites? All the Quranic commentators? The history of Jihad-conquest and of the treatment of non-Muslims?

MYTH – ISLAM IS COMPATIBLE WITH THE WEST

A quick run through Muslim websites can teach you a lot about Islam. Just make sure you are able to read between the lines, or read Arabic as I do. I like www.Islamweb.net. But you, as a Westerner, do not know how to read Arabic or understand the sermons. I can access and listen to some of the most popular religious speakers in the Arab world, including one of my favorite speakers when I was Muslim – Abdil Hamid Kishk at:

http://audio.islamweb.net/audio/index.php?page=lecview&sid=374&read=0

The man speaks like Hitler – very mesmerizing, poetic, enchanting, and he knows how to capture the minds and souls of millions all over the Muslim world. He delivers sermons on global Jihad, martyrdom, glory days of Islam, and he emphasizes that we need to replicate it through Jihad warriors, in order to establish a global Islamic rule.

But you have to know Arabic. The English translation is tamed down.

The site also has all sorts of Fatwas on how Muslims conduct their lives in the West. I will give one example. One fatwa (religious decree) is regarding a Muslim living in the West:

> *I am living in a non-Muslim country where there is a very small non-Arab Muslim community and I am fearful of being tempted into Zina (adultery). I want to get married but I do not feel ready (emotionally) for marriage and its responsibilities because I am still continuing my studies. I am financially able to marry a Muslim woman from my country but I am not ready for a real marriage and I need someone to help me with my loneliness in this foreign country. I am thinking of marrying an older (as I am 28 years old) non-Muslim woman (40-50) who can keep me away from Zina (adultery) and at the same time be a help (financially, emotionally and socially) to me rather than a worry. The woman I intend to marry is Christian but she does drink alcohol occasionally. Also, I am not sure if she will obey me in covering her arms or lower legs when out of the house. After, finishing studies I plan to marry a Muslim woman from my country.*

> *1. Can I marry such a woman?*

> *2. If she stops drinking and she covers most of her body (except putting the hijab) can I marry her then?*

> *3. Should I have to tell her about intending to marry another woman? (she probably will not mind but she will ask for a divorce before I get married).*

> *4. Do I have to tell my Muslim wife that I am married to another woman?*

> *5. Since she is old and she probably would not want to live in another country, can I divorce her? or must I have to travel back and forth to be with her? When answering the questions please keep in mind that*

I may be successful to get her to accept Islam. Jazakumullah Khairan for your help.

The response from the Muslim leader with the Fatwa is typical:

"Our answer to your questions will be summarized in the following:

1. Allah permitted Muslims to marry women from the People of the Book provided they are chaste as clarified in <u>Fatwa 3039</u>.

2. We do not advise you to marry the said woman even if this is permissible in principle, as this could lead to many disadvantages because the women from the People of the Book, in this present day and age, are not chaste. For more benefit on the disadvantages of marrying women of the People of the Book and the problems that arise thereof, please refer to <u>Fatwa 3604</u> and <u>8298</u>.

   Furthermore, since you are able to marry a Muslim woman, then you should not exchange that which is better for that which is lower and worse.

3. If it happens that you do marry this woman, *you are not obliged to inform her that you are planning to marry a second wife, and you are not obliged to inform the second wife that you are already married with one wife.* For more benefit, please refer to <u>Fatwa 948</u>. As regards divorcing her in the future, then please refer to <u>Fatwa 3306</u> and <u>2337</u>.

   Finally, for more benefit on the ruling of residing in a non-Muslim country, please refer to <u>Fatwa 5285</u>. Allah Knows best."

Westerners are unaware that most of the Arab youth that come to the U.S. have obtained their permanent status by marrying American women, then, of course, divorcing them for a better Muslim wife. All of my cousins obtained their status by doing this. Many take the kids back to the Middle East, and if, God forbid, they have a daughter, in Islam, a Muslim girl better marry a Muslim. A Muslim girl marrying out of her faith could be killed, which is why it's rare for a Muslim girl to marry a non-Muslim. From a social aspect, Islam is not compatible with the West. In the Middle East, most countries have a Sharia Family Code, which prohibits Muslim women from marrying non-Muslim men but places no restrictions on who Muslim men can marry.

Chapter 19
How to Deal With Islamic Fundamentalism

Islamic Fundamentalism has been brewing for centuries with slow, long-term planning by the many clergy fighting a political struggle with the dictatorships that were appointed by Western powers. In fact, this is the main argument that Islamists use against the West. This will continue for as long as Mecca, Medina and the Ka'aba stay wealthy and strong and radicals are allowed to sit in comfortable mosques brainwashing millions via madrassas and mosques worldwide.

The key to defeating terrorism lies in the economic and political manipulation of Saudi Arabia, yet this is unlikely, since the oil interests so far have not allowed the West to disturb Saudi Arabia.

Consequently, the Islamist belief is that God protects Mecca and Medina, until it burns in the end of days and in accordance to their eschatological teaching, but for now, it serves as a morale booster for Islam worldwide.

Yet, Al-Saud is hated by the Islamists, and it's a delicate subject, since the fear is that any change might disrupt the whole delicate balance, and the oil will fall into the hands of Islamists, if indeed Saudi Arabia is not Islamist enough.

If we find an alternate source of energy, which is not tough to do, Arabia will quickly revert to tribalism, and the West cannot be blamed if feudal and tribal wars erupt. So far, we are blamed for the sectarian war in Iraq. Jihad must be proven as un-divine, and the wars between Muslims must not be blamed on the West.

America helped liberate Afghanistan, and what happened after was that the Jihadists attacked each other over power. The same has happened in Iraq, yet the American presence seems to muster worldwide blame for the sectarian violence.

Experts in the West break down the Jihadists into two ideological types: Salafists, radicals who developed within Sunni societies, and Khomenists, radicals who developed within Shia communities. The Salafists have various ideological and political branches: Wahabis, Muslim Brotherhood, Tablighi and others. From this "tree" came al-Qaeda, Hamas, Islamic Jihad, Jemaa Islamiya, Salafi Combat Group, and dozens of smaller groups around the world. The Khomeinists are the radical clerics in control of Iran. They have created Hezbollah in Lebanon, along with the latter expanded cells around the world.

The head of Salafi Jihadists today is al-Qaeda; the head of Khomeinist Jihadism is the Iranian regime.* The problem with experts that Western government agencies seek is that they define the enemy as the organization (al-Qaeda) or the state (Iran) instead of the driving principles behind their movements. In the war against Russian Communism, the West had a clear understanding that our war was against Communism. But now, we have yet to determine who our war is against – is it Islamo-Facism? Radical Islam? Islamo-Nazism? Fundamental Islam? Islam? And as soon as anyone defines the enemy, they are pressured to retract. Let me say this again, living in the Middle East, I never heard anyone address each other as Salafi or Wahabi!

The misperception of the enemy and coddling a supposed liberal Muslim agenda just gives the Jihadists more time and opportunity to further penetrate and infiltrate the West. This is why it is dangerous that Sheikh Al-Qaradawi, who is not a member of al-Qaeda, holds to the

---

* See Committee on International Relations, U.S. House of Representatives, Washington, D.C. 20515-0128, Subcommittee on International Terrorism and, Nonproliferation, Edward R. Royce [CA], Chairman, "9/11: Five Years Later, Gauging Islamist Terrorism," page 7.

same principles as al-Qaeda and heads up The European Council for Fatwa and Research and would be invited by the E.U. to act as an advisor, and be called "a respected scholar and religious leader worthy of the deepest respect." (Andrew C. McCarthy, The myth of a vibrant "moderate Islam." National Review Online, February 15, 2006)

Little wonder that the moderate, influential Muslim Council of Britain refers to Qaradawi as "a voice of reason, understanding and wisdom." Indeed, with moderates like these abounding, how surprised should we be to find Secretary Rice herself – while very publicly hosting an Iftaar dinner to mark the end of the "holy month" of Ramadan – bestowing a federal promotion on the Muslim Umma, whose creed, she announced, is now the "religion of love" as well as the firmly entrenched "religion of peace?" "We in America," Rice effused, "know the benevolence that is at the heart of Islam." (Ibid)

The contemporary vision of "moderate Islam" as a meaningful force for good is a mirage. Certainly, there are moderate Muslim individuals. There are large pockets of them, here and there, who have assimilated into the modern world and want only to live in ecumenical peace. But many of the people we call "moderates" are flat-out phonies – the bagmen who rise on the shoulders of the leg-breakers. (Ibid)

Americans want to intercept the Jihadists before they engage in terror acts and intercept the ideological threat before it can produce the Jihadists. Yet how can that be done without defining the sources that produce them and declaring them as the enemy? We try to learn from the UK and Australia and their counter-terrorism tactics. We do not produce the proper laws to stop the influx of Jihadists, as we did to Communists in the war against Communism. We were at war against Communism, and we should be at war with Islamism and not just with the terror organizations.

STOP THINKING IN WESTERN TERMS

Every time I view media publications or political decisions regarding the Middle East, I see that Westerners view Middle East issues through their Western mindset. Westerners compare their thinking to that of a Middle

Easterner and compare moderates from the Middle East to the Western understanding of what a moderate is, as if Palestinian Mahmoud Abbas or Iranian Rafsanjani are real moderates in the true Western sense.

Western concepts of heroism and sacrifice are different from Muslim culture. The 9/11 hijackers are heroes to Arabs, yet from the Western mindset, the heroes are the firemen and policemen who died risking their lives to save others from the burning Twin Towers.

The problem of a lack of understanding is still dominant, even in Israel. Professor Louis Rene Beres of the Department of Political Science at Purdue University has correctly explained the Israeli-Palestinian conflict in this way:

> *Jewish supporters of the Oslo "Peace Process" still do not understand the true sources of terrorism against Israel. Projecting their own very generic conceptions of Western history upon the contemporary Middle East, they naively identify these sources within the standard theoretical frameworks of economic disenchantment and rising expectations. Palestinian terrorism is a conscious expression of blood sacrifice, including the blood of "the Jews," and violence against "the Jews" is always an expression of what is sacred. For Palestinian terrorists, violence and sacred are inseparable."* (Louis Rene Beres, *The Meaning of Coming Violence Against Israel,* June 10, 1999, pp. 1-2)

It is vital for Westerners to realize that, in Muslim countries, religion can never be divorced from politics. This marriage between politics and religion may vary from one Muslim country to the other, depending on the volume of Sharia they use. Yet, Westerners need to know that Sharia laws are complex and have substantial control in every Muslim country in which Sharia has shaped the civilization.

This is not the main problem, since religion plays an intricate roll in the political process in America as well. Yet, the American Constitution separates church and state; and Christianity, from a biblical perspective, believes that followers of the faith must act as good citizens, regardless of the government in which they live, as long as those laws don't conflict with God's laws.

This is not the case with Sharia law or with the Muslim desire to establish it. This struggle never died in the Middle East. It simply remained dormant for several decades, attempting to rise every now and then, but it was stopped by dictators who wanted to keep their power. The West, however, instead of keeping its hands out of Iraq or Palestine, interceded in the name of their global efforts to establish democracy, and the end result was aiding the very system they were fighting against. In Iraq, Islamist influence is at work, and in Palestine we pressured Israel to allow Arabs in Jerusalem to vote, and now we have Hamas.

So how can America deal with the Middle East and, at the same time, deal with its global desire to establish free societies and democratic governments?

This effort is viewed by the Muslims as a Western and International Zionist aspiration to occupy the Middle East and rob it of its resources, especially oil.

Yet, the ignorance, whether intentional or not, continues unabated in Western media. Regarding the serious fighting in Somalia, The BBC coverage predominately sides with the argument of Muslim apologetics – that Islamic laws will result in less lawlessness. This careless approach ignores the fact that the Somali Islamic Courts Council (SICC), which has used its military might to spread Islamic Sharia law across most of southern Somalia, would be a major threat to Ethiopia next door, because what comes after establishing these Sharia communities is an expansion ideology that would engulf the whole region in chaos, war, and persecution of non-Muslims, and, ultimately, a global Jihad.

The way to see this unfold is to monitor Osama bin Laden. The Islamists accuse Ethiopia, Washington's top counter-terrorism ally, of invading Somalia and have threatened holy war against any foreign troops there. Al-Qaeda leader Osama bin Laden has publicly encouraged jihadists to join such a war – Sharia expansion ideology at work.

STOP THINKING THAT THEY DEFINE GOD AS WE DO

NAMES OF ALLAH

You always hear this phrase whenever you have a religious discussion: "We all worship the same God."

I could have written an entire book on the different views of God in today's world, but some concepts of God, if one digs deep, are dragons in sheep clothing. Some of the names of Allah pack a meaning that Westerners need to learn. Here are a few:

KHAYRUL MAKIREEN *(Arabic)*

THE GREATEST DECEIVER

SCHEMER

CONNIVER

All four main interpreters of the Quran, Ibin Katheer, Al-Tabari, Al-Jalalyn, Al-Qurtubi, interpret this as Allah, the "great deceiver." According to the text, Allah deceived everyone by making observers believe that Christ was crucified, yet a likeness of Christ was crucified and not Christ himself. Through this, Allah proclaims he has removed the path of salvation, since Christ never died for sin.

AL-MUMEET *(Arabic)*

THE CREATOR OF DEATH

THE SLAYER

THE LIFE-TAKER

AL-DHARR *(Arabic)*

THE DISTRESSER

THE AFFLICTER

THE PUNISHER

AL-MUTAKABBIR *(Arabic)*
PRIDE FILLED
THE MOST PROUD

"Allah's Prayers and Peace be upon him," "Allah says: "Pride is My Wear, Supremacy is My Dress, I will break anyone who vies with Me for them and I do not care." (Hadith)

"Glory be to the One who rightfully deserves to be called the Most PROUD, He is Allah." (Islambasics Library)

From the verses above, Muslim apologists declare that: "This proves that Allah is the truth, and any idol they set up beside Him is falsehood," and "Allah is the Most High, Most Great (Al-Kabeer)." Quran 31:30

The very statement yelled by Jihadists in every operation Allah Akbar (Allah is greater), is described by Muslim scholars:

"Majesty and glory belong to Allah alone. From this quality comes the command to magnify Allah by saying the takbîr, Allâhu akbar, Allah is Greater. This is pride in the purest sense of the word. It is inconceivable of anyone except Allah, in an absolute sense." (Sahij Muslim, Hadith collector, Transliteration Beautiful names)

AL-MALEK *(Arabic)*
THE KING

Regarding his kingdom, it includes both humans and demons, a concept rejected by a Judeo-Christian perspective:

"Say: I seek refuge with [Allah] the Lord of the Dawn from the mischief of the evil He created...the mischievous evil of Darkness as it becomes intensely dark." (Quran 113:1-3)

The "evil <u>he</u> created" refers to the Muslim god, Allah. Seeking refuge in the lord of the dawn (morning star) who created evil and mischief is contrary to Judeo-Christian theology, which considers such descriptions better suited to satan than to God.

"Say: I seek refuge with the Lord of the multitudes, The King of multitudes, The God of multitudes, From the mischief of the Whisperer (of Evil), who whispers into the hearts of the multitude, the multitude of demons and people." (Quran 114:1)

The Quran further defines this king and lord:

"This is a Message sent down from the Lord of men and jinn [demons]." (Quran 69:43)

"I only created jinn [demons] and man to worship Me." (Surat adh-Dhariyat, 56)

"Say: It has been revealed to me that a band of the jinn [demons] listened and said, 'We have heard a most amazing Recitation. It leads to right guidance so we believe in it and will not associate anyone with our Lord.'" (Quran, chapter of the Jin)

Here demons heard the Quran recited and followed Allah their lord:

"An imp of the jinn said, 'I will bring it to you before you get up from your seat. I am strong and trustworthy enough to do it." (Quran, The Ant)

Here, demons are serving King Solomon.

There is a difference in the Judeo-Christian concept of God. The pride-filled god, the causer of death and affliction is none other than satan who afflicted Job, caused the death of mankind in the garden of Eden, and hailed himself as the most proud. Satan is described in Isaiah as son of the dawn who brings all evil and destruction. Yet in Islam, Allah is described as the "bringer of evil."

"Nay, verily: By the Moon, And by the Night as it retreateth, And by the Dawn as it shineth forth..." (Quran 74:32-34)

"So, since we [Jinn/Devils] have listened to the guidance (of the Quran), we have accepted (Islam): and any who believes in his Lord (Allah) has no fear of loss, force, or oppression." (Quran 72:13)

How could God as understood in Judeo-Christian cultures be one who would "violently tear out the soul and drag them to destruction? Yet the Quran describes Allah as:

"I swear by those who violently tear out (the souls), and drag them to destruction." (Quran 79:1)

"I swear by the dawn, and the ten nights, and the even and the odd, and the night when it departs." (Quran 89:1)

"This is a Message sent down from the Lord of men and jinn [demons]. (Quran 69:43)

HE IS A WAR GOD

The concept of God in the West has developed from the Judeo-Christian heritage. One cannot deny the influence of Christian thinking in the West. Yet, the attributes of God from a Western tradition have come as a result of a rich background in Christian and Jewish concepts.

God as defined in the Quran is different. In many ways, the concept of god from Islamic traditions conflicts with the biblical God. We do not have attributes of God in the Bible as great deceiver, or the Lord of demons. This lord in the Quran is different in many aspects, and he requires bloodshed and war:

> "Believers! Wage war against such infidels as are your neighbours, and let them find you rigorous." (Sura 9:124)

This war is also against the people of the Bible:

> "Make war upon such of those (Christians and Jews) to whom the scriptures have been given as believe not in God and His Apostle, and profess not the professor of truth, until they pay tribute out of hand, and they be humbled." (Sura 9:29)

And instead of reaching out to unbelievers as prescribed in the New Testament, the Quran calls for fighting them in Jihad wars:

> "Fight against them until idolatry is no more and Allah's religion reigns supreme. But if they desist, fight none except the evil doers." (2:193)

> "Those who believe, fight in the Cause of Allah, and those who disbelieve, fight in the cause of Taghut (satan, etc.). So fight you against the friends of Shaitan (satan); Ever feeble indeed is the plot of Shaitan." (satan) (4:76)

"SAY to those Arabs of the desert, who took not the field, ye shall be called forth against a people of mighty valour. Ye shall do battle with them, or [other translations have "until"] they shall profess Islam." (Sura 48:16)

"O Prophet! Strive hard against the disbelievers and the hypocrites, and be harsh against them." (9:73)

"O you who believe! Fight those of the disbelievers who are close to you, and let them find harshness in you, and know that Allah is with those who are the Pious." (9:123)

"kill the disbelievers wherever we find them." (2:191)

"fight and slay the Pagans, seize them, beleaguer them, and lie in wait for them in every stratagem." (9:5)

"slay or crucify or cut the hands and feet of the unbelievers, that they be expelled from the land with disgrace and that they shall have a great punishment in the world hereafter." (5:34)

"Be harsh with unbelievers," (48:29)

The Quran also allows them to be "disobedient towards the disbelievers and their governments and strive against the unbelievers with great endeavour." (25:52)

Muhammad even prescribes fighting for Muslims and tells them that:

"it is good for us even if we dislike it." (2:216)

Then he advises Muslims to "strike off the heads of the disbelievers"; and after making a "wide slaughter among them, carefully tie up the remaining captives." (47:4)

Jihad is mandatory and warns us that "unless we go forth, (for Jihad) He will punish us with a grievous penalty, and put others in our place." (9:39)

"And He orders us to fight them on until there is no more tumult and faith in Allah is practiced everywhere." (8:39)

"God has bought from the faithful their selves and their belongings against the gift of paradise; they fight in the way of Allah; they kill and get killed; that is a promise binding on Allah." (Repentance, 9:110)

"And that God may test those who believe, and destroy the infidels." (3:141)

"Relent not in pursuit of the enemy." (4:104)

"O Prophet! MAKE WAR on the infidels and hypocrites, and deal rigorously with them." (Sura 66:9)

The concept of Jihad is foreign in the Judeo-Christian view. With Islam, one is not dealing with a mere religion for personal use but a system of war. Some argue that these verses were fulfilled for a specific time in Muslim history. However, since the advent of Islam through today, that is not what is being taught at the religious academies in the Middle East:

"O you who believe! Fight those of the disbelievers who are close to you."

Ibin Kateer, interprets this verse in Sura 9:

The Order for Jihad against the Disbelievers, the Closest, then the Farthest Areas. Allah commands the believers to fight the disbelievers, the closest in area to the Islamic state, then the farthest. This is why the Messenger of Allah started fighting the idolators in the Arabian Peninsula. When he finished with them and Allah gave him control over Makkah, Al-Madinah, At-Ta'if, Yemen, Yamamah, Hajr, Khaybar, Hadramawt and other Arab provinces, and the various Arab tribes entered Islam in large crowds, he then started fighting the People of the Scriptures. He began preparations to fight the Romans who were the closest in area to the Arabian Peninsula, and as such, had the most right to be called to Islam, especially since they were from the People of the Scriptures...After his death, his executor, friend, and Khalifa, Abu Bakr...he started preparing the Islamic armies to fight the Roman cross worshippers, and the Persian fire worshippers. By the blessing of his mission, Allah opened the lands for him and brought down Caesar and Kisra and those who obeyed them among the servants. Abu Bakr spent their treasures in the cause of Allah, just as the Messenger of Allah had foretold would happen. This mission continued after Abu Bakr at the hands of he whom Abu Bakr chose to be his successor,...With 'Umar, Allah humiliated the disbelievers, suppressed the tyrants and hypocrites, and opened the eastern and western parts of the world. The treasures of various countries were brought to 'Umar from near and far provinces, and he divided them according to the legitimate and accepted method. 'Umar then died as a martyr after he lived a praise worthy life. Then, the Companions among the Muhajirin and Ansar agreed to choose after 'Umar, 'Uthman bin 'Affan, Leader of the faithful and Martyr of the House, may Allah be pleased with him. During 'Uthman's reign, Islam wore its widest garment and Allah's unequivocal proof was established in various parts of the world over the necks of the servants. Islam appeared in the eastern and western parts of the world and Allah's Word was elevated and His religion apparent. The pure religion reached its deepest aims against Allah's enemies, and whenever Muslims overcame an Ummah, they moved to the next one, and then the next one, crushing the tyranical evil doers. They did this in reverence to Allah's statement, (O you who believe! Fight those of the disbelievers who are close to you,)

It is clear, from the highest scholars of the Quran, how Muslims view the interpretation of these verses.

STOP BUILDING THEIR CONFIDENCE

The U.S. has always viewed political Islam – both the radical oppositions and the Islamic regimes – as natural partners in the task of suppressing the left and, in the context of the Cold War, of weakening the Soviet Union's influence in the region. With few exceptions (most notably the Shiites in Iran), organizing, arming, training and funding Islamist groups as a reactionary weapon against the rising tide of mass upsurge and social revolution became a cornerstone of U.S. foreign policy. This was especially true after the defeat of the British and French imperialists in the Suez Canal dispute of 1956. The plethora of fundamentalist offshoots from the main Islamist organizations in particular, were the perfect tool for the low-intensity combat that the U.S. Central Intelligence Agency (CIA) uses. (*The Nature of Islamic Fundamenalism*, Lisa McDonald, presented to a DSP and Resistance Educational Conference in Sydney in January 2002)

With the support of the CIA, Saudi Arabia organized an "Islamic front" to build a more effective capitalist political alternative to pan-Arab nationalism and socialism. This network included the Muslim Brotherhood in Egypt, Hamas in Syria and Palestine, Sarekat-e-Islam in Indonesia, the Front for Islamic Salvation (FIS) in Algeria and Jama'at Islami in Pakistan. (Ibid)

Finding it difficult to build a mass base as wave after wave of left-wing currents swept across their countries, many of the Islamist groups, despite their anti-imperialist rhetoric, fell into the lap of imperialism for their survival. This brought them into alliance with most of the regimes in the region, which were heavily dependent on help from the U.S. to crush the mass revolts they faced. The Islamic fundamentalists' vigilante groups became a major tool of reaction and counter-revolution for the right-wing states in connivance with imperialism. (Ibid)

In Indonesia, Sarekat-e-Islam provided many of the foot soldiers in the coup against the left nationalist President Sukarno, wiping out the Communist Party and murdering as many as two million leftists. (Ibid)

In Egypt and Syria, Islamist organizations like Akhwan-ul-Muslimeen were used to destabilize left-wing regimes. Egyptian President Anwar Sadat protected the radical Islamists in the 1970s to neutralize the left-leaning Nasserites and the Communists, and later to recruit to the anti-Soviet campaign in Afghanistan. (Ibid)

Jordan's King Hussein, backed by the U.S., often relied on Islamists' support in combating left opponents, and Yemen's President Abdallah Saleh was supported by Islamists in clashes with Marxists in South Yemen. (Ibid)

In Bangladesh (then East Bengal), during the 1971 independence war, the Jama'at-e-Islam, Al-Shams and Al-Badar groups played a similar role in league with the Pakistani army, murdering hundreds of thousands of leftists leading the mass upsurge there. (Ibid)

In Pakistan, during the dictatorship of General Zia-ul-Haq, Jama'at-e-Islami was the main tool of imperialism and the Pakistani state to curb anti-dictatorship leftists. (Ibid)

The process reached its peak during the 1980s, when thousands of Islamists were trained and sent to Afghanistan to try to overthrow the Soviet-backed People's Democratic Party of Afghanistan (PDPA) government, which took power after the 1978 revolution there. Afghanistan is estimated to be the largest covert CIA operation involving Islamic fundamentalists (in 1987, U.S. military assistance to the mujaheddin reached

$700 million – more than Pakistan received – much of it sent via Saudi Arabia to keep the extent of U.S. support hidden). (Yacov Ben Efrat, *Afghan boomerang,* Challenge, No. 70, November 9, 2001.) In the mid-1990s, the U.S. cozied up to the anti-left Sudanese regime of General Omar Bashir, the product of a coup in 1989 by Bashir and Sheikh Hassan Turabi against the democratically elected government. Shortly afterwards, Bashir allowed the CIA to open offices in Sudan.

In 1978, the U.S. National Security Council set up, in collaboration with the CIA and the Saudi and Turkish intelligence services, Islamist propaganda networks intended to infiltrate the nationalist Muslim organisations in the Soviet republics of central Asia. Large quantities of weapons and Korans printed in the Gulf states were introduced into Uzbekistan, Tajikistan and Turkmenistan.

Likewise, the Israeli intelligence agency, Mossad, under successive Israeli governments, discreetly supported the Muslim Brotherhood in the Occupied Territories in the 1960s and 1970s, while the Brotherhood was exclusively attacking Yassar Arafat's left nationalist Palestine Liberation Organisation (PLO). (Eric Rouleau, *Politics in the name of the prophet,* Le Monde Diplomatique, November 2001.)

What makes and breaks the stock market is confidence. The same goes for any system of government.

When it comes to the Middle East, the West needs to know that it is playing a game of chess with the devil and, in this case, every time they make a move, the costs are tremendous. In Afghanistan, the shortcomings of the PDPA and the U.S./Pakistan/Saudi-sponsored war against the Soviet-backed government eventually resulted in the Taliban coming to power. The U.S. had thought that Communism was the enemy, so they aided Jihadist movements in Afghanistan, and when they defeated Communism, the Jihadist confidence that *victory comes from Allah* and *Islam is the answer* grew tremendously. To remove one satan – Communism – seems to only give birth to another – Islamic fundamentalism.

Yet, the American government still hasn't learned. We continue to carry out our policies of tolerance towards Islamic fundamentalism. Yet by ignoring the rise of Islamic fundamentalism, partly because of these policies in the Middle East, we will end up discovering that we've been aiding and abetting the Islamist enemy.

The confidence build-up reached a new level when Israel's arm was twisted by the United States to force Israel to allow the Jerusalem Arabs to vote – after all, democracy and free elections must prevail. Then, after the elections were over, Hamas received the victory, democracy was thrown out, and Islamism entered in.

Still, the U.S. did not learn. When it came to the withdrawal of Jews from Gaza, the United States insisted on establishing peace by dismantling Jewish communities in Gaza. Israel complied with the requests and removed all Jewish residents from Gaza. The results were catastrophic – the destruction of a vibrant Jewish community by mobs intent on mayhem and violence.

Gaza is the capital headquarters of Hamas. Islamists in the Hamas movement had always argued *"La Tu'adu Filisteen Illa Bil-Islam"* – "we can never re-take Palestine unless we revert to Islam" totally. (Islamic Association of Palestine, Hamas Branch, from *The River to The Sea,* video conference in the U.S.)

They acquired Gaza, and, as a result, their argument that Islam is the solution prevailed. This gave Hamas the victory in the elections, which, in turn, caused the Islamist confidence to swell.

The rapid transformation of Gaza into the most active terror base in the Arab world has not led to any calls by the international community for Israel to take military measures necessary to destroy the emerging threat. To the contrary, the international community, led by the Bush Administration, has greeted Gaza's mutation into, what Palestinians refer to as, a new Somalia, with even more strident demands for continued Israeli appeasement of Palestinian terrorists. The latest testimony to Israel's unprecedented diplomatic weakness in Washington came when President George W. Bush demanded that Israel allow Arab residents of Jerusalem to vote in the upcoming Palestinian elections –

elections in which Hamas is expected to receive a plurality, if not a majority, of votes. Al-Qaeda has now become an actor in the Palestinian areas and in south Lebanon. Israel's security brass has no policy for contending with the manifest links between the Iranian regime and Palestinian terror groups. (Caroline Glick, The Jerusalem Post, Israel's New Era, Jan. 5, 2006)

Yet, the confidence buildup did not stop there. During the Lebanon-Israeli fiasco, The State Department insisted that we must have a cessation of hostilities. Israel pulled back, and Nassrallah declared victory.

Iranian Guardian Council Secretary, Ayatollah Ahmad Jannati, stated in a Friday sermon, which aired on Channel 1, Iranian TV, on September 1, 2006:

> *The Muslims should learn that they too can stand up to the enemy. As Hassan Nasrallah said, Israel is weaker than a spider web. This is based on the Quran, according to which their plots and schemes are weaker than a spider web. This goes for America as well. It too is weaker than a spider web. But it requires real men...If the Islamic countries are to act like Hezbollah, and stand up to America like men, America will be humiliated, just like Israel.*
>
> **Crowd:** *Allah Akbar*
>
> *Allah Akbar*
>
> *Allah Akbar*
>
> *Khomenei is the leader.*
>
> *Death to those who oppose the rule of the Jurisprudent*
>
> *Death to America*
>
> *Death to England*
>
> *Death to the hypocrites and Saddam*
>
> *Death to Israel*

A Friday sermon by Hamas to military parades in abandoned Israeli settlements in Gaza aired on Al-Jazeera TV, September 16, 2005:

> **Sheik Nazzar Rayan:** *The vanquishing of the enemy in Gaza does not mean this stage has ended. We still have Jerusalem and the pure West Bank. We will not rest until we liberate all our land, all our*

Palestine. We to not distinguish between what was occupied in the 1940's and what was occupied in the 1960's. Our Jihad continues, and we still have a long way to go. We will continue until the very last usurper is driven out of our land.

[...]

Speaker: *If the Palestinian Authority is weakened by the pressures, and tries, or even makes a decision to collect the weapons, we will reject this decision, and we have the actual capabilities to reject it. We will not give these weapons in – After Allah, we have these weapons to thank for being where we are today, having liberated this place in honor and dignity. On the contrary, we say that these weapons will grow in strength. We will improve our ability to manufacture and buy weapons in order to continue the liberation. We stand at the gates of Hirbiya, Barbara, and Ashkelon, which we aspire to liberate. The liberation can progress only with these weapons and their improvement. So we say that on the contrary...Oh you who bear arms but refrain from using them for liberating (our land) – we call upon you to join us in the liberation effort. On the contrary – it is you who should give your weapons to us, so we could use them honorably.*

[...]

Speaker: *It will be written in history that the Palestinian people knew [their] way and knew for certain that this enemy understands only one language – the language of blood, the language of sacrifice, the language of martyrdom. This enemy has never fought a real battle throughout its history. It met (Arab) armies that were submissive, weak, and defeatist. It faced (Arab) leaders who were collaborators, cowards, and traitors. But then, when it faced a different kind of group – when it faced people who compete with one another for martyrdom, people who encourage their sons to die...A mother gets her son ready, and then receives the news of his martyrdom with cries of joy. A father receives the news of his son's martyrdom with pride and honor. Our women push our children (to martyrdom), in a way that confused the occupation.*

[...]

Hamas spokesman Mushir Al-Masri: *We stand here on our liberated land, near the armistice borders. We remember when Sharon* *said that Netzarim is like Tel Aviv. Hamas has said, through the lion of Palestine (Rantisi), that Gaza is like Tel Aviv. The promise that has been fulfilled and will be fulfilled in the future, oh Sharon, is the promise of Allah, and the promise of Hamas. Behold, Palestine is being liberated, Allah willing.*

We have come here in multitudes to proclaim that Hirbiya and Ashkelon will be taken by the mujahideen. We have come here to say that the weapons of the resistance that you see here will remain, Allah willing, so that we can liberate Palestine – all of Palestine – from the (Mediterranean) Sea to the (Jordan) River, whether they like it or not.

[…]

Speaker: *What is your goal?*

Crowd: *Allah.*

Speaker: *What is your goal?*

Crowd: *Allah.*

Speaker: *Who is your leader?*

Crowd: *The Prophet Muhammad.*

Speaker: *Who is your leader?*

Crowd: *The Prophet Muhammad.*

Speaker: *What is your constitution?*

Crowd: *The Koran.*

Speaker: *What is your constitution?*

Crowd: *The Koran.*

Speaker: *What is your path?*

Crowd: *Jihad.*

Speaker: *What is your path?*

Crowd: *Jihad.*

Speaker: *What is your greatest desire?*

Crowd: *Death for the sake of Allah.*

Speaker: *What is your greatest desire?*

Crowd: *Death for the sake of Allah.*

Speaker: *What is your greatest desire?*

Crowd: *Death for the sake of Allah.*

Speaker: *What is your movement?*

Crowd: *Hamas.*

Speaker: *What is your movement?*

Crowd: *Hamas.*

Speaker: *Oh multitudes, which are your brigades?*

Crowd: *Al-Qassam.*

Speaker: *Oh multitudes, what is your army?*

Crowd: *Al-Qassam.*

Speaker: *What is your army?*

Crowd: *Al-Qassam.*

Speaker: *With the blessings of Allah, our land will be liberated, and we will walk in Tel Aviv, Haifa, and Jaffa.*

[...]

Speaker: *I hope you will not listen to those who tremble in fear, to those who have disappointed (you), whom we have not heard in five years, to those who did not fire a single bullet, to those whose business and profits were not affected, to those who sent their children to universities in Europe, far from the heat of battle.*

The Iraq Report is now being introduced, and several recipes for disaster are embedded in it. Israel, the world's favorite scapegoat, must negotiate more territory. The U.S. must sit down with Syria and negotiate...

If, indeed, the United States is at war with terrorism, then what is there to negotiate with Syria? Mustafa Tlas, the head of the Syrian Ministry of Defense wrote *The Matzoh of Zion,* which justifies ritual murder charges brought against the Jews in the Damascus blood libel of 1840. Syria, along with Iran, gives the Lebanese militia, Hezbollah, "substantial amounts of training, weapons, explosives, political, diplomatic, and financial and organizational aid." (U.S. State Department, Council On Foreign Relations, State Sponsors – Syria)

Hezbollah has:

1. Destroyed much of northern Israel.

2. Humiliated the IDF in the eyes of the world.

3. Undermined U.S. confidence in Israel as a strategic asset.

4. United the Muslim world against Israel.

5. Strengthened the Shiite position in Lebanon.

Hezbollah may soon gain control of the government, in which case Sheikh Hassan Nasrallah will become Lebanon's prime minister. Iran will then be on Israel's northern border. (The Foundation of Constitutional Democracy, August 14, 2006)

Here is his proposal, made at a graduation ceremony in Beirut on October 22, 2002: "If they [the Jews] all gather in Israel, it will save us the trouble of going after them worldwide." (Cf. Wikipedia, H.N.)

Ahmadinejad in Iran, Hamas in the Palestinian Authority, Hezbollah in Lebanon, and all jihadists are more confident than ever, and they believe that they are closer than they have been in ages to realizing the Muslim Prophet Muhammad's prediction that:

> *The last hour would not come unless the Muslims will fight against the Jews and the Muslims would kill them until the Jews would hide themselves behind a stone or a tree and a stone or a tree would say: Muslim, or the servant of Allah, there is a Jew behind me; come and kill him.* (Sahih Muslim, bk. 41, No. 6985)

So, in summary, sheer ignorance surged a global Islamist confidence for terrorists:

- Gaza was given back to Hamas. Islamism as a result mushroomed and gave birth to an Islamist Palestinian state.

- Afghanistan's Jihadists were assisted to oust Russia, which caused Islamists to take over Afghanistan, and we are still in the clean-up phase to no end.

- Lebanon's Hezbollah terror organization was spared due to a weak Israeli government and world pressure for Israel to pull back. As a result, more Islamist confidence was built up.

- Now, Americans are asking to pull out of Iraq, which will proclaim victory for the terrorist "insurgents." This will cause Islamism to mushroom throughout the Middle East.

I have even heard arguments from prominent experts on the Middle East, that Hamas' victory was a good thing – after all, at least now we know our enemy!

Ridiculous

Building the mold for any Islamic state, like Palestine and Iran, will only create a ripple effect. If they succeeded in Palestine and Iran, indeed, Islam is the way to go, and the ripple effect will move towards Syria, Turkey, the C.I.S. nations, Pakistan (in which the majority already wants radical Islam), Libya, Algeria, Sudan, Egypt...

To Islamists, it's victory – victory over Russia in Afghanistan, victory over Israel in Gaza, victory over Israel in northern Lebanon, and now, victory over America in Iraq. Never before, since the beginning of Islam, have they had such confidence, and to them, we are prostrating, handing it to them on a silver platter. To them, this is submission. Welcome to Islam.

LIKE DRUG ADDICTS, THEY NEED DETOX

Self Detoxification

I began my self detoxification when I began to realize that we had insufficiency in the way we think. We need to start with basic things in order to help the terrorist mind to think straight. Most Westerners think that the way to reason with the Jihad mindset is not to offend them. Big mistake! The Jihad mindset needs to deal with the reality that what he thinks is untrue and destructive. One can start with sharing a documentary on the Holocaust, then follow through with questions. Listen to the typical denials – the Holocaust is a fabrication, a Zionist invention, a myth.

Denial of truth is not an issue that affects only the ignorant or the uneducated. In fact, most terrorist minds are quite educated. Ahmadenijad would hold an entire conference questioning the Holocaust as a fabrication and an exaggeration. He is quite educated. The issue has nothing to do with truth, but the spiritual conditioning of the masses. In the Middle East, information is introduced and tailored to specific standards. Anything that goes against the standard is viewed with suspicion. So, be ready. For when you deal with the Jihad mindset, you will immediately be viewed with suspicion. Remember, to them, you are the enemy, the occupier, the invader, the conspirator, the Kafir who wants to destroy their religion and their way of life, while the truth of the matter is that all you want is to be left alone – live and let live.

Yet, it's even more than racism that holds him back from seeing you as a friend. He views you as a corrupted individual, a morally bankrupt person. After all, your country created Hollywood, porn, Las Vegas, prostitution...

He is holier than you in every aspect of life.

Perhaps his hatred even could stem from spiritual bigotry more than racism. He is morally superior. As one Muslim Imam stated, "A Muslim is superior to all others, more superior than the Christians, more superior than the Jews, more superior than the Hindu, they are Kaffers. No Kaffer is innocent. You might say, no no no, Christians are innocent – no Kaffer is innocent." (*Obsession* by Waynne Kopping)

One exchange I had with Dr. Khalil Muhammad, a professed Muslim moderate and a professor at San Diego University argues:

> *Why did Egypt, Persia etc. become Muslim? The answer is simple; the intellectuality of Islam was way above and beyond what they had.*

In other words, Islam supersedes the religions of these countries, as well as what we have in the United States. It is no wonder why Khalil religiously protects the Islamic world from Western ideologies.

Khalil Muhammad further commented, "Peace ceased when the crusades were launched, and which have not yet ended."

In other words, Dr. Khalil is stuck in the Middle Ages and claims that the West is on a crusader war against Islam. This is hardly a "moderate"

Muslim. He contends that the war that needs to be fought is between Islam and the Crusaders.

He then further explains:

> What is wrong with fighting against tyranny and oppression, whether it be intellectual or otherwise? Is this not what the U.S. forces are supposedly in Iraq to do? What makes it right for these predominantly Christian soldiers to do, and not for Muslims to have a similar philosophy?

Yet, Khalil Muhammad duped many intellectuals into believing he was a moderate Muslim. In fact, he was invited to the funeral of Daniel Pearl, the American journalist who was beheaded in Pakistan.

This type of thinking is rare among Westerners, who are used to minority white supremacists. This is religious bigotry, which is new to Western minds yet so old in the East. To dehumanize the enemy by taking away the compassion instinct that is within us, is an art carried out by religious extremists. It prepares the followers to kill without compassion.

What needs to be done is to heal the millions of them who are infected with this mindset. You will encounter them for sure, either by email or in the workplace.

You might think that the Jihad mindset is only abroad. But it is here, too. They are amongst us. Have I made you paranoid? If so, that's good. When I first learned defensive driving at traffic school, I was told that the best way to drive defensively is to be a paranoid driver. It worked. I have been driving for twenty-eight years and so far, not a single accident. I have prevented several cars from hitting me by being a paranoid driver. I have only had two accidents, and they were intentional. They are long stories, but to make them short, we were attacked by a gang once in Fullerton, California. This was during the time when I was a Jihadist. I got into my Pontiac Lemanz and followed their van, and then I smashed their van with my tank. Those old Pontiacs were solid metal. Another accident occurred when I was driving down Big Bear Mountain in California and a gang of Samoans didn't allow me to pass. When I tried to pass, they attempted to drive me off the cliff. I ended up doing to them what I did to the other gang – I smashed the side of the car until I was able to pass. Then they started shooting at me. A bullet hit two inches under my head and hit the double layer rim on the back window of my Datsun Pickup truck. Anyone who has driven downhill on Big Bear in California would know how dangerous that drive is.

Let's return to the subject at hand, the much bigger gang, the fanatic Muslims. You can start by proving to him that he is a racist. First, ask him if we as humans should be justified by our actions or by our words? Of course, he will say our actions. Then, probe him – why was he silent when Saddam lobbed scuds at the holiest land to Islam – Saudi Arabia? Why was he silent and did not rush to help Muslims when Saddam killed hundreds of thousands of them? The reality is that the Jihad mindset is racist. Yes, he hates it that Saddam killed Muslims, but it's not such a major issue on his agenda. The only thing he cares about is that, in his mind, a non-Muslim is killing them. He is conditioned to remain silent regarding Muslims killing other Muslims. He usually gives you light responses, that he hates what these Muslims have done. Keep at it. Do not let him escape the argument – what have you done, as a Muslim, for your brother? I am not interested in what you have to say. I will judge your motives by your actions. You stated yourself that what counts is action, so what about Darfur? What have you done for the persecuted Muslims there?

Muslims do nothing for Darfur Muslims. First of all, they are black, yet this is not the major reason. The main reason is that evil is not interested in ridding the world of evil. Evil is simply interested in ignoring the problem at hand. Blame someone else (Israel, America) by creating additional enemies to keep the sheep from paying attention to the wolves.

Perhaps you have a problem with me using the word evil. If so, it is your problem and not mine. No mind can fathom Hitler and his Holocaust project unless one is confronted to understand the reality of evil. Just look around. There is evil everywhere.

STOP THE CYCLE OF PEACE

Peace demonstrators always carry leaflets that say "Stop The Cycle of Violence," yet, violence in the Middle East comes as a result of false treaties, which are never kept and are always the stepping stone to escalate more violence.

"Hudna" is a new term all Westerners must learn. After 9/11 Westerners learned the word Jihad. Well, not exactly, they still divide on whether the term means "self struggle" or "struggle within." Again, Jihad means "struggle," or "my struggle," just as *Mein Kampf* means "my struggle," but struggle with what? In time, the "struggle within" camp will understand – it just takes more lessons until they see.

But the word *Hudna* needs to be understood as well. Simply put, it is a ceasefire. But a more thorough definition would be that it's an Arabic term for a truce meant to produce a period of calm with an enemy in order to gain concessions, regroup, rearm, and re-attack at an appropriate time. This has been its purpose throughout Muslim history. A particularly famous early Hudna was the Treaty of Hudaybiyyah between Muhammad and the Quraysh tribe.

According to *Umdat as-Salik*, a medieval summary of Shafi'i jurisprudence, hudnas with a non-Muslim enemy should be limited to ten years:

> *If Muslims are weak, a truce may be made for ten years if necessary, for the Prophet made a truce with the Quraysh for that long, as is related by Abu Dawud.* ('Umdat as-Salik, o9.16)

Take, for example, the *Oslo Peace Accords*. Arafat relied on the term when he spoke about his commitment in 1994 to the Oslo Peace Accords.

At a mosque in Johannesburg, just a month after the signing, Arafat again declared (not realizing that he was being taped) that the Accords were merely a way to facilitate his jihad against Israel. Later, when challenged about this, he wiggled out of it by declaring that he was using the term jihad in its most positive sense: a struggle against inner negative forces. So, Arafat presented himself as a "jihad" fighter for peace. (Discoverthenetworks.com, *a guide to the political left,* Yasser Arafat)

Even Faisal Husseini (one of the PLO's highest level spokespersons) clarified the meaning of the Oslo Accords for the world in an interview with the Egyptian newspaper el-Arabi (June 24, 2001):

> *Had the U.S. and Israel realized, before Oslo, that all that was left of the Palestinian National movement and the Pan-Arab movement was a wooden [Trojan] horse called Arafat...they would never have opened their fortified gates and let it inside their walls...The Oslo agreement, or any other agreement, is just a temporary procedure, just a step towards something bigger...distinguish the strategic, long-term goals from the political phased goals, which we are compelled to temporarily accept due to international pressure...Our ultimate goal is the liberation of all of historic Palestine, from the [Jordan] River to the [Mediterranean] Sea. – In other words, across the entire existing State of Israel.* (Discoverthenetworks.com, *a guide to the political left,* Yasser Arafat)

The story of the *Trojan Horse*, in other words, is synonymous to *Hudna*.

Whether secular Arabist or Muslim fundamentalist, the application is the same. Hamas agreed to several ceasefires between 1993 and 2003, none of which was honored. The West must understand these offers are tactical maneuvers to allow the militant groups time to live to fight another day. At root, the current ceasefire between Israel and Hezbollah will eventually fail because, like all *Hudnas* to date, they are always broken, and it would be sacrilege to keep them.

The Hamas Charter states:

> *For renouncing any part of Palestine means renouncing part of the religion; the nationalism of the Islamic Resistance Movement is part of its faith, the movement educates its members to adhere to its principles and to raise the banner of Allah over their homeland as they fight their Jihad: "Allah is the all-powerful, but most people are not aware."*

So, any land deals as part of a Hudna are absolutely an anathema.

Yet, the circular logic continues, and the West keeps biting the bait – every time.

Hamas' Mahmoud Zahar reiterated after the electoral victory:

We have no peace process. We are not going to mislead our people to tell them we are waiting, meeting, for a peace process that is nothing.

Zahar echoed the Hamas Charter's declaration:

"[Peace] initiatives, the so-called peaceful solutions, and the international conferences to resolve the Palestinian problem, are all contrary to the beliefs of the Islamic Resistance Movement.

And even though it seems that Hamas might reject any peace plan, rest assured that, in the near future, they will sign a Hudna. Except this time, you my Western friend, knows the difference – another Trojan horse.

I have set this on record so that when it happens, you remember.

What the West fails to understand about Islamism is that jihad has stages. If Muslims have the upper hand, then jihad is waged by force. If Muslims do not have the upper hand, then jihad is waged through financial and political means.

Since Muslims do not have the upper hand in America or Europe, they talk about peace in front of you, while supporting Hamas and Hezbollah in the back room. The whole idea of Islam being a peaceful religion emanates from that silent stage of jihad. When Sheikh Qaradawi taught Muslims in conferences in the U.S., (on video), he gave the example of Salahu-Deen Al-Ayubi (Saladin), when he was asked to concede to peace with the verse from the Quran 8:61, "And if they incline to peace, then incline to it and trust in Allah."

However, from Quran 47:35, he replied, "And be not slack so as to cry for peace [when] you have the upper hand."

In Islam, conceding to peace means that the Islamic Umma (nation), is weak. So, as soon as Islam becomes the dominating force, it switches into war gear.

WATCH THE NEXT GENERATION

When I was a terrorist supporter, I made outlandish statements – The Jews run the Congress, the Jews run the media, the Jews kill the innocent...

Yet, similar statements are made at our universities – Richard Falk taught that "Iran is a model for a humane government," Andres Steinberg: "Israel destroys Christian shrines," Rashid Khalidi: "Israel is racist," DeGenova: "Patriot Americans are white supremacists," Hamid Dabashi: "Jews are vulgar."

All of these are so similar to what I learned as a terrorist. However, these professors are not labeled as terror supporters, but I am being labeled as a racist.

In another speech at a Los Angeles Jewish synagogue, one Rabbi critiqued the New Testament as "riddled with violence." I had no problem with his right to state this, yet when I confronted him, I asked, "Why do you feel free to critique the New Testament, but afraid of critiquing Islam's well documented violence?" to which he could not reply.

It didn't matter that I stated in my speech that a Jew had the right to critique Christianity, a Christian had the right to critique Mormonism and Islam, and a Muslim had a right to critique the Bible and Christianity. I was still accused of racism and bigotry against Islam. One can say almost anything against any other religion but Islam. Why?

The critique of religion is not racism but freedom. Racism is when someone attempts to stop another from expressing his religious opinion. In this case, the objection in itself was racist. Yet, the racists accuse the non-racist of racism. Explain that one.

Earlier I mentioned my experience at Colombia, but the problem is not only at Colombia. Conservative commentator David Horowitz, a self-professed reformed lefty, who founded the influential news-critiqued website FrontPageMag.com (see: www.frontpagemag.com), shook up the halls of higher learning with the publication of his book, *The Professors: The 101 Most Dangerous Academics in America*. The list makes a persuasive case that universities are overrun by left-wing professors, and they're far from mild, aging hippies. As the jacket blurb sums up: "Far from being harmless, they spew violent anti-Americanism, preach anti-Semitism, and cheer on the killing of American soldiers and civilians – all the while collecting tax dollars and tuition fees to indoctrinate our children." (Horowitz's worst offender? University of Colorado ethnic studies professor, Ward Churchill, who made news last year after publicly referring to the 9/11 World Trade Center victims as "little Eichmanns" – arguing that they were complicit in America's global genocide by virtue of their work in the finance business.)

Horowitz says universities were deliberately targeted by lefties in the 1960s after they realized the academy was ripe for transformation. The preponderance of liberals in disciplines, such as sociology and anthropology – where U.S. studies show something approaching a 30:1 left-right ratio – is proof they've succeeded. "How do you get a skew like that unless there's a political litmus test [in hiring practices], which there is?" he asks.

Those on the far left are able to exercise their control through domination of hiring committees, he says, stacking the faculty with fellow travelers, as well as the imposition of politically correct speech codes to exterminate dissent. "They have political control in universities because they are willing to destroy a person's career at the drop of a hat," says Horowitz.

But the brilliant master plan may have one big flaw, he notes: the more radical that universities have become, the more they've alienated the public, politicians and alumni–putting their funding in jeopardy. "If universities allow themselves to become political, then they'll become subject to the laws of politics," says Horowitz. "And a fundamental law of politics is, you don't fund your opponents." That the ideological takeover of America's schools may one day collapse, may provide some comfort to those who hope for a return to more enlightened institutions–that is, if it doesn't bring the entire university system down with it. (*Canada's Nuttiest Professors*, Terry O'Neill, Monday, September 25, 2006)

STOP LISTENING TO FALSE MODERATES

"A fanatic is one who can't change his mind and won't change the subject." – Winston Churchill

Are we hearing from moderate Muslims? If so, where are their Arabic websites? If there are a few, how many are there? Why are they only in English? Why, when they make statements about certain Muslim jurisprudence, will you find only parts of all that was said – just what is palatable to Western minds.

Take Al-Ghazali, the famous theologian, philosopher, and paragon of mystical Sufism, who is regularly quoted by the so-called moderates as a prime example of moderate Islam. Yet, he is never quoted by the so-called moderates regarding his view on Jihad and other religions. Al-Ghazali wrote about jihad war and the treatment of the vanquished non-Muslim dhimmi peoples:

> *...one must go on jihad (i.e., warlike razzias or raids) at least once a year...one may use a catapult against them [non-Muslims] when they are in a fortress, even if among them are women and children. One may set fire to them and/or drown them...If a person of the Ahl al-Kitab [People of The Book – Jews and Christians, typically] is enslaved, his marriage is [automatically] revoked...One may cut down their trees...One must destroy their useless books. Jihadists may take as booty whatever they decide...they may steal as much food as they need...*(Andrew Bostom, quoting Wagjiz, 1101 A.D., *Islamic Holy War* and *The Fate of Non-Muslims*)

Contemporary scholar Bassam Tibi, sums it up as follows:

> *At its core, Islam is a religious mission to all humanity. Muslims are religiously obliged to disseminate the Islamic faith throughout the world. "We have sent you forth to all mankind" (Q. 34:28). If non-Muslims submit to conversion or subjugation, this call (da'wa) can be pursued peacefully. If they do not, Muslims are obliged to wage war against them. In Islam, peace requires that non-Muslims submit to the call of Islam, either by converting or by accepting the status of a religious minority (dhimmi) and paying the imposed poll tax, jizzieh. World peace, the final stage of the da'wa, is reached only with the conversion or submission of all mankind to Islam...*

Muslims believe that expansion through war is not aggression but a fulfillment of the Quranic command to spread Islam as a way to peace. The resort to force to disseminate Islam is not war (harb), a word that is used only to describe the use of force by non-Muslims. Islamic wars are not hurub (the plural of harb) but rather futuhat, acts of "opening" the world to Islam and expressing Islamic jihad. Relations between dar al-Islam, the home of peace, and dar al-harb, the world of unbelievers, nevertheless take place in a state of war, according to the Quran and to the authoritative commentaries of Islamic jurists. Unbelievers who stand in the way, creating obstacles for the da'wa, are blamed for this state of war, for the da'wa can be pursued peacefully if others submit to it. In other words, those who resist Islam cause wars and are responsible for them. Only when Muslim power is weak is Hudna "temporary truce" allowed (Islamic jurists differ on the definition of "temporary"). (Tibi, Bassam,. *War and Peace in Islam,* in *The Ethics of War and Peace: Religious and Secular Perspectives,* edited by Terry Nardin, 1996, Princeton, N.J., pp. 129-131)

Under Sharia, after Islam takes over, there is no equality or rights for non-Muslims. These edicts differ little between Sunni or Shia. The Tabandeh Tract became the core ideological work upon which the Iranian government based its non-Muslim policy today:

Thus if [a] Muslim commits adultery his punishment is 100 lashes, the shaving of his head, and one year of banishment. But if the man is not a Muslim and commits adultery with a Muslim woman his penalty is execution...Similarly if a Muslim deliberately murders another Muslim he falls under the law of retaliation and must by law be put to death by the next of kin. But if a non-Muslim who dies at the hand of a Muslim has by lifelong habit been a non-Muslim, the penalty of death is not valid. Instead the Muslim murderer must pay a fine and be punished with the lash. (Tabandeh, Sultanhussein, *A Muslim Commentary on the Universal Declaration of Human Rights,* p. 17.)

Since Islam regards non-Muslims as on a lower level of belief and conviction, if a Muslim kills a non-Muslim...then his punishment must not be the retaliatory death, since the faith and conviction he possesses is loftier than that of the man slain...Again, the penalties of a non-Muslim guilty of fornication with a Muslim woman are augmented because, in addition to the crime against morality, social duty and religion, he has committed sacrilege, in that he has disgraced a Muslim and thereby cast scorn upon the Muslims in general, and so must be executed. (Tabandeh, Sultanhussein, A Muslim Commentary on the Universal Declaration of Human Rights, pp. 18-19.)

Islam and its peoples must be above the infidels, and never permit non-Muslims to acquire lordship over them. The marriage of a Muslim woman to an infidel husband (in accordance with the verse quoted: "Men are guardians over women") means her subordination would be to an infidel. That fact makes the marriage void because it does not obey the conditions laid down to make a contract valid. As the Sura says: "Turn them not back to infidels: for they are not lawful unto infidels nor are infidels lawful unto them (i.e., in wedlock)." ("The Woman to be Examined," LX v. 10; Tabandeh, Sultanhussein. *A Muslim Commentary on the Universal Declaration of Human Rights,* p. 37.)

STOP DEALING WITH MODERATE STATES, INSTEAD, APPLY PRESSURE

Take Turkey for example, in 1923, the victory of Kemal Ataturk in Turkey dealt a heavy blow to pan-Islamism as the Ottoman Empire, in which Islam was an official religion, was brought down. Muslim apologists argue that the problems between East and West started when imperialist powers carved up the remains of the Ottoman Empire into nation-states after World War I, more radical Salafis began to argue that Islam was in danger of being extinguished by Western influences and developed the idea that Western culture was equivalent to jahiliyah (the barbarism that existed before Islam) and must be brought down by a Jihad.

In Turkey, the main Sunni Islamist parties have been coalition partners in successive secular governments, and some "Islamic democrats," as they call themselves, are part of the movements for human rights, democracy and, albeit less consistently, for the national rights of Kurds. Turkey had to go through four successive Islamist political parties – National Order, National Salvation, Welfare, and Virtue – which have tried to represent the Islamist cause. In Turkey, Islam had to play a flexible or pragmatic approach to gaining mass support in the transformation of the rhetoric and platform of Turkey's Islamic Welfare Party when it relaunched itself in 1997 as the Virtue Party.

Today, Adolf Hitler's notorious racist creed *Mein Kampf* is a bestseller in Turkey these days and so is a novel about an imminent U.S. invasion of Turkey. 100,000 copies of *Mein Kampf* have been printed in Turkey. The German Government has raised its concerns about the publication of "Mein Kampf," which is banned in Germany. Anti-Semitism is rising in the nationalist Turkish press. Thirty-one percent of Turks believe the United States will invade Turkey. Turkish public opinion was almost unanimously against the war in Iraq. If Iran's nuclear program were left unchecked, this could encourage Tehran's Arab neighbors and Turkey either to seek nuclear capabilities of their own (i.e., Israel) or to import nuclear technologies (i.e., Saudi Arabia).

Anti-Americanism and Islamic fundamentalism are faring quite well in Turkey today. (Armenian News, Aris Babikian, Canada, 13.10.2005)

On February 14, 2006, the New York Times published an article entitled, "If you want a film to fly, make Americans the heavies." The article described the success of a film shown in Turkish movie theatres entitled, "Valley of the Wolves – Iraq." This film depicts American soldiers (as well as a Jewish American doctor) as carrying out atrocities and massacres against Turkish and Iraqi Muslims. Since 1994, the myth of a secular, Westernized Turkey has been undermined by the Islamic upheaval in Turkey. Kemal Attaturk was a brutal dictator, who completed the genocide of Greek, Armenian, and Assyrian Christian populations and ultimately, established a ruthless dictatorship, which abolished the Islamic Caliphate and secularized Turkey. The secularization of Turkey, however, was never any stronger or more secure than that in Nasser's Egypt, Asaad's Syria, or Saddam's Iraq. The Islamists, in fact, were underground, and when opportunistic politicians, such as Prime Minister Adnan Menderes, needed them to participate with Turkish nationalists in the infamous anti-Greek pogroms of 1955, they were readily available. In November 2002, one year after the 9/11 attacks, the Justice and Development Party finished first with an outright majority in Turkey's national elections. This should have been perceived by American officials and media as a blatant insult, following the 9/11 attacks and the exposure of the fanatical excesses of the Taliban. A genuinely secular society does not elect Islamists following 9/11 and when the Taliban, Iran, and Saudi Arabia serve as models for an Islamic State.

In April 2004, there was a referendum held in the free and occupied parts of Cyprus. The citizens of the free parts of Cyprus voted against the United Nations plan that would have, in effect, sealed the Turkish occupation and denied native Cypriots such basic rights as freedom of movement. (homeboynet.wordpress.com, Turkey's Anti-Americanism, July 28, 2007)

Greek Cypriots, voting in free Cyprus, were blamed, while "Turkish Cypriots" were praised for allegedly accepting the U.N. Plan. Secretary General Kofi Annan's plan for Cyprus was intended to legitimize the Turkish occupation, but the Greek majority of Cyprus apparently irritated Annan and his supporters by practicing democracy. The United States should not count on the Kemalists displacing the Islamists. The Islamic movement in Turkey is too strong, and, ultimately, the Kemalists, who ruled for eighty years, opened the door for the Islamists by suppressing democratic opposition. (homeboynet.wordpress.com, Turkey's Anti-Americanism, July 28, 2007)

It is in the interests of the United States to contain and isolate the hostile Turkey that is emerging. Washington should push for the expulsion of all Turkish troops and Muslim settlers from Cyprus. The world needs buffer zones from Islamists. The United States should also give maximum support to democratic Greece, whose border with Turkey is the border between the West and militant Islam.

Prime Minister Rejep Tayyip Erdogan is undoubtedly a fundamentalist Muslim. He was imprisoned for writing a poem in which he praised "our minarets, which are our rockets, our domes, which are our helmets." To call him a "post-Islamist" is rather funny. It's like calling someone a "post-Nazi." The problem with Turkey is that it is currently in a situation somewhat comparable to Iran in the 1970s. It has a narrow stratum of the Westernized middle class and technocracy. It has an army that is always ready to intervene if the Islamic tendency asserts itself too strongly, but it also has a simmering volcano in the countryside, where the majority of people share the sentiment of their coreligionists elsewhere. Even the most European of Turkish cities, Istanbul, the megalopolis of six million people, has a city council dominated by Erdogan's party. In the opinion of many experts, the problem with Turkey is not if, but when – when will it happen. Right now, among the junior ranks of the Turkish army, (the lieutenants and the captains), there is the emergence of Islamist cells for the first time. In the past such tendencies would have been dealt with quite rigorously, but it is to be feared that once the Turkish army is infected with this syndrome, it will no longer be able to intervene –as it had done in the past – to replace the government if it displays Islamist tendencies too heavily and to protect the legacy of Kemal Ataturk. The additional problem is that the U.S. government is still insistent that it is desirable for Turkey to join the European Union. This is completely inexplicable! If Turkey joins, then you can kiss Europe goodbye. Overnight it would become the second most populous country in "Europe," after Germany, with a far greater fertility rate, both in terms of cultural identity and demographic trends. The Turks would finally achieve what they failed to do back in 1683 at the gates of Vienna. (Sunday, April 16, 2006, *Understanding the Terrorist Mind-Set,* News and Views, Srdja, Trifkovic)

Turkish aspiration to join the E.U. is fading and they're beginning to focus on other Middle Eastern nations. King Abdullah visited Turkey during August of 2006 – the first visit there by a Saudi monarch in four decades. The shift has strategic implications for Washington, which views Turkey as a bridge to the Muslim world, a partner in the war on terrorism, and a model for how Western democratic values can coincide with Islam. Since the Ottoman Empire crumbled in the early 20th century, Turkey has fixed its gaze on the West – and Erdogan has brought his nation closer to its dream of being part of Europe than at any time.

But now, as the E.U. questions whether it wants to let in such a large, relatively poor, and overwhelmingly Muslim nation, Erdogan has increasingly been courting Middle Eastern nations.

The prime minister visited Qatar, Bahrain, and Pakistan in 2006. In February, he hosted Khaled Mashaal, the political leader of the Palestinian militant group Hamas. The next month, Erdogan became the first Turkish leader to address a meeting of the Arab League. And he recently condemned Israel's attacks on Lebanon in deeply emotional terms. (Suzan Fraser, Associated Press Writer, Wednesday, August 9, 2006)

Turkey is an important player to Jihadists. This region of Asia Minor includes Turkey, Uzbekistan, Tajikistan, Girgestan, and this was the heart of the vast Islamic Ottoman Empire for many centuries.

The simmering Islamic volcano in the villages of Anatolia and in the poor neighborhoods of the sprawling cities makes us wonder...If and when Turkey becomes a fully-fledged democracy, that instant it will become Islamic and anti-Western..." (Serge Trifkovic, *Islam, the Sword of the Prophet,* p. 203)

Turkey has the largest standing army of the European NATO powers. A Turkish professor of political science says, "if you read the Islamists newspapers, you'll see that what they're telling their voters is: 'You haven't given us enough votes to govern alone. We have to act like this.' Their argument is, 'Give us more power and then see what we can do." (John Hooper, "Islam on Probation," The Guardian, August 7, 1996).

Western appeasement of Islam in Turkey is based on the false assumption that Turkey, with its Kemalist views, is moderate. This view provoked fighting against Christian Serbs and Macedonians in order to support Bosnian and Albanian Muslims in Bosnia and Kosovo. These groups were aided by Iranian Islamists and Chechens in an attempt to re-Islamize the Balkans.

There is a general, but incorrect, belief that these nations were peaceful and friendly with Israel because the newly liberated Muslim Republics of Central Asia (C.I.S.), which split from Russia and Communism, seemed to embrace a pro-Western policy, reinforced by diplomatic ties with Israel and the West.

Against all hopes, expectations, and predictions of the "experts," Necmettin Erbakan, the head of the Islamist Party, won a plurality of the vote in 1996. The Turkish government today is openly pro-Islamic and is awaiting control over the military machine, which is still pro-Western. The Islamists, in contrast, looked increasingly to the Muslim states for economic and security assistance. Although Erbakan's stated intentions were not to replace NATO membership or hoped-for participation in the European Union (EU), he visited Libya and Iran soon after taking office, concluded an agreement to purchase Iranian gas, and was instrumental in creating the so-called Developing Eight, whose members include Egypt, Libya, Iran, Pakistan, Indonesia, Malaysia, Nigeria, and Turkey.

Erbakan denounced Israel and joined with Saudi Arabia and other Muslim states and organizations in opposing the peace process. Prime Minister Tayip Erdogan, following Erbakan, with his newly created Islamic Party, which ran for elections in 2002, won a sweeping majority of the vote. The Islamic party in Turkey today is the most popular since the times of Kemal Attaturk.

Turkey's desire to fight terrorism and maintain economic ties with Israel duped the world. Everything changed in March 2003 during the preparations for the Iraq War, when Turkey decided to ban the United States from using its territory and openly showed favor to the Palestinian cause. In time, the Islamists will appoint their own leaders in the Turkish military.

In 1974, Turkey invaded Cyprus, moved in Muslims, and ordered the Greeks to move out within twenty-four hours. Churches went up in flames or were converted into mosques. Seventy percent of Cyprus' industry is now under Turkish control. Yet it's still considered part of NATO and a "friend" of the U.S., despite the fact that Turkey's past is rising up, as from a wounded beast, and turning into a ravishing monster.

It is no wonder that the CIA's 1997 State Failure Task Force report identified Turkey as a nation in danger of collapse. The West needs to come to grips with the realization that Turkey is not a democracy, and any efforts to establish a democracy in it will prove fatal since democracy, like the attempts in Iraq, will only be used for electing an Islamic Sharia-driven system. (Stanley Cohen, Professor of Criminology, Hebrew University, Jerusalem, *Law and Social Inquiry, Vol. 20, No. 1,* winter, 1995, pp. 7, 50)

TURKEY'S DARK HISTORY

In 1915, Talaiat Basha, the Minister of Interior in the Ottoman government sent an order to the governor of the city of Halab Nuri Bek:

> *Despite a previous decision concerning the elimination of the Armenian Race, as the necessities of time did not allow the fulfillment of this holy intent, and now, after we eliminated all obstacles, and seeing that the time has come to redeem our nation from the dangerous race. We have entrusted you, and we insist, that you do not surrender yourselves to the feelings of pity, as you face their miserable situation.*

> *For the cause of putting an end to their existence, you need to work with all your strength, to completely destroy the Armenian name in Turkey, once and for all.* (Na'aeem Bek, *The Armenian Atrocities,* p. 43)

Yet Turkey is typical of the Jihadist mindset, with it's collective denial regarding it's past history. Stanley Cohen, Professor of Criminology at The Hebrew University in Jerusalem:

> *The nearest successful example [of "collective denial"] in the modern era is the 80 years of official denial by successive Turkish governments of the 1915-17 genocide against the Armenians in which some 1.5 million people lost their lives. This denial has been sustained by deliberate propaganda, lying and coverups, forging documents, suppression of archives, and bribing scholars. The West, especially the United States, has colluded by not referring to the massacres in the United Nations, ignoring memorial ceremonies, and surrendering to Turkish pressure in NATO and other strategic arenas of cooperation."* (Stanley Cohen, *Law and Social Inquiry,* Vol. 20, No. 1, Winter 1995, pp. 7-50 [quote from pp. 13-14,] published by the American Bar Foundation, University of Chicago Press.)

The Turkish Government is spending millions of dollars in pursuit of a false, offensive, and, above all, dangerous historical revisionism through the outright purchase of scholars and university chairs within our nation's most prestigious universities.

Heath Lowry, for example – the Princeton academic praised in the Ledger's May 13th letter – is now the subject of a scandal involving his surreptitious employment by the Turkish Government and his clandestine communications, coaching the Turkish Embassy on how to most effectively deny the Armenian Genocide within academic circles. Lowry was appointed head of the "Ataturk Chair of Turkish Studies" at Princeton University after a $1.5 million endowment from Turkey, but he was recently removed as department head after the scandal. ("Princeton Is Accused of Fronting For The Turkish Government," The New York Times, 5/22/96)

An example of this type of denial and war on truth would be if Germany were to deny any part in the Holocaust. Yet, unlike the West and continuing even until now, despite monumental evidence, the typical Jihadist denial continues. If Germany confessed the Holocaust and made it illegal to deny it, then in the Middle East, they will deny it by any silly means and simplistic explanations from revisionists and neo-Nazis like David Duke.

STOP BELIEVING THAT ISLAM OFFERS EQUALITY

In the *Revival Of The Religious Sciences* and the *Book of the Counsel for Kings,* the moderates favorite, Al-Ghazali defines the "role" of women, warns of their guile, mischief, meanness, and immorality, and outlines what women must endure because of Eve's actions in the Garden of Eden:

> *A woman should stay at home and get on with her spinning, she should not go out often, she must not be well-informed, nor must she be communicative with her neighbors and only visit them when absolutely necessary; she should take care of her husband and respect him in his presence and his absence and seek to satisfy him in everything; she must not cheat on him nor extort money from him; she must not leave her house without his permission and if*

given his permission she must leave surreptitiously. She should put on old clothes and take deserted streets and alleys, avoid markets, and make sure that a stranger does not hear her voice or recognize her; she must not speak to a friend of her husband even in need...Her sole worry should be her virtue, her home as well as her prayers and her fast. If a friend of her husband calls when the latter is absent she must not open the door nor reply to him in order to safeguard her and her husband's honour. She should accept what her husband gives her as sufficient sexual needs at any moment...She should be clean and ready to satisfy her husband's sexual needs at any moment.

As for the distinctive characteristics with which God on high has punished women, (the matter as follows): "When Eve ate fruit which He had forbidden to her from the tree in Paradise, the Lord, be He praised, punished women with eighteen things: (1) menstruation; (2) childbirth; (3) separation from mother and father and marriage to a stranger; (4) pregnancy; (5) not having control over her own person; (6) a lesser share in inheritance; (7) her liability to be divorced and inability to divorce; (8) its being lawful for men to have four wives, but for a woman to have only one husband; (9) the fact that she must stay secluded in the house; (10) the fact that she must keep her head covered inside the house; (11) the fact that two women's testimony has to be set against the testimony of one man; (12) the fact that she must not go out of the house unless accompanied by a near relative; (13) the fact that men take part in Friday and feast prayers and funerals, while women do not; (14) disqualification for rulership and judgeship; (15) the fact that merit has one thousand components, only one which is attributable to women, while 999 are attributable to men..." (Ibn Warraq, *Why I Am Not a Muslim,* 1995, Amherst, NY, p. 300.)

The Andalusian Maliki jurist Ibn Abdun (d. 1134) offered these telling legal opinions regarding Jews and Christians in Seville around 1100 A.D:

No...Jew or Christian may be allowed to wear the dress of an aristocrat, nor of a jurist, nor of a wealthy individual; on the contrary they must be detested and avoided. It is forbidden to [greet] them with the [expression], "Peace be upon you." In effect, 'Satan has gained possession of them, and caused them to forget God's warning. They are the confederates of satan's party; satan's confederates will surely be the losers!" (Quran 58:19 [modern Dawood translation]). *A distinctive sign must be imposed upon them in order that they may be recognized and this will be for them a form of disgrace* (Vajda, G. "À propos de la situation des Juifs et des Chrétiens à Séville au début du XIIe siècle," Revue des Études Juives, 99 [1935], pp. 127-129)

STOP BELIEVING IN ISLAMIC REFORMATION

You cannot fight Islamic terrorism by denying what the Quran or Islam actually says or by twisting and re-interpreting verses. Instead, combat the Islamic principles of violence.

Reform was successful in the Christian church, but the success came as a result of adhering to the Biblical text and not doing away with it and by challenging the institutions that abused their authority.

The opposite is true when it comes to Islam. Adhering to the text means acting out of violence and hate. Peace starts when we make it illegal to follow text that conflicts with our international laws, and ultimately, we must de-fang Islamism and jihad and their governments, just as we did to the Islamic Ottoman Empire, which the Islamists are trying right now to revive.

We find nothing in the tenets of Christianity or Judaism that comes even close to Islam's form of government. Of course, the Jewish and Christian faiths have nothing to do with government.

Also, the Bible clearly states that the faithful need to "obey the laws of the land," making it clear that the Biblical God is not enforcing a theocracy on earth by the sword of any mortal being, be it vicar or king.

We simply cannot compare the reforms in the Judeo-Christian culture with reforms in Islam. I have heard the term "Islamic democracy."

It's an oxymoron, like "capitalistic communism."

Islam is many things: a moral code, Khilafa, civil law, and a global government. Learning Arabic is crucial to Muslim worship, since Muhammad the prophet clearly taught *"La-Yuta'abbadu Illa Be-Tilawateh"* – one cannot worship Allah unless he recites the Quranic verses in Arabic. Arabic would unite the Islamic world. There are groups such as the Free Muslim Coalition Against Terrorism that are working toward change, but what do they intend to change?

Any change of the text would be a corruption. Are these groups speaking of reformation, re-writing, re-interpreting, or creating a new kind of Islam? True reformation must come from within.

Islamic reformation is not the business of the West. The fifty-five Muslim states need to deal with each other, on their own turf. Then, they cannot accuse the West of interfering in their business. If we stay out of it, there can be no liberal accusations of imperialism and no conservative cries about working with the enemy.

Contemporary Islam is indistinguishable from fundamental Islam. And I want you to know that ignorance of Islam, and toleration of it, will cost us our freedoms, our property, and our lives. Communism and Nazism were not defeated because they were made more moderate. Rather, they were defeated by attacking their principles.

UNDERSTAND THE TRUE OCCUPATION

I choose to speak out because I know what is wrong. And what is wrong has nothing to do with Israel's occupation of the land or America's occupation of Iraq. What is wrong is Islam's occupation of the mind. There are other victims just like me, hundreds of millions of them, and like Hitler's *Jugend* – they all started as children. They are taught the same songs about killing Jews as I was. When will we get rid of the education propaganda promoting both destruction and self destruction? Will it take a generation? Ten? Until then, there will be no peace, no matter what kind of land settlement the world tries to enforce, not when Muslim children undergo this occupation of the mind, there is no solution unless we liberate the children from this evil, growing menace and stop the cycle.

STOP ELITIST WESTERN MINDSET

We keep hearing from various political leaders – not only in the United States, – that the same syndrome is present on both sides of the Atlantic Ocean, the almost desperate attempt to make a distinction between terrorism and the allegedly peaceful and tolerant real Islam. We've all heard President Bush making references to that effect. In his speech to the National Endowment for Democracy last October, he went a step further and said that terrorists were "distorting the idea of jihad!" He advanced from claiming that Islam was *essentially* peaceful to effectively asserting that jihad, from a purely Islamic view, was *inherently* peaceful. In Europe, the greatest culprit is Tony Blair, who says that we cannot even use the term "Islamic terrorism" because Islam is inherently peaceful, and it would be a contradiction of terms to put those two words together.

This elitist mindset is probably the greatest enemy of the Western world, because the war cannot be won unless we clearly define the terrorist as the enemy. (Sunday, April 16, 2006, *Understanding the Terrorist Mind-Set*, News and Views, Srdja, Trifkovic)

The war against terrorism must entail the rediscovery of our spiritual and moral roots and the reassertion of our civilizational identity and worth. Unless, and until, the Western world does so, waging the war on terror in the name of putrid, lukewarm "multi-culturalism" is doomed to fail. In addition, the sleepwalking is continuing not only among the political leaders but even more outrageously in the academic and mainstream media.

For instance, only a short time ago, the Chicago Tribune had an article by a De Paul law professor by the name of Cherif Bassiouni. Bassiouni claimed that Islam does not mandate a death penalty for apostates and converts to Christianity – which is a white-faced lie. In Arabic, the mandated dissimulation by Muslims of non-Muslims is called taqqiya. Lying to infidels is desirable and recommended. The real Islam has had thirteen centuries of violent interaction with its environment. The real Islam is the one that has left a trail of blood from its birthplace into all four areas of major conquest: into North Africa and Europe, into today's

Pakistan and India, into the Caucasus, and into the Balkans. If, and when, there is a massive Quranic revision that would relativize violent suras and verses, which would require a critical attitude towards the traditions of the "prophet," then, perhaps we could lower our guard. But in the meantime, just taking the pronouncements of the Western bien-pensants and politicians at face value would be dangerous. (Sunday, April 16, 2006, *Understanding the Terrorist Mind-Set,* News and Views, Srdja, Trifkovic)

STOP THINKING THAT ISLAM IS SIMPLY A RELIGION

You might ask, "What does a religion have to do with war? What is Jihad? Isn't it self-struggle?" Islam is not simply a religion but a set of laws called Sharia and a system of governance to be established in the whole world.

In terms of the Islamic world outlook, the notion of dividing the political sphere from the religious sphere is utterly alien. Islam is a totality of existence: it is a religion, and a legal code, and the blueprint for political action. Any attempt to pigeon-hole the human experience into politics, religion, society, etc., from the Islamic point of view, would be heretical. (Sunday, April 16, 2006, *Understanding the Terrorist Mind-Set,* News and Views, Srdja, Trifkovic)

Westerners need to know that the desire to re-establish Khilafa is immense these days. One Muslim expresses it as follows:

> *Today Muslims started to wake up from the ashes of the Arab-Isreali war of 1967, from the ashes of the Bosnian war, the Chechnian war, the Kashmir wars. Muslims are starting to realize that they will not stand unless they are united and attached to the bond of Islam. Muslims are starting to return to Islam and the West is alarmed again, after several years of Turkish Athan (call to prayer) in the mosques of Istanbul returned to declare "Allah Akbar" in clear Arabic. A sign of the coming back of a great civilization.* (Biography Of Sultan Abdul Hameed The Second, and *The Fall Of The Islamic Khilafa,* Dawanet.com)

STOP THE INFLUX OF MUSLIM IMMIGRATION

Muslims must be treated equally with non-Muslims – in no manner should Sharia Law that conflicts with Western values be tolerated. We must also insist on integration with the host society, not self-imposed ghettos to isolate the women and children from the benefits of freedom. (*Muslim Immigration Must be Halted,* by Lewis Loflin)

In France, the rapidly increasing numbers of unassimilated Muslims – in particular, slum-dwelling unemployed young men – have led to an upsurge of extreme violence. This article notes that when professional robbers from these communities rob a bank or armored car, they do so with bazookas and rocket launchers. Many of those French citizens who voted for Le Pen in April 2002 did so on account of "crime," a term often used broadly to indicate society spinning out of control. While much of the media coverage around that election verged on hysteria about jack-booted right-wingers, this BBC piece listened to several residents of Paris in a reflective mood. One Jewish woman said she considered voting for Le Pen because she feared the violence and disorder from the immigrant Muslims. And there is plenty to fear. During the "summer of violence" in 2001, the town of Trappes, near Paris, experienced cars being set on fire nearly every night and the police station was fire-bombed several times. (Daniel Pipes, August 12, 2003)

According to a new study from the Crime Prevention Council, Brå, it is four times more likely that a known rapist is born abroad, compared to persons born in Sweden. Resident aliens from Algeria, Libya, Morocco and Tunisia dominate the group of rape suspects. According to these statistics, almost half of all perpetrators are immigrants.

In Norway and Denmark, we know that non-Western immigrants, which frequently means Muslims, are grossly overrepresented in rape statistics. In Oslo, Norway, immigrants were involved in two out of three rape charges in 2001.

The numbers in Denmark were the same and even higher in the city of Copenhagen, with three out of four rape charges. Sweden has a larger immigrant population than any other country in northern Europe. The numbers there are likely to be at least as bad as those of Scandinavian neighbors. The actual number is probably even higher than what the authorities are reporting now, as it doesn't include second generation immigrants. Lawyer Ann Christine Hjelm, who has investigated violent crimes in Svea high court, found that eighty-five percent of the convicted rapists were born on foreign soil or by foreign parents. (Fjordman, December 15, 2005, Front Page Magazine)

Some Muslim immigrants admit their bias quite openly. An Islamic Mufti in Copenhagen sparked a political outcry after publicly declaring that women who refuse to wear headscarves are "asking for rape."

Apparently, he's not the only one thinking this way. "It is not as wrong raping a Swedish girl as [it is] raping an Arab girl," says Hamid. "The Swedish girl gets a lot of help afterwards, and she had probably [been with a man] before, anyway. But the Arab girl will get problems with her family. For her, being raped is a source of shame. It is important that she retains her virginity until she marries." (Ibid)

It was no coincidence that a Swedish girl was gang raped in Rissne – this becomes obvious from the discussion with Ali, Hamid, Abdallah and Richard. All four have disparaging views on Swedish girls and think that this attitude is common among young men with immigrant backgrounds. "It is far too easy to get a Swedish whore...girl, I mean," says Hamid, and laughs over his own choice of words. "Many immigrant boys have Swedish girlfriends when they are teenagers. But when they get married, they get a proper woman from their own culture who has never been w-ith a boy. That's what I am going to do. I don't have too much respect for Swedish girls. I guess you can say they get [screwed] to pieces." (Fjordman, December 15, 2005, Front Page Magazine)

I've seen the future of Eurabia, and it's called Sweden. Malmø is Sweden's third largest city, after Stockholm and Gothenburg. Once-peaceful Sweden, home of ABBA, IKEA and the Nobel Prize, is increasingly looking like the Middle East on a bad day:

> *ALL of the 600 windows at one of the schools in Malmø have been broken during the summer holiday. Window smashing alone costs the city millions every year. City buses have been forced to avoid the immigrant ghetto, as they are met with youths throwing rocks or*

bottles at them if they enter. Earlier this year, a boy of Afghan origin had made plans to blow up his own school.

People working in the emergency ward at the major hospital in Malmø receive threats every day, and they are starting to get used to it. Patients with knives or guns are commonplace. They have discussed having metal detectors at the emergency entrance, but some fear this could be seen as a provocation. (Taken from an exclusive series of translations from the Swedish press, made for Jihad Watch by Ali Dashti)

Rapes in Sweden, as a whole, have increased by seventeen percent just since the beginning of 2003 and have had a dramatic increase during the past decade. Gang rapes, usually involving immigrant Muslim males and native Swedish girls, have become commonplace. Two weeks ago, five Kurds brutally raped a thirteen-year-old Swedish girl.

In Norway, Muslims make up less then two percent of the population, yet they use forty-five percent of the welfare. These statistics are similar throughout Scandinavia.

Elite opinion ascribes the French intifada *only* to faults in French society, such as unemployment and discrimination. When one leading intellectual, Alain Finkielkraut, dared bring Islam into the discussion, he was criticized savagely and threatened with a libel lawsuit. So, he backed down. (Daniel Pipes, The New York Sun, December 20, 2005)

In Britain, the July transport bombings seemingly highlighted the dangers of homegrown Islamism. Five months later, however, lessons learned from this atrocity have been nearly forgotten. For example, the Blair government appointed an Islamist who had been banned from entering America, Tariq Ramadan, to a prestigious taskforce; and it abandoned efforts, even temporarily, to close down extremist mosques. Tariq Ramadan is the grandson of the founder of the Muslim Brotherhood in Egypt, with a long history that sparked the Islamist movement worldwide. As Israel's population lurches leftward, led by a defeatist government ("We are tired of fighting, we are tired of being courageous, we are tired of winning, we are tired of defeating our enemies," Vice Prime Minister Ehud Olmert declared), it forgets the lessons of Oslo, appeases its enemies, and virtually invites more violence against itself. (Ibid)

Rudolph Giuliani worries that we are "going backward in the fight against terrorism." Andrew McCarthy concludes that "the September 10th spirit is alive and well." Steven Emerson tells me that "pre-9/11 political correctness has reasserted itself." (Ibid)

And I worry that not even a catastrophic act of terror will return a desensitized West to its post-September 11 alarm, solidarity, and resolve. (Taken from a blog by James Wolcott, quoting Daniel Pipes, New York Sun, December 2005)

John Kerry's notion of terrorism as a nuisance similar to prostitution or gambling has taken hold, suggesting that future acts of violence will be shrugged off. And, even if mass murders do awaken the public, a next round of alertness will presumably be as ephemeral as the last one. (Ibid)

If there ever was a crisis, it is over. Life is good, dangers are remote, security appears adequate...sleep beckons. (Daniel Pipes' blog, December 20, 2005)

In the U.S., I recall my days when I started in Chicago, Illinois, which some claimed had more Muslims in residence in the early 1990s than any other American city. Today, Muslims in Chicago are from the Middle East, India, Central and Southern Asia, and many other parts of the world. They are active in promoting their faith, providing a range of services to the Islamic community and interacting with one another as well as with non-Muslims. More than forty Muslim groups have been established in greater Chicago.

Similarly, Muslims in the California cities of Los Angeles and San Francisco have found an agreeable climate in which to flourish. They too represent most areas of the Muslim world, most recently, Afghans, Somalis, and citizens of other African countries. The Islamic Center of Southern California is one of the largest Muslim entities in the United States. It's well-trained staff have become widely known for their writings and community leadership. The center's impressive physical plant provides virtually every service that the immigrant Muslim community might possibly need. (USINFO.STATE.GOV, *Patterns of Muslim Immigration,* by Jane, I. Smith)

I recall making trips to Dekalb county for PLO fundraising events, advertised by the Arab Student Association at Loop College in Chicago, which was a haven for all types of groups – the PLO (Palestinian Liberation Organization); PFLP (Popular Front to Liberate Palestine); and Muslim Brotherhood, which later gave birth to the IAP (Islamic Association of Palestine), a front for the Hamas terror organization.

Americans have been unaware of the large volume of students rushing in from all parts of the Arab world beginning around the early 80's. Since then, immigration into the United States from Arab states has become a threat to the security of the U.S.

Dearborn, Michigan is a good example. Of the 25,000 American citizens and green-card holders in Lebanon, at least 7,000 are from Dearborn, Michigan, the heart of Islamic America, especially Shia Islam in America. These 7,000 are mostly Shiite Muslims who openly and strongly support Hezbollah. The same is true for many of the other 18,000 American citizens living in Lebanon. (Congressman Mark Steven Kirk, July 18, 2006)

Many of the more than 7,000 Detroit residents currently in Lebanon supported the murder of 300 U.S. Marines and civilians and are active in Dearborn's Bint Jbeil cultural center. In Southern Lebanon, Bint Jbeil is a Hezbollah-dominated city and a frequent destination of Hezbollah's leader, Sheikh Hassan Nasrallah, who is very much at home there. Bint Jbeil is a frequent source of the shellings on Northern Israel. (The Lebanese American Heritage Club also features mostly Hezbollah fans) (Debbie Schlussel, July 18, 2006 www.debbieschlussel.com)

Racketeering and financial aid to terrorism comes from the funds and money raised here in the United States. I recall one of my own family members funneled money from schemes to sell contraband cigarettes and Enfamil products. Yet, after he was reported, nothing was done. He still freely moves in and out of the country. There are numerous examples such as this. A Dearborn Heights, Michigan man, thirty-six-year-old Youssef Aoun Bakri, recently pleaded guilty to charges of conspiracy to violate the Racketeer Influenced and Corrupt Organizations Act (RICO) and using illegally obtained funds to help finance the terrorist group Hezbollah. (The Conservative Voice, 12,27,2006)

The Detroit/Dearborn area is a major financial support center for many Mideast terrorist groups, according to a Michigan State Police report obtained by Newsweek. "Southeast Michigan is known as a lucrative recruiting area and potential support base for international terrorist groups. It is also conceivable that 'sleeper cells' may be located in that area of the state...Almost every major terrorist organization has operatives in Michigan," according to this report. Citing information received from the Detroit office of the FBI, the report states that "most of the twenty-eight international terrorist groups recently identified by the State Department...are represented in Michigan. Examples include such well-known terrorist organizations as Hezbollah, Hamas, Islamic Jihad, Egyptian Brotherhood, Al-Gama'at, Al-Islamiyya, and Osama bin Laden's terrorist organization – al-Qaeda." (By Keith Naughton, Newsweek, October 20, 2001)

The West needs to understand that an influx of Muslims into non-Muslim areas is costly. One can see this from several examples throughout the Middle East. Lebanon was once a vibrant country with a mostly Christian population. Now it is a center for terrorism.

The same issues can be mentioned regarding Christian dominated communities in Israel. Take Bethlehem, the birthplace of Christianity. When the Palestinian Authority took control in 1995 it immediately expanded the city's boundaries to ensure a Muslim majority. 30,000 Muslims from adjacent refugee camps were incorporated into the expanded boundaries. Between October 2000 and November 2001, nearly 3,000 Christians fled the West Bank. Arafat has Islamicized Bethlehem and the nearby towns of Beit Jala and Beit Sahur. As a result, in 2003, only twenty percent of Bethlehem's Christian population remained – as opposed to sixty percent in 1990. Bethlehem, which was once considered a Christian town, now has a population of 30,000 Christians – dominated by 120,000 Muslims. The Christian minority faces constant Muslim hostility, as Jeanine Hirschhorn wrote in 2003:

*Off the record, Bethlehem's Christian spokesmen speak of harass-
ment and terror tactics, mainly from the gangs of thugs who have
looted and plundered Christians and their property under the
protection of Palestinian security personnel.*

Hirschhorn wrote: "Christian homes and real estate have been arbi-
trarily expropriated, including a school in Beit Jala that the P.A. turned
into a terrorist training center. Christian women have been intimidated,
abducted, and raped, with many becoming terrorists to save family
honor,…Those brave enough to speak out publicly, risk P.A. accusations
of 'collaborating with Israel,' [and are] subject to arrest, extensive inter-
rogation, imprisonment and [even] execution."

The Palestinian Authority appropriated lands of the Greek Orthodox
Church in Bethlehem through a combination of violence, forged documents, and bribes. In some cases, elements within the church cooper-
ated with Arafat's forces. Mosques are often built on formerly
Christian-owned land.

The P.A.'s thoroughly corrupt "judicial system" adds to the persecution of
the Christians in Bethlehem by simply lifting all protection. For example,
a Christian family owned a plot of land with a business center on it.
When a Muslim family took possession of the building and began using
it without permission, the Christian family filed a claim. After long and
arduous court hearings, the Christian family's claim was upheld. But the
verdict was never enforced by police, and later, a new court verdict
appeared, signed by the same judge, that canceled the previous verdict
and ratified the Muslim's claim to the land.

Information is difficult to gather because Christians live in a constant
state of terror, but the statistics speak for themselves.

Palestinian terrorists took over the Church of the Nativity, using it as a
fortress from which to fire upon Israeli troops. While holding nuns,
priests and monks hostage, they also stole or destroyed virtually everything of value inside the building. And they got away with it. Those
terrorists, including some wanted for the murders of Israeli civilians,
were permitted to leave the country unscathed and unmolested – all in
an effort to avoid further destruction at the holy site.

The Christians' position has become so tenuous that even Pope John Paul II told them, "Do not be afraid to preserve your Christian heritage and Christian presence in Bethlehem" when he visited the city in 2002. Nevertheless, Christians are fleeing Bethlehem in large numbers. If this trend continues, "the only Christian presence in Bethlehem may be foreign tourists," Hirschhorn wrote. "Bethlehem's revered Christian shrines may one day become tourist curiosities, like the Nabetian city of Petra or the Roman amphitheater at Caesarea."

A document captured by the Israelis in Bethlehem during Operation Defensive Wall shows that Arafat's Fatah/Al Aqsa Martyrs, the same criminals who broke into the church, demanded monetary support of Bethlehem municipal officials for its "military" campaign.

Such a demand is just an extension of a larger extortion racket being perpetrated on the remnant of Christians, who represent a dwindling and tiny minority among the burgeoning, Muslim population in Arafat's territory. Men of the Bedouin Taamra tribe, based near Bethlehem, are used by Arafat's forces to shake down Christian businessmen. They take from the Christians and give to the terrorists – keeping some for themselves and terrorizing civilians with impunity under the corrupt Arafat regime.

When senior Fatah terrorist Atef Abayat was killed in a car explosion, he was found to be wearing gold rings on his fingers that had been stolen from Christian businessman George Nissan. It's a routine matter for Fatah members to extort money from businessmen who operate souvenir shops, real estate offices, and gas stations in Bethlehem. This campaign is carried out in cooperation with the Palestinian security apparatus, according to captured documents.

Last spring, a Bethlehem woman named Saadah Hamidan was raped and murdered by a senior Fatah/Tanzim official, Iman Ali Azmi al-Kadi, a close friend of Abdallah al-Nu'ura (Abu Hadid), one of Tanzim's leaders in Bethlehem. Al Kadi was brought to trial. But, according to local Christian sources, the judge was bribed, and the rapist was acquitted.

As you may have read in the World Net Daily dispatches by William Murray from the West Bank, the terrorists' favorite game is placing the

Christians in the crossfire – firing at Israelis from within and behind churches and Christian businesses that are then destroyed by tanks and rocket fire.

All this goes on while the Christian world remains silent. A months-old letter to the Vatican from Bethlehem's Christians, pleading for help against the onslaught of rape, murder, and plunder at the hands of Arafat and the Muslim majority, has not even been answered.

Such is life for Christians now in Bethlehem and other formerly Christian towns in the West Bank. Just imagine what it will be like when Palestine becomes a real state. (World Net Daily, *Christian persecution in Arafat-land*, Posted: July 22, 2002)

Yet, the mixed reports still flood the media, blaming Israel and the Separation Wall for Christians leaving the Holy Land. The problem is that Christian representation in the Holy Land is either by "leaders" who kowtow to the Hamas government or by those who are too afraid to speak up.

While the Mayor of Bethlehem calls on his people to trust Hamas, there is talk about a tax, or Jizzieh taxation that could be leveled on non-Muslim, second-class citizens. A Hamas member of the Bethlehem City Council, Hassan El-Masalmeh, told the Wall Street Journal in late December 2005: "We in Hamas plan to implement this tax some day. We say it openly, everyone is welcome in Palestine, but only if they agree to live under our rules." The tax they plan to implement some day is the humiliation tax – established in Muslim history against Dhimmi (Jews and Christians) – will, and must, be implemented.

Christian businesses used to flourish in Bethlehem. Muslim terrorists beat Christian merchants or made them pay protection money. Many Christian stores were forced to close. Other Christian businesses failed because of a Muslim boycott.

While Christian Arabs continued to flee Palestinian-controlled areas, since 1948, the Christian community in Israel has more than quadrupled. Christians enjoy far more safety and freedom in Israel than they do in Palestinian lands. Bethlehem, once a comfortable home to

Christians, has become inhospitable, yet the denial of negative events by Christian leaders in Bethlehem, who sell out their people for political gain, still circulate through the media.

CONFRONTING DENIAL

"No people will tamely surrender their Liberties, nor can any be easily subdued, when knowledge is diffused and Virtue is preserved. On the Contrary, when People are universally ignorant, and debauched in their Manners, they will sink under their own weight without the Aid of foreign Invaders." Samuel Adams

> **Argument:** *"The occupation in Iraq is costing American lives and hampering our ability to fight the real global war on terror."* (Howard Dean)

> *Ann Coulter responds to the above statement with: "This would be like complaining that Roosevelt's war in Germany was hampering our ability to fight the real global war on fascism. Or anti-discrimination laws were hampering our ability to fight the real war on racism. Or dusting is hampering our ability to fight the real war on dust" (What Part of the War on Terrorism do They Support?* by Ann Coulter, August 23, 2006)

> *Coulter continues, "The Guantanamo detainees are not innocent insurance salesmen imprisoned in some horrible mix-up like something out of a Perry Mason movie. The detainees were captured on the battlefield in Afghanistan."*

Finger pointing and the blame-game debates continue in the U.S. Yet, the best way to fight radical Islam is to not support their favorite candidates or legislations. Support those candidates, or legislations which take a stand against terrorism. Consider the Patriot Act, for example. The USA Patriot Act, a landmark of post-September 11 cooperation between the military and law enforcement, passed 98-1 in the Senate in October 2001. Ann Coulter points out: "The vast majority of Senate Democrats (43-2) voted against renewing the Patriot Act last December [2005], whereupon their minority leader, Sen. Harry Reid, boasted: 'We killed the Patriot Act' – a rather unusual sentiment for a party so testy about killing terrorists."

In 2004, Sen. John Kerry – the man that the Democrats wanted to be president – called the Patriot Act "an assault on our basic rights." At least, all "basic rights" other than the one about not dying a horrible death at the hands of Islamic fascists. Yes, it was as if Congress had deliberately flown two commercial airliners into the twin towers of our Constitution. The mainstream press does not take Islamist aspirations seriously and sees the war on terror as basically over, as shown by Maureen Dowd's comment in the New York Times that the Bush administration is trying "to frighten people with talk of al-Qaeda's dream of a new Islamic caliphate."

It wasn't until Hitler started his Jihad, *Mein Kampf,* did the world recognize their folly. History will repeat itself.

STOP BLAMING OURSELVES

The civil war, now in its early stages in Iraq, was not caused by the American presence. It could not have been prevented by anything done, or not done, by the Americans. It reflects many things. It reflects the new demographic balance. Just as in Lebanon, the Shia Arabs have outnumbered the Sunnis. At the beginning of Saddam Hussein's regime they constituted less than fifty percent of Iraq's population. They now constitute sixty to sixty-five percent. (Jihad Watch, Fitzgerald, *What Did The Bush Administration Not Know about Sunnis and Shia and When Did It Not Know It*, Posted at August 4, 2006 12:26 PM)

Yet, the blame continues regarding the Iraq War and the WMDs. Americans need to stop listening to Barbra Streisand, Michael Moore and Brad Pitt. Our duty is to preserve, protect and defend the Constitution of the United States. The Congress of the United States voted, in joint resolution, shortly after 9-11, to give the president the power to do whatever he deemed necessary to defeat terrorism. How can he possibly do that without proper intelligence data? And how can he be authorized to kill the terrorists but not to listen to their phone calls? It is notably unhelpful for Democratic Party leaders to engage in endless bitter, mocking criticism while actively undermining virtually every tool the president has at his disposal for preventing another attack on America – including NSA wiretapping, data mining and the Patriot

Act – without producing any real and substantive evidence that he's damaging the Constitution or curtailing the civil rights of Americans. (David Wilson, Bangor Daily News, 10/10/2006)

STOP GIVING THEM DEMOCRACY

"Democracy is the worst form of government except all those other forms that have been tried from time to time." (Winston Churchill)

The West thought that everyone wanted democracy. It ignored a major factor that, in the Muslim world, democracy was never in existence, and even today, in the fifty-five Muslim nations, democracy was never established. What did the West expect when they insisted that Arabs in Jerusalem vote? Did they expect that a mini-America would be established? Can't they see what we have is a mini-Iran instead?

The only time democracy was used in the Middle East was during elections, and after the elections were over, democracy was thrown out the window.

These days especially, if democracy is introduced in the Middle East, the majority would elect Islamic fundamental states. The writing on the wall in Iraq is obvious – the United States is fighting a terrible war in order to institute a Shiite government that will soon become a proxy for Iran.

The Muslim world is broken in two major sects – Shia and Sunni. The only time when there was relative peace and harmony between the two is when one would subjugate the other. In Iraq, under Saddam's Ba'ath party, which had a Sunni majority, Shia either pledged allegiance or were subjugated by the majority Sunni faction.

Yet, American leaders are late to confess the mistake:

"Mr. McCain had pointed exchanges with both generals, who conceded that events had taken them by surprise."

"General Pace," the senator said, "you said there's a possibility of the situation in Iraq evolving into civil war. Is that correct?" "I did say that, yes, sir," the general replied.

"Did you anticipate this situation a year ago?"

"No, sir."

"Did you, General Abizaid?"

"I believe that a year ago it was clear to see that sectarian tensions were increasing," General Abizaid said. "That they would be this high, no."

It has been said that George Bush pooh-poohed the notion that Sunnis and Shia would be at each other's throats. After all, it seems reasonable to Western men that Saddam Hussein's killing of Kurds and Shia Muslims was not supported by the vast number of "good Sunnis" and certainly not by that silent Sunni majority that had also suffered from the cruelties of Saddam's regime. Just as soon as that cruel regime was removed, everything would be all right. Just as soon as the promise of American money, tens of billions lavished all over the country, was received, things would take a turn. Those Americans – the biggest construction and oilfield companies, and all those American soldiers – had been made to believe that if only those Iraqis had new schools and hospitals and roads and bridges and power grids, if only Umm Qasr was dredged, if only the Americans kept putting out oilfield fires and rebuilding things, so that Iraq would be – would be as it had never been, in fact – then all manner of things would be well. (Jihad Watch, Fitzgerald, *What Did The Bush Administration Not Know about Sunnis and Shi'a and When Did It Not Know It,* Posted at August 4, 2006 12:26 PM)

After a week or a month of celebrating when the regime fell, the Iraqis soon reverted to type. They complained. They whined. They watched and watched as the Americans tried to get them to organize, tried to get them to cooperate with each other and not merely hold out their hands, pushing each other aside in order to claim more, more, more of the endless American funds and goodies and never satisfied with what those American soldiers, risking their lives even to go from Point A to Point B, did for them. "But where's the air-conditioning?" said a teacher to a stunned American soldier who had just proudly showed her the building he and his men had totally rebuilt and refurbished. The soldier had thought she would be pleased. (Jihad Watch, Fitzgerald, *What Did The*

Bush Administration Not Know about Sunnis and Shi'a and When Did It Not Know It, Posted at August 4, 2006 12:26 PM)

What a surprise, then, to keep being surprised. What a surprise to find out that the Shia, who made up the entire delegation of influential Iraqis-in-exile (Chalabi, Allawi, Makiya, all the others), were not set on creating a "new Iraq" but on merely creating an Iraq in which the Ba'ath, and with the Ba'ath the Sunnis, would be put permanently in their place, and the Shia Arabs would dominate. What a surprise for the American policymakers, who continually ignored or misinterpreted the evidence. That first purple-thumbed election was interpreted as "democracy on the march." It was nothing of the sort. The Shia were keenly aware that they constituted sixty to sixty-five percent of the population. They knew that obtaining power through this "democracy" would please the Americans, and the Americans were useful for a good while longer. Americans were useful because they would keep distributing largesse, billions and billions of it, and because it was always hoped they would train the Shia (thinking all the while that they were training "Iraqi" police and "Iraqi" soldiers). Of course, wasn't it pleasant to have the Americans fighting and dying in the Anbar Province, putting down the Sunnis, both the followers of Al-Zarqawi, who regarded the Shia as Infidels, and the local Sunnis, who simply opposed the Shia because they wanted to retain political power, and, hence, every other kind of power, for themselves, for the Sunnis. Let the Americans do as much of the fighting and dying as possible – why not? (Jihad Watch, Fitzgerald, *What Did The Bush Administration Not Know about Sunnis and Shi'a and When Did It Not Know It,* Posted at August 4, 2006 12:26 PM)

Americans, ignorant of the Sunni-Shia relations, will be quick to blame the current administration, if not themselves. The current administration cannot be blamed for causing the inevitability of the war that would result, at whatever level, using whatever means, once it was clear that the Sunnis were losing political and economic power and would not be getting it back. (Jihad Watch, Fitzgerald, *What Did The Bush Administration Not Know about Sunnis and Shi'a and When Did It Not Know It,* Posted at August 4, 2006 12:26 PM)

Still, the U.S. is pursuing its democracy campaign to its logical conclusion. Washington is signaling a willingness to deal with Islamists in Lebanon, the Palestinian Authority, Egypt, and elsewhere, thereby bolstering radical Islam's power. Islamists are getting what they have been looking for – recognition.

STOP JEWISH FEAR

"I would rather have my fellow Jews die in Germany..."

Said on the eve of the Nazi genocide by "Reform Rabbi Stephen Wise, the undisputed leader of organized American Jewry," and "probably the most influential and well-respected American Jew of his generation" in reply to British prime minister Neville Chamberlain's suggestion that Jewish refugees from Hitler might settle in Tanganyika.

As George Santayana famously said, "Those who cannot remember the past are condemned to repeat it." For the Jewish people, this means repeating Catastrophe. Therefore, if you are a member of the Jewish community, which has been subjected to genocidal attacks for over 2000 years, the rational thing is to expect another such attack and prepare for it, the better to mount an effective self-defense and, ideally, to prevent the next mass killing altogether. (*Historical and Investigative Research* – 17 Jan 2006, by Francisco Gil-White)

An example of what I mean is that most Jews are unable to recognize the signs indicating that their own mainstream leaders are taking them down the path to destruction, just as mainstream Jewish leaders did the same prior to and during World War II. The same mainstream leaders who betrayed the Jewish people in WWII created the mainstream Jewish organizations that hold sway over the Jewish people today. (Ibid)

There is a story told of two Jews, right before they are killed:

"Sam and Irving are facing the firing squad. The executioner comes forward to place the blindfold on them. Sam disdainfully and proudly refuses, tearing the thing from his face. Irving turns to him and pleads: 'Please Sam, don't make trouble!'"

By telling this story Jews demonstrate that they are – at some level – aware that a certain pathology of reasoning makes their self-defense difficult.

WHAT ABOUT JOSEPH-NACHT

I have spoken at many Jewish events, and the same pathology that existed prior to Nazi Germany is prevelant today. The comments I get from Jews are usually fearful. Jews have spent hundreds of millions in building Holocaust memorials to remind the world to never forget. One of the events of which they like to remind the world is Kristallnacht – the night Nazis burned the synagogue in Berlin. Yet, when Joseph's Tomb was burned in Israel, a synagogue much more important to Jewish history then the Berlin Synagogue, little was said about it in the West. Nothing in these Holocaust museums even mention the event.

In general, Jews (especially those in the West) are plagued with fear – fear of reprisals, fear of being noticed, and fear of the reality that is at hand.

For any Jew who wants to say never forget Kristallnacht, I must say – "what about Joseph's Tomb? You simply want to fight dead Nazis, yet are afraid to stand up and fight the living Nazis – Islamic Jihad."

Pierre Van Passen was a famous journalist whose career spanned from the 1920s to 1968. He reported during the time of Nazi Germany. Van Passen's book, *The Forgotten Ally,* published in 1943, of an extraordinary meeting he had in January 1932 with Rabbi Steven Weiss, where he gave a lecture at Temple Emanuel on 5th Avenue and warned of the menace of Hitler, who he had recently interviewed for his newspaper. He warned the Jewish people to get their people out of Europe. He predicted in 1932 that Hitler would try to kill all of the Jews in Germany and Europe. Rabbi Steven Weiss, then the most prominent leader of the American Jewish community at that time) complained to Pierre Van Paassen about his statements on Germany and Hitler: "What you said was preposterous, take it from me, young man, Germany is still Germany. Civilization is not going to be wiped out like that. America and

England will have something to say," Van Paassen responded. "I hope they will but I am not so sure as you are."

Today, Jews are again relaying on America and the UK, but so far, I do not see any real action on the parts of these countries to do what is necessary to bring down Iran or the Islamic fundamentalist terror threat. The Jewish community leaders are paralyzed with fear, and Israel buckles to every pressure brought upon them by so-called friendly nations. Van Paassen's words need to be heeded again, and now. Doing nothing about Iran and appeasing the Islamic threat is a recipe for another holocaust, which will be much more devastating than the holocaust of World War II.

Jews must keep all of their holy places sacred, protect them and keep them intact. Without Jewish heritage, there is no Jewish connection to the land of Israel. This is why Muslims are trying relentlessly to convert all Jewish holy places into mosques. Concentrating on Holocaust memorials while ignoring Jewish historic landmarks is in contradiction of the very basic principles of Jewish survival. The issues concerning the living need to be vocalized so much more. Instead, we only think of the dead, and we say "never again," while the "never again" happens right in front of our eyes and despite all of the Holocaust memorials.

Here are other issues to consider:

- Most Jews act as they see other Jews react around them. They seem to seek more to be accepted in order to get respect, instead of gaining respect by strength and honor.

- Jews seek Arab love like a farmer who plants seeds on rocks and daily pours water on stones, leaving the good soil untouched.

- Jews are ashamed to quote the truth but object when Muslims quote Khaybar massacre from their Islamic references, yet they refuse to quote verses from The Good Book regarding their right to the land. No one on earth can tell a Muslim that he has no right to Mecca or the right to quote his Quran to claim it.

Every Jew who has told me that they are not religious, has a Menorah, a religious symbol. If I ask them how Israel won against all odds they always say, "It was a miracle." How is it that someone who believes in miracles refuses to acknowledge the source of these miracles? Yet, they celebrate with a Menorah, which is a symbol of another biblical miracle. When I ask them, "Do you believe that the Bible predicted these miracles?" they always pause and show no emotion.

Even many of the Rabbis object. One Rabbi in Florida said that he liked my speech, but I lost his support the moment that I objected to giving land for peace. "Why?" I asked. He said that giving land to the Arabs is the most logical solution. I asked him if he kept Kosher, to which he said, "Of course, I am a Rabbi." Then I asked him, "Rabbi, is it logical to keep Kosher in today's world?" He replied, "No." Then I asked him, "Why do you observe this 'illogical' commandment and refuse to observe the other? The land was given to you to posses forever. Why do you always pray as a Rabbi, 'If I forget thee, oh Jerusalem, let my right hand...' yet you want to give up East Jerusalem? Why not cut your hand Rabbi?" He became speechless, of course. He would object to the messenger instead of viewing his inner heart. He prays, thinking that he doesn't really mean it and hates the messenger for stating what he supposedly believes in.

Speaking to Jewish audiences is like speaking to a dead branch with no fruit. The only thing that grows on it is thorns from the past, and every time you touch it, it pricks you and causes you to bleed – inside. They react and forget to act. They simply want to respond to newspaper editors complaining about some anti-Israel article, yet they forget that acting is better then reacting. It was the pre-emptive strikes that won their 1967 Six Day War.

Then, they get into so many programs attempting reconciliation, bridge building, and interfaith dialogues. It's like a farmer who plants his seed on a stone. He waters it and waits patiently, hoping it would grow into a tree. A bird flying by picks it up and fly's away. Instead, Jewish communities need to find the soft soil, plant many seeds, then rest. It will grow on its own and bare much fruit.

The West can understand their plight. They suffer the same terror. They need to educate others and stand up in a grass root effort without fear. Pre-emptive strikes win wars. Responding to strikes allows tremendous casualties. Just look at Yom Kippur. When Israel hesitated to strike first, they nearly lost their state and all of their lives, collectively.

They fear persecution. But I have said it before, and I say it again, in life we all have two choices – to die for something or die of something.

They always invite me to tell my story, yet they forget to tell theirs, not the same old ones, but the current suffering and persecution they have to deal with.

In history, it's always the few who made all the difference and not the grumbling crowds. I am an Arab, and, as an Arab, I must say we are tired of the complaining Jews.

What we need to do is reach out to hearts and not just present intellectual arguments. Most Jews do not want us to speak out our message but are glad to speak through us. Just as Muslims proclaim Mecca by divine right, the Jewish people must proclaim their right, first their divine right, secondly, their historic right – a right to live without world persecution. This is all outlined in my book *Why I Left Jihad,* in which I show the irrefutable biblical and historic Jewish right to the land.

LEARN FROM THE BEST

Sir Winston Churchill wrote the following about Islam:

"How dreadful are the curses which Muhammadanism lays on its votaries! Besides the fanatical frenzy, which is as dangerous in a man as hydrophobia in a dog, there is this fearful fatalistic apathy. The effects are apparent in many countries. Improvident habits, slovenly systems of agriculture, sluggish methods of commerce, and insecurity of property exist wherever the followers of the Prophet rule or live. A degraded sensualism deprives this life of its grace and refinement, the next of its dignity and sanctity. The fact that in Muhammadan law every woman must belong to some man as his

absolute property, either as a child, a wife, or a concubine, must delay the final extinction of slavery until the faith of Islam has ceased to be a great power among men." (*The River War* [1899], Winston Churchill's account of the Sudanese campaign)

"Individual Muslims may show splendid qualities. Thousands become the brave and loyal soldiers of the Queen: all know how to die – but the influence of the religion paralyses the social development of those who follow it. No stronger retrograde force exists in the world. Far from being moribund, Muhammadanism is a militant and proselytizing faith. It has already spread throughout Central Africa, raising fearless warriors at every step; and were it not that Christianity is sheltered in the strong arms of science, the science against which it had vainly struggled, the civilisation of modern Europe might fall, as fell the civilisation of ancient Rome." (Ibid)

"The religion of Islam above all others was founded upon the sword...Moreover it provides incentives to slaughter, and in three continents has produced fighting breeds of men – filled with a wild and merciless fanaticism." (Ibid)

John Quincy Adams:

In the seventh century of the Christian era, a wandering Arab of the lineage of Hagar [i.e., Muhammad], the Egyptian, combining the powers of transcendent genius, with the preternatural energy of a fanatic, and the fraudulent spirit of an impostor, proclaimed himself as a messenger from Heaven, and spread desolation and delusion over an extensive portion of the earth. Adopting from the sublime conception of the Mosaic law, the doctrine of one omnipotent God; he connected indissolubly with it, the audacious falsehood, that he was himself his prophet and apostle. Adopting from the new Revelation of Jesus, the faith and hope of immortal life, and of future retribution, he humbled it to the dust by adapting all the rewards and sanctions of his religion to the gratification of the sexual passion. He poisoned the sources of human felicity at the fountain, by degrading the condition of the female sex, and the allowance of polygamy; and he declared undistinguishing and exterminating war, as a part of his religion, against all the rest of mankind. THE ESSENCE OF HIS DOCTRINE WAS VIOLENCE AND

LUST: TO EXALT THE BRUTAL OVER THE SPIRITUAL PART OF HUMAN NATURE [Adams's capital letters]...Between these two religions, thus contrasted in their characters, a war of twelve hundred years has already raged. The war is yet flagrant...While the merciless and dissolute dogmas of the false prophet shall furnish motives to human action, there can never be peace upon earth, and goodwill towards men. (John Quincy Adams, Sixth President of The United States of America, 1830)

The precept of the Koran is, perpetual war against all who deny, that Mahomet is the prophet of God. The vanquished may purchase their lives, by the payment of tribute; the victorious may be appeased by a false and delusive promise of peace; and the faithful follower of the prophet, may submit to the imperious necessities of defeat: but the command to propagate the Muslim creed by the sword is always obligatory, when it can be made effective. The commands of the prophet may be performed alike, by fraud, or by force. (Ibid)

John Wesley:

Ever since the religion of Islam appeared in the world, the espousers of it...have been as wolves and tigers to all other nations, rending and tearing all that fell into their merciless paws, and grinding them with their iron teeth; that numberless cities are raised from the foundation, and only their name remaining; that many countries, which were once as the garden of God, are now a desolate wilderness; and that so many once numerous and powerful nations are vanished from the earth! Such was, and is at this day, the rage, the fury, the revenge, of these destroyers of human kind.

Hilaire Belloc:

Will not perhaps the temporal power of Islam return and with it the menace of an armed Muhammadan world, which will shake off the domination of Europeans – still nominally Christian – and reappear as the prime enemy of our civilization? The future always comes as a surprise, but political wisdom consists in attempting at least some partial judgment of what that surprise may be. And for my part I cannot but believe that a main unexpected thing of the future is the return of Islam. (1938)

Bishop Fulton J Sheen:

Today (1950), the hatred of the Muslim countries against the West is becoming hatred against Christianity itself. Although the statesmen have not yet taken it into account, there is still grave danger that the temporal power of Islam may return and, with it, the menace that it may shake off a West which has ceased to be Christian, and affirm itself as a great anti-Christian world Power.

Gregory Palamus of Thessalonica:

For these impious people, hated by God and infamous, boast of having got the better of the Romans by their love of God...they live by the bow, the sword and debauchery, finding pleasure in taking slaves, devoting themselves to murder, pillage, spoil...and not only do they commit these crimes, but even – what an aberration – they believe that God approves of them. (1953)

Vernon Richards:

The true Islamic concept of peace goes something like this: "Peace comes through submission to Muhammad and his concept of Allah" (i.e. Islam). As such the Islamic concept of peace, meaning making the whole world Muslim, is actually a mandate for war. It was inevitable and unavoidable that the conflict would eventually reach our borders, and so it has. It's time for you, and many millions more Westerners to wake up and finally grasp the enormity of what we're up against. This is Islam's latest attempt to conquer the infidel world. Why do you suppose they waited until three centuries after the siege and battle of Vienna before they tried again? Was it because they saw an opportunity to get after us for the first time since 1683, because political correctness and the apologists it brought in train softened us up, and made us totally unaware of how evil and intolerant Islam really is, and gave them that window of opportunity to once again threaten our civilization with doom. (2001)

"the time cometh, that whosoever killeth you will think that he doeth God's service." (Jesus, The Bible, John 16:2)

STOP IGNORING HISTORY

Name-calling is a poor substitute for actually considering the ideologies in question. Churchill was accused of being a Naziphobe. In fact, Lady Astor (Nancy Witcher Langhorne Astor, Viscountess, 1879-1964) was known as a fierce debater. There is a famous exchange between Winston Churchill and Lady Astor when they were both staying at Blenheim Castle visiting the Marlboroughs. The two politicians had been at each other's throats all weekend when Lady Astor said, "Winston, if I were your wife I'd put poison in your coffee." Whereupon Winston said, "Nancy, if I were your husband I'd drink it." (Famous Quotes & Stories of Winston Churchill, The World Book Encyclopedia, 1958)

Yet, today, no one in their right mind argues that Churchill and his Naziphobe attitude was wrong.

I believe that today we are at as decisive a turning point as we were in 1935, when the democracies failed to be honest about the nature of Hitler and failed to have courage.

Churchill says he was asked by Franklin Delano Roosevelt, the American President, "What should we call this war?" Churchill replied, "The Unnecessary War." He went on to write an entire section of the book called *The Years the Locusts Have Eaten,* and he said if the democracies had had any courage, any intellectual honesty, any willingness to act in 1935, they could have replaced Hitler's regime at a remarkably low cost, but because they lacked that courage, they lacked that intellectual honesty, over 100 million people died in the Second World War, and the Holocaust inflicted enormous wounds upon Jews, Poles, gypsies, and Russians. Had Hitler won, I suspect that an unending number of people would have died. (Atlanta Journal Constitution, March 8, 2006, Bob Kemper, AIPAC, 2006, newt.org)

THE RESULTS OF IGNORANCE

What happenes if the West ignores this trend? Many would claim that the fear of Islamic fundamentalism is xenophobic since these groups are backwards and cannot compete with Western capitalism. But that is not the West's fear. The West would welcome the Muslim world to enter the fold of modernization. America defeated Japan's military might yet welcomed its industrial exchange. We should be worried about the military capabilities that these nations might obtain. Because of the close geographical and political relationship with Islamic Taliban rulers in Afghanistan over the last decade, Pakistani Islamic fundamentalism is undoubtedly making progress towards gaining state power.

In Pakistan, the US/NATO strategy rests on the survival of one man: Pervez Musharraf. This dependence may prove short-lived. After the loss of a reported 3,000 troops, Pakistan has ceded the tribal areas of Waziristan (population: 800,000) to pro-Taliban local rule. Weapons will be returned, outposts will be abandoned, and compensation will be paid. Pakistan has negotiated a ceasefire with the Taliban's Mullah Omar. Pakistani troops will no longer hunt down the Taliban (and likely al-Qaeda) in Pakistan. This ceasefire also prevents US/NATO troops from crossing the border to pursue Taliban forces. That, compounded with releasing al-Qaeda and Taliban prisoners, shows that Musharraf is in a retreat mode. Musharraf's retreat clearly demonstrates that he is in a survival mode. Should Musharraf fall, there are likely no Pakistani generals who would survive a coup and stand between Pakistan's nuclear weapons and the Islamist-dominated, and al-Qaeda entangled, Pakistani Inter-Service Intelligence (ISI). India has long held that the South Asian arm of al-Qaeda, Lashkar-e-Taiba, is both responsible for the deadliest terrorist attacks in India and directly supported by Pakistan's ISI. The fall of Musharraf would likely mean ISI control over Pakistani nuclear weapons. Not many seem to notice just how close al-Qaeda and Bin Laden are to wresting a nuclear power into their control.

In addition, there is a desire for a U.S. pull out of Iraq, which would increase Iran's control in the region. The U.S. indirectly aided the establishment of a pro Shia dominance which will backfire. Iran will then rule, by proxy, Iraq via a majority Shia government, Syria's Alawite Shia, and Lebanon's Hezbollah Shia military. Iran would have full access to Israel's northern border.

To remain silent about Iran, which has become the military super power in the Middle East, would create competition for Sunnis, who comprise eighty-five percent of the Muslim world. There are several candidates –

Turkey, Egypt, or even Pakistan. In order to gain support, this Sunni candidate would have to unite Muslim masses by representing Islam. The Western ignorance about the Sunni-Shia divide will cause the whole Muslim world to be transformed into an arms race for nuclear weapons. Yet, with this divide, they could easily unite on a dash for Israel, as we have seen with Hezbollah and Hamas during the last war between Israel and Hezbollah. A form of defeatism has taken over the White House. Israel cannot sit idle each time the U.S. signals possible compromise with Iran, which has purchased $1 billion of mobile, surface-to-air TOR-M1 missiles and other hardware. Israel recently announced a successful test of its Arrow defense system, which intercepted a simulated Iranian long-range Shahab-3 missile.

Israel is also reported to be building up the long-range capability of its air force. Experts say that Israel's intention to increase its fleet of German-built Dolphin submarines is aimed at establishing a "second-strike" nuclear capability. The trend is definitely moving towards a cold war in the Middle East between the two most powerful nations in the region, Israel and Iran. If Iran develops nuclear weapons, it could spark a regional arms race because Turkey, Saudi Arabia and Egypt would consider acquiring atomic bombs. Recently announced plans by Egypt and Turkey to build nuclear power plants are raising a ripple of concern about the long-term prospect of a nuclear arms race in the Middle East. Turkey, which produces 50,000 barrels of oil per day yet it consumes 700,000 barrels per day, can make a good case for the use of nuclear energy. Turkey plans to build three nuclear plants by 2015. The environmentalist pressure to minimize the use of fossil fuels gave these nations the argument that nuclear energy is an environmentally-friendly option.

CONCLUSION

Let me state this from the start – Islamic terrorism uses cult-like conditioning techniques to convert masses into becoming remorseless killers. They commit acts of violence intentionally perpetrated on civilian non-combatants with the goal of furthering their ideological laws to the whole world.

That's what Islamic terrorism is. Yet, terrorism is brain washing American Muslim children, and we are silent – all in the name of peace and political correctness. However, we will not get this peace. We will only have peace when Americans love their children more than they love false peace.

This type of terrorism is a self-destructing cancer. The problem is that it will destroy us in the process. We must speak out while we have the chance, without fear of death. We are all destined to either die for something or die of something. It is said, that Vigilance is the price for freedom, yet vigilance will begin when we remove the terror-cancer that is within our land.

The process of changing terrorists to become tolerant, accept different views and dialogue, and use critical thinking, is done by creating logical questions for them. It was this process that caused me to weed through fact and myth. I recognized that doubting and questioning can be good by following basic instincts.

Yet doubting and questioning by extremists is viewed as a weak faith. My doubts arose after I started thinking about the Dead Sea Scrolls. They were written in Hebrew. How could I have hated my own mother. That God was LOVE. That God valued LIFE. Started examining Holocaust Books which angered my family (brother taught his daughter that American flag is not their flag), why such anger?

I began to shatter the myth of a Jihadist God. I developed anger against my spiritual abusers. I began to recognize that the problem is not the occupation of land, but the occupation of the minds of children. I began to see my mentors as drug pushers. I began a movement to combat it. I began to fight appeasement in schools and universities. My children were frustrated and hesitant to express their views, and they were faced with hatred for standing up for the U.S. and Israel. I began to recognize that love has limits. Obedience pressure has limits.

What needs to be done:

- Remove all fanatical leaders.
- Destroy the group's unity by dismantling the hate-filled mosques.

- Resist rejection from the peer groups in school.
- Declare the extreme Islamic view as a political movement and not simply a religion.
- Establish TV programs with opposing views, present the truth, and air it throughout the Muslim world.
- Stop importing Saudi oil.
- Stop immigration from countries that have a high population of Islam and predominantly Islamist views.
- The same for schools – watch our universities and protect the next generation of Americans. Understand that the threat is not only Islamic Jihad but Islamic extreme Sharia laws which conflict with our ways of life
- Stop the production of terrorist operators.

Terrorist groups use cult-like conditioning techniques to convert normal individuals into remorseless killers. The premise of this book is that the limited global counter-terrorism resources should focus on eradicating the terrorist group training camps where the conditioning takes place (fanatic mosques), rather than trying to find terrorists after they have already been conditioned. Change the political spectrum. Democracy in areas that cannot comprehend it should not have elections, as we have seen from the outcome with Hamas. Be careful how to remove thugs in the Middle East. What will replace it? Stop the confidence building by giving concessions to terrorists.

– Walid Shoebat